# THE UNKNOWN
# KIMI
# RÄIKKÖNEN

## KARI HOTAKAINEN

# THE UNKNOWN
# KIMI
# RÄIKKÖNEN

## KARI HOTAKAINEN

SIMON &
SCHUSTER

London · New York · Sydney · Toronto · New Delhi

A CBS COMPANY

First published in Finland by Siltala Publishing, 2018
First published in Great Britain by Simon & Schuster UK Ltd, 2018
A CBS COMPANY

3 5 7 9 10 8 6 4 2

Simon & Schuster UK Ltd
1st Floor
222 Gray's Inn Road
London WC1X 8HB

www.simonandschuster.co.uk
www.simonandschuster.com.au
www.simonandschuster.co.in

Simon & Schuster Australia, Sydney
Simon & Schuster India, New Delhi

A CIP catalogue record for this book is available from the British Library.

Hardback ISBN: 978-1-4711-7766-8
Trade Paperback ISBN: 978-1-4711-7767-5
eBook ISBN: 978-1-4711-7768-2

Typeset in the UK by M Rules
Printed and bound by CPI Group (UK) Ltd, Croydon, CR0 4YY

*Thank you, Sami Visa*

Don't give me facts, tell me what they mean.

Even bad memories can be good ones.

# CONTENTS

\*   \*   \*

# PREFACE

**There are many sports** in the world which only a few take up as a hobby, but which have been accepted as Olympic sports. We get detailed descriptions and expert commentaries on someone lying in a sled, sliding along a frozen chute at an insane speed. I don't know anybody whose hobbies include sledding – perhaps because few nations can afford to build sledding tracks on mountainsides. There are seventeen such tracks in the world. After the Olympics, these tracks become sad museums.

Ski jumping is an important sport for the Finns, but how many actually do it? Perhaps a minuscule fraction of the people who watch it on television. In theory, it's possible to take it up as a hobby. A failure to do so doesn't deter anyone from expressing confident opinions and analyses of what went wrong at the takeoff stage.

No one has Formula 1 as their hobby. No one would say

they're going to a Formula practice in the evening. All the same, at every bar and petrol station you find experts who will tell you that the Sepang circuit simply doesn't suit such and such a driver.

We're not ski jumpers ourselves, we don't fly, carried by our skis, for a single second, but that doesn't stop us from being experts. Being on the outside makes us infallible.

This book has been written from an outsider's perspective. There aren't many other perspectives around. This is not a biography; it couldn't be because the protagonist is only halfway through his life. This is the story of a racing driver who could have become a car mechanic. But he didn't; he became world-famous instead. It happened quickly and with luck on his side, thanks to his mother, father and the man himself. All he wanted to do was to drive as fast as possible. Most such people remain unknown – something he would have liked – but it's too late now.

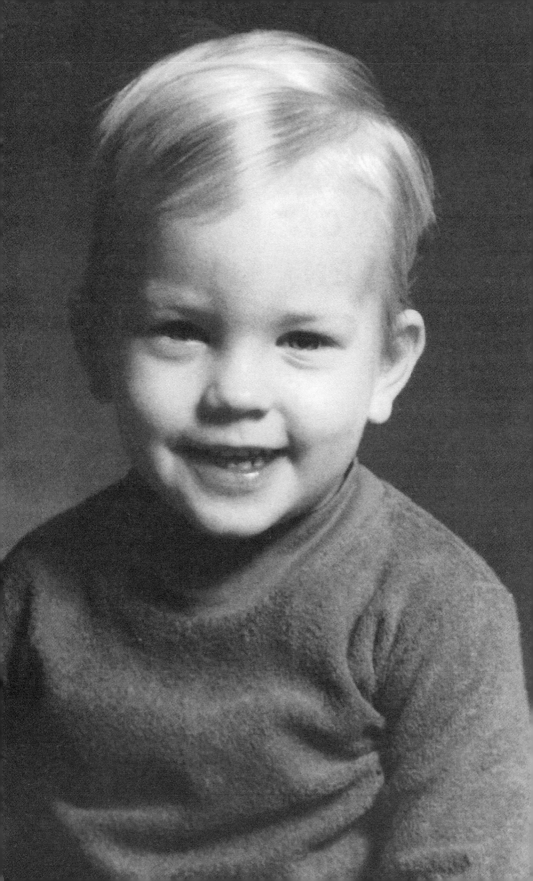

# A CAR IS A
# SILENT SPACE

**It's 1981 in Karhusuo,** Espoo. It's night time; the boy is restless, he can't get to sleep. His mother is trying to soothe him, picks him up again; the boy has always liked being held. He's very different from her other son, who is two years older; he's more sensitive, with his feelers out. At last the boy falls asleep in the early hours of the morning.

The next day, on her way to work, the exhausted mother thinks of what she and her husband have already been concerned about for a long time: the boy doesn't speak, not a word, even though he's nearly three.

The parents take the boy to be examined. There's nothing wrong with him; he performs all the tasks quickly, actually more quickly than is average for his age. He just doesn't speak. Maybe it'll come later.

The speech comes in the end and, after saying goodbye to cuddles, the boy takes off at breakneck speed. Action beats words 10–0. His legs work faster than his tongue; the flaxen-haired boy has broken loose.

Thirty-six years on, his forename has lost its second half. He's just Kimi today; Kimi-Matias has vanished in a cloud of dust, and no one remembers his official first name any longer. It's unlikely that many people even know it, only perhaps one or two of the dozens of fans in the foyer of the Sama-Sama Hotel in Kuala Lumpur on Friday at 9.10am. At least they know he'll come out of the lift soon – and won't say a word.

The fans come from Malaysia, Japan and China. They speak Formula English among themselves, with a scant vocabulary but with a lot of noise. Screaming and cooing know no language barriers. They flit from one lift door to another, and their simultaneous, ringing utterances sound as if exotic birds had flown to the scene to peck at the same morsel: a taciturn driver.

The fans glance expectantly at a familiar figure, Kimi's affairs manager, Sami Visa, who comes down to the foyer in lift number two. He's carrying a Ferrari rucksack with the numbers 007 printed on it. The fans are not deceived by the James Bond reference; seven is Kimi's race number. They know what Visa's appearance in the foyer means: Kimi will be down soon, and we'll be the first ones to see him.

The doors of lift number four open. The man in red has arrived.

Kimi wears a T-shirt with a collar covered in sponsors' logos, a pair of shorts, a cap and black glasses. Mark Arnall, his physiotherapist, also in red, comes out of the lift at the same time. He has accompanied Kimi for the past sixteen years, ensuring the driver has all he needs. Peace and privacy are the only things that Arnall can't supply.

Kimi sees the fans and stops. He knows what he has to do before diving into the Maserati waiting outside. A couple of minutes, forty metres, then the encounter will be over.

Sami Visa tries to keep the cooing fans at arm's length. They hand over one cap and one shirt at a time for Kimi to sign – they mustn't be allowed to touch him. Kimi writes 'KR', or something like it, scrawling his initials quickly. Then the next one. Is there one more? Very well, one more. His face remains expressionless, except for a fleeting change, a twitch round the lips: a smile, a silent present to the faithful supporters who have travelled a long way to be there.

The fans shriek for joy. They've got something, and something is better than nothing. The main doors slide open, and Kimi walks quickly to the Maserati and sits down in the driver's seat – which has been adjusted to the lowest possible position, the back reclining as far as it can. This is the way he sits in all cars. It's a work-related habit: the driver of a Formula car sits in an almost horizontal position.

Mark Arnall occupies the passenger seat and passes

Kimi a bottle of carefully selected liquid. The weather is humid and warm, 34°C. The air conditioning ensures we are immune to the outside temperature. The car leaps forward. As soon as we're over the hotel ramp and on the motorway, Kimi accelerates to over 100 km/h. His left hand shakes the half-litre bottle of some grey, thick substance, a smoothie. His right hand holds the wheel, the middle finger changes gear; the car jerks. I catch a glimpse of the speed limit: 70 km/h. When the limit becomes 100 km/h, Kimi accelerates to 140. I glance at Sami Visa. His expression says: 'Don't say anything; this is how it always goes.'

The distance from the hotel to the Sepang circuit is just under ten kilometres. Kimi's team-mate Sebastian Vettel left with his trainer, Antti Kontsas, before us but we arrive at the circuit at the same time.

**He goes where no one has any business or the keys to enter: his own world. What might look like introversion from the outside is simply concentration.**

Apart from 'good morning', Kimi hasn't said a word on the way there, even though his closest colleagues, Mark and Sami, are in the car. I recall what Sami said to me earlier: 'Kimi becomes a racing driver first thing in the morning. He goes where no one has any business or the keys to enter: his own world. What might look like introversion from the outside is simply concentration.'

We get out of the car. Visa reminds us that, before we go to the pit area, there's a brief meeting with fans. Around a couple of hundred of them have been enclosed behind a wire fence, and they hand over caps, cards, their arms and T-shirts. Kimi jots his vague 'KR' scrawl on the caps, poses for a mobile phone swaying at the end of a selfie stick, and does all he can to ensure he won't need to do anything more.

To the fans, this meeting means a lot. They've paid a great deal of money to get here to look at the cars – normally just glimpsed fleetingly – and the drivers they hardly ever see at such close quarters. They want a great deal, but get little. They want facts that become fiction as time goes by. The stories change; rumours emanating from the pit area are more plentiful than exhaust fumes. The drivers, inside their large helmets, are spied on TV screens looking like men on the moon. The scoreboard displays the truth, and the drivers repeat what happened in a few short words. But the fans want a piece of the man himself; they want to see him, maybe to touch him, to look into his eyes, hidden behind dark glasses. Into those ice-blue eyes, which they've only ever seen in photos and which scan the racetrack for a passage, a gap for overtaking – or hiding.

Hard to say what they get out of Kimi, who during his eighteen-year career has given as many interviews as Lewis Hamilton, the four-time world champion and social media king, gives in a week.

It's all over in ten minutes and Kimi skips towards the pit area. His way of advancing is somewhere between running and walking. The nimble figure darts like a hare through the area and he finds his way into the depths of Ferrari's garage. He's gone. Mysterious are the ways of this man.

His room within Ferrari's quarters is sparse: a space of some twelve square metres built of a chipboard-like material. Every centimetre is utilised to the full: a narrow bed suitable for massage; a table on which Mark Arnall has arranged three helmets, a pair of driving gloves and shoes, towels and several bottles of carefully blended drinks. A corner of the room contains a small, blue bathtub made of reinforced plastics, full of ice-cold water. The driver sits in it for a short while before the race and after the race. His body temperature has to be regulated because the sun heats the 700-kilo racing car to an unforgiving heat. Glamour has abandoned this room in favour of the media, where it thrives.

We move on to Ferrari's hospitality quarters, which are located in the paddock area, a long alley reserved for guests and the press. The teams have all erected their miniature worlds along it. The paddock is also accessible to those who have paid around €6,000 for a package covering the whole weekend. For that price, you get good food and something that is unimaginable to the holder of a standard ticket. And what exactly is that something? It's a glimpse of the driver, a seat in a restaurant built above the pit garages, plus a feeling of importance. People have, throughout the history of mankind, paid substantially more than the recommended price for that feeling.

Ferrari's hospitality quarters smell of basil, garlic and freshly baked white bread with a thin crust. Ferrari has brought Italy to Malaysia. That's what the team always does, whatever the cost. All the delicacies on the laden tables are traditional Italian dishes created by the head chef and his assistants. Sergio Bondi, Ferrari's chief of logistics, says that everything possible is brought along from Italy: pasta, coffee, chairs, tables, even the flour for the bread rolls. The chef sources the best raw materials in each country two days before the race. China, Abu Dhabi, Australia – no matter which country it is, Italy will be constructed there. In Europe, Ferrari requires thirty trucks for transport. Other locations entail flying 300,000 kilometres each year. After every race, the 44,000-kilo circus is dismantled and packed up in the space of seven hours. Annual coffee consumption amounts to 70,000 cups. This year, 170 Ferrari employees were present at the testing of the new car in Barcelona. All this boosts the yearly budget to well over €400 million. If you think about it, the amount is hardly rational.

And all this money to enable two young men to drive for about an hour and a half, defying death and with no destination – that is, they return to the very same spot they started at, soaking wet and panting, their necks on fire, short of words but alive.

**And all this money to enable two young men to drive for about an hour and a half, defying death and with no destination – that is, they return to the very same spot they started at, soaking wet, panting, their necks on fire, short of words but alive.**

I'm deep in thought when Sami taps me on my shoulder. It's time to go into the garage to observe the beginning of the first practice session. We approach the heart of the matter in the labyrinthine pit area: two red cars. An island between the cars is full of computers and men in red wearing ear protectors. We stand further away, so earplugs are enough for us.

Kimi is already ensconced in his car – only his helmet and right hand are visible; the hand reaching out for a bottle handed over by Mark Arnall. Arnall's left hand carries another one. There must always be two bottles, in case one goes missing or breaks. A parched driver is a useless driver.

It's time to start the cars. The Ferrari sounds like a 700-kilo pig being slaughtered, stabbed with a hundred knives on both sides. The noise comes from an angry and injured beast that wants to get the hell out of the garage, away from the tyranny of the men in red into the freedom of the start/finish straight, onto the enclosed track.

The screeching penetrates the earplugs and pierces the head like molten steel. The car hurtles out of the garage onto the track, where it accelerates to 200 km/h in five seconds. It takes under a minute and a half to drive around the 5.5-kilometre circuit. The cars dash past the pit garage like low, barely recognisable missiles. The monitor is your best source for getting the whole picture, even though everything takes place before your eyes.

I mention this infernal racket to Kimi later. He comments drily that the sound of the modern-day cars is reminiscent of a lawnmower, while the models of a few years ago made a proper noise.

There are two free practice sessions; both last for an

hour and a half and are for examining set-ups and testing tyres. Everything is geared to preparing for tomorrow's qualifying. By the afternoon, the track is quiet, but the working day continues with technical discussions. These are followed by what Kimi learnt at the age of three, but what is awkward in front of strangers: talking. He stands before ten microphones, rubbing his neck with his right hand. His mother Paula knows what that means: the boy's pissed off. He's got to say something, form sentences that sound clear but mean nothing. The world is full of such sentences, but the compost heap for them has an unlimited capacity. They're left to decompose on the internet, while hard copies of newspapers are recycled or wrapped round fish and chips. No one – no editors, fans or drivers – remembers after a fortnight where those sentences were uttered. Was it in Malaysia, Japan, China, or perhaps in Austin, Texas? They don't remember because they're the same words, repetitions of the same thing, verbal confirmations of the numbers displayed on the scoreboard.

You were the fifth fastest in the free practice. What does that bode for tomorrow's qualifying? 'Hmm. I'm not sure.'

You were three-hundredths of a second faster than your team-mate. Why do you think that was? 'Hmm. Hard to say.'

Did the car feel good for tomorrow's qualifying? 'Hmm. It was OK. We'll see tomorrow.'

Are you confident about tomorrow? 'Hmm. Yeah.'

You haven't yet given up on the Constructors' Championship? 'Hmm. No.'

He looks up, down, past the reporters, anywhere except straight at them. For him, dark glasses were invented to protect a man from other people's eyes, not the sun.

The interview is over. Kimi skips off and disappears back into Ferrari's garage, where the team will dissect the technical aspects of the day's events.

Finally he reappears and weaves his way purposefully through the crowd. You could easily lose sight of him. It's dusk by the time we're driving towards the hotel. Kimi accelerates till he's over the speed limit and fumbles for the drink with his free hand.

It's quiet, apart from a humming sound; only the Maserati growls from time to time, and that's to order.

I can't see into Kimi's mind but I can guess at its general drift. *Another day's over, home is over 10,000 kilometres away in Switzerland, another fortnight before I get there. The new fellow at the back is writing a book about me. Soon I'll be able to have a shower and go to bed. I'll sleep as late as possible. I wonder how they're doing at home, if everything's all right, if Robin has learnt new words. Does Rianna allow Minttu to sleep, or is the little girl restless? I'd like to be there but I can't. The car was good today; it felt good to be inside it. I like driving best; the problems start as soon as I get out of the car. Nobody asks questions when you're racing.*

Kimi backs the Maserati into a parking space and starts

striding towards the doors. A few tenacious fans are keeping vigil in the foyer. The tired driver has taken off his sunglasses; his blue eyes look straight at them and his right hand does the familiar gesture of scrawling 'KR' on a cap. The lift door whirrs and he's gone.

Late at night, I log onto the internet in the hotel room. Thursday's press conference about the coming weekend catches my eye. The drivers were asked what sort of memories they have about the Malaysian race, now to be run for the last time. The drivers answer dutifully and politely – that means boringly. Then it's Kimi's turn. He had his first race win here in 2003, and a reporter asks what he'll miss most. A brief silence is followed by words that drop like stones on a tiled floor. Kimi says that, to be honest, he doesn't know if he'll miss anything. It's a nice circuit. But the airport, the hotel and the circuit are all you see here. You can choose if you'll miss any of them or not.

Some of the reporters crease up; others are silent. This is the essence of humour: when all else fails, try the truth. Every driver and every reporter knows that there's no chance of getting to know the city, the people or the local dishes during a race weekend. Everyone knows it; no one says it. Apart from one man, who learnt to speak at the age of three.

'We travel pleasantly, over the speed limit.' In Kimi's car in Kuala Lumpur. PHOTO: KARI HOTAKAINEN

# NOT A SINGLE METRE

**It's 9.10 on Saturday** morning at Kuala Lumpur's Sama-Sama Hotel. The pole for tomorrow's race will be decided today. We're due to leave the hotel at 9.30. The driver stays in bed till the last minute.

I'm sitting in the foyer bar, having a coffee. The adjacent table is occupied by a loud-mouthed trio wearing caps; the two women and one man have experienced life and lots of beer. Their Ferrari-red T-shirts have dark stains – no doubt faded memories of cheap and tasty Tiger beer. They're around fifty years old, have hoarse voices, and exude the smell of stale alcohol, which has been marinating their innards for days on end. It turns out they're Australian and flew over from Sydney on Wednesday to watch the race through a glass of beer.

One of the women, the one with strikingly ginger hair, asks if they had pissed me off the night before. I say that I wasn't in the bar, so they still had the option open to them. The man of the group – he has tiny holes on his pink cheeks – asks gruffly if I'm a fan of Kimi or a fan of Lewis Hamilton, the English earring-wearing character. In his opinion, I clearly look like a Lewis Hamilton man. I say I'm heterosexual and a fan of nobody. The women burst into laughter, relieved that they haven't pissed me off.

The man demands to know my opinion of Kimi Räikkönen. I say that I don't know the man but appreciate the way he defies death. I also say that I've never watched an entire Formula 1 race and I was never interested in motor racing. The women want to know more about my shortcomings, but the man silences them by means of a searching look at my face. I sense his gaze both on my throat and my ears because of the way his eyes swivel. He asks where I come from and what I am doing in a hotel close to the Sepang circuit if I'm not into Formula. I say I'm from Finland and on a perfectly ordinary holiday. The group is galvanised. I come from the same country as Kimi Räikkönen; my stock goes up. They order more beer to toast my home country. They all talk at the same time, each giving their own opinion of Kimi, who is like a family member to them. Kimi is the only driver who doesn't spout inanities after a race. They know he lives in this hotel but haven't managed to spot him because he arrives so late that the heavily intoxicated group forgets to keep an eye on the lift. They think that they'll have to see Kimi; it isn't enough to glimpse him as he whizzes past on the main straight at 290 km/h. You don't get any kind of impression of the person in those circumstances. I agree.

The man wants to buy me a stiff drink; after all, the Finns drink liquor for breakfast. I decline and thank them for a pleasant chat. I get up, and the man wishes me luck, though he doesn't think I need any because I'm fortunate enough to hail from the same country as Kimi.

All the members of the group are suddenly gripped by an urgent need to empty their bladders and rush to the toilets with their open-toe sandals flapping and colourful shorts rustling. As soon as they've disappeared, the lift doors open, and the man in red skips towards the Maserati.

We travel pleasantly, over the speed limit, until we reach a roundabout. Kimi mutters a warning to himself about not taking the roundabout at full tilt. He's impatient to get to work, into the small space, inside the helmet.

We arrive at the circuit. It will be decided in three hours' time who will start Sunday's race on pole. One of Kimi's favourite songs is called 'Pole Position', which he likes to sing in karaoke. The interpretation requires a drink or two, after which the last word of the refrain shoots out like a bolt from the blue: 'in my ... pole position'. The country song was written by Hector, who also penned the lyrics, and recorded by the late Kari Tapio. Like so many of the karaoke favourites, it says, as if by accident, a great deal about the singer's own life: 'Time went by, often pulled the rug away/crazy youth and all powerful/Devil gave me the day, God the night/every day like a small eternity./I would've been content with much less/because I know how well I've been blessed/I'm here and now perhaps to stay/with what I've got/in my pole position.'

The pursuer of the pole position strides away; the song stays in my head. Sami and I walk to Ferrari's hospitality area. Workers dressed in red drink strong coffee, buzzing with excitement. Team boss Maurizio Arrivabene, a slender man with a grey beard, sucks at a tubular smoking device decorated with the Ferrari logo, and puffs out smoke to one side. The product is Philip Morris' latest invention, Iqos, which heats a small dose of tobacco to a fiery temperature and releases the nicotine to its user without paper – that means one poison less. I notice other important characters holding the same device.

Arrivabene is a man of experience. He can store the tension inside as if it were a jam jar in a cellar. His distracted eyes reveal some essential truths about motor sport: if the driver succeeds, the engine may fall apart. If the driver makes even one mistake, he'll be in fifth place. If someone is in front of the driver at a crucial moment, half a second will be lost. In this sport, half a second is a tediously long time. There's no other sport in which the time differences are so small. In F1, tiny is massive.

The team boss pulls three centimetres of tobacco from his Iqos and pushes it into the device's own ashtray, which looks dainty and elegantly designed, quite unlike the usual smelly object. Arrivabene swings round towards the garage, hoping that the clock will favour his drivers today.

Sami Visa brings me the day's third bottle of water and a small cup of strong coffee. He has known Kimi for twenty-two years, or since 1996. He's old enough to be Kimi's father; now he acts as the driver's affairs manager. Kimi has always been bad at accepting anyone's advice, even when it is good and appropriate. He's always done his own thing, though the road has occasionally morphed into a path, a ditch or a wilderness. A driver is a driver even without a road underneath him. He does listen to Sami, though, and the reason is clear. Sami doesn't bullshit him, nor will he ever. The promise was given in Villa Butterfly's sauna two years ago when a verbal contract was agreed for the affairs manager's post: 'If you bullshit me, I'll kill you.'

Sometimes a verbal agreement is more binding than a piece of paper. I've seen far too many Italian films about families and begin to wonder about the threat included in the contract when a big, jet-black man sways into the terrace. He greets Sami in a deep, gravelly voice. He shakes my hand, assuming I recognise him. I hide my ignorance by fidgeting with my coffee cup. The man jumps off his chair to embrace the head chef. The man and the chef gesticulate so wildly that Sami gets the chance to give me some basic info: the man is Moko, a well-known Senegalese jewellery designer, one of the founders and owners of the jewellery and fashion firm Chrome Hearts. Everybody here knows him except me. His company has worked with Madonna, Lenny Kravitz and many other stars. Moko has a lifelong pass to F1 races. He got it originally from Jean Todt, Ferrari's team boss, who is currently President of the International Automobile Federation (FIA).

Moko returns to our table, and when I tell him I'm writing a book about Kimi Räikkönen, a fire lights up in his eyes. 'Listen, white captain,' he starts, and wants to tell me everything. He began following Formula 1 in 1979, when apartheid was still alive and kicking. It was highly incongruous for a black man to support a white racing driver. In Moko's native country of Senegal, the popular sports were soccer and rugby, but he chose Formula 1. He thinks Kimi Räikkönen can be compared to artists who allow their work to do the talking. Before I ask more questions, I catch myself staring, rather impolitely, at his colourful midi-length kaftan. Moko notices my gaze and is prompted to praise the achievements of Marimekko, the Finnish textile firm. He has bought Marimekko fabrics and used them to sew unique garments for himself.

He says he started following Kimi when the driver was still with Sauber. 'The boy came in from the shadows and switched on the lights straight away. I just watched, followed and imprinted him on my mind,' Moko reminisces. They didn't meet until Kimi moved to Ferrari. At the opening race of Kimi's first season with the team at Melbourne, Australia, Moko was sitting in the paddock area under a tree when Kimi walked by. Moko said: 'Good afternoon, Mr Räikkönen. Welcome to Ferrari.' Kimi stopped, looked at Moko, smiled and said: 'Thank you.' 'Some photographers nearby were watching us; they laughed as they commented that it evidently took an African to make Räikkönen smile.' Moko laughed and added: 'I gave him an amulet from my collection, and he did, indeed, win the race.'

## The helmet contains a perspiring head, which in turn contains a brain working at a considerably higher number of revolutions than the car.

'What you see is what you get. Kimi's got no hidden agenda.'

Moko arrived at the race from his home in Paris in a private jet and will later head for Stockholm to attend a Rolling Stones concert (because 'the boys' asked him to). The company he represents has produced a sizeable fashion and jewellery range based on the Rolling Stones' tongue logo. He doesn't tell me this himself; I hear it from others. When I ask about it, Moko says that he doesn't talk about his work but tries to do it so well that others do. Moko thinks Kimi is more of a wise man than an iceman. 'A wise man doesn't come out with everything but leaves something concealed inside, in storage. He reminds me of writers like Marcel Proust and Albert Camus, who kept quiet and let their pens do the talking.' I don't quite see the connection between their activities and Kimi's, but Moko does. He tells me that he has also met people in the driver's inner circle, including Kimi's parents and grandmother.

Moko falls silent and looks at the crowd.

He thinks that I'll come up against major difficulties halfway through the book at the latest. I ask what sort of difficulties, but he remains enigmatic. Finally, he says I should have a detailed chat with Kimi's mum, because a man has got only one mother. I promise him I will.

I'm jolted out of my thoughts by a familiar sound about 100 metres away. A pig is being slaughtered. It's time to move to the slaughterhouse. The men in red have started the monster. Who will be the fastest over five and a half kilometres? The practice session has begun and will last for an hour, followed by a break and then the day's main business: an hour's qualifying to determine the grid for Sunday.

The helmet contains a perspiring head, which in turn contains a brain working at a considerably higher number of revolutions than the car. Thousands of repeat drives facilitate the job: the bends become straighter, the neck gets used to the vibrations, old data is stored in the spinal cord. I, an outsider, believe that a driver is used to the proximity of death. Kimi thinks I'm exaggerating – the cars today are safe.

The first qualifying session is promising, the second even more so. A tiny error at the end of the last section costs Kimi the pole. He'll be second on the grid. The prospects for tomorrow are good; the car and the driver are in harmony.

Microphones appear in front of Kimi's mouth. He has got to say how he feels and what he can expect from tomorrow. He's red-faced and scratches his neck. This time he's not pissed off; it's a matter of sheer physical pain. He suffers from an atopic rash, which sometimes flares up. The reporters are given a brief, matter-of-fact statement to the effect that the swerve, barely visible in slow motion, cost him the pole, but he's optimistic about tomorrow. He says only what is absolutely necessary, and that means: very little. When the person you're interviewing says hardly anything, you've got to read his body language. They decipher that the car is good enough for a win if nothing unexpected happens – except that the unexpected is precisely what often happens in this sport.

We drive from the circuit to the hotel in silence. The race is tomorrow – tomorrow is the reason why we travelled 10,000 kilometres to get here. Because of Sunday, Kimi arrived here on Tuesday. He lowers his eyes at the hotel entrance and walks to the lift as fast as he can. This time, he doesn't stop but signs caps as he passes. His room is on the seventh floor, third door on the left. He goes in, has a shower and something to eat. Then it's time to contact Switzerland and Skype his family: Minttu, Robin and Rianna. Has Robin learnt new words?

The foyer bar is quiet. The three Australians have slumped with a total of four eyes open. That'll do; enough to see me. They want to know what happened on the track while they were on their own racetrack leading to the bar. I tell them. The other two eyes open. Kimi will win tomorrow; they're quite sure about that – as sure as they are of having to get to the scene of the action tomorrow.

I exchange another few words with the trio, who have lost their sense of time. I can't help thinking how the press has written copiously, though inaccurately, about Kimi Räikkönen's bibulous leisure pursuits. Nowadays, Kimi drinks in a year what these Aussie fans knock back in twenty-four hours.

Sunday morning is sweltering. The temperature is 36°C in the shade, and in the racing car it's double that. The pit garage is full of buzz and bustle. Something is not right during the warm-up lap. Kimi's car is losing power; ten men in red rush to the scene, strip the car of its fibreglass parts, and push their heads inside. Minutes tick by; the race start is imminent. A camera captures a close-up of team boss Arrivabene's uncertain, worried face. There's a gasp. Kimi's car is pushed into the garage; the men in red push people out of the way – there's no time. Or if there is, it has stopped. A huge quantity of invisible banknotes float in the area; all that money will be lost if the fault is not found. It's found, but there's not enough time to repair it. Kimi gets out of the car and walks into the garage with his helmet on. There's an empty spot on the grid next to Lewis Hamilton. Kimi travelled to the ends of the earth for nothing. He didn't drive a single metre this time, though he's done it here before, back in 2003, when he recorded the first race win of his career on this circuit.

Today's fault was in the turbo hose, but it won't be announced until tomorrow. The man performed well but to no avail. And he has got to stay put, has to watch the others drive on without him. He has got to answer when reporters ask what it feels like, not driving a single metre. He has got to hang around the workplace till the end even though he can't do his job.

At last, when it's already getting dark, we're able to leave the circuit.

The Maserati transports a bunch of silent men at a snail's pace, caught in the big city's endless traffic jam. Kimi spots an opportunity: a motorcade ahead of us – a Malaysian government minister appears to be leaving the circuit. A line of three official cars is led by two policemen on motorcycles. Kimi begins to follow the procession, which makes its dignified and privileged way through the congestion in a lane of its own. The police are waving at us to indicate we're not allowed to follow. Kimi snorts, weaving his way after the motorcade. I glance at Sami Visa. His expression tells me not to say anything this time either; this is the way it goes today.

We arrive at the quiet hotel. The driver with no race vanishes into the lift.

Sami and I remain in the foyer. The sense of frustration has spread to us; words are in short supply, our silent fury directed at the turbo hose: why didn't you work? Are you worth even €100 in a €7 million car?

Kimi's leaving tonight for Bangkok to attend an event for sponsors. The race at Japan's Suzuka circuit will follow. All positive energy is directed towards that race. Everything is as it was before: he's just got to concentrate on the next race and hope the engine won't play up. No, everything's not as it was before. He's got a family now: a wife and two children. He's got something to lose.

# TWO SECONDS
# IS AN ETERNITY

**It's Baar in Switzerland;** it's home. Dad lies on the sofa holding a bottle of water in his left hand, a toy car of Robin's in his right. Robin is tuning his cars on the floor. There's no rush. He won't need to leave for the season's last race in Abu Dhabi for another three days; this time the whole family will go. Then the season is over.

On this sofa, Kimi is a father, not a racing driver. He talks vivaciously, comments on Robin's chatter, takes part in the game, talks nonsense, laughs, catches his son out in the middle of a prank, carries on with it. The 38-year-old man has been a father for almost three years. His second child, a girl called Rianna, was born six months ago. Everyday life is more eventful than an F1 race. On the racetrack, events are repetitive; one race is much like another.

With young children, moments retain their uniqueness; tomorrow everything may have changed: a new word is added to Robin's vocabulary, a new expression appears on Rianna's face. Formula 1 makes way for number one people.

There he sits, the Iceman, yet there's no sign of coolness. 'Iceman' is a nickname coined by Ron Dennis, the team boss of McLaren. It's an alias, a shield, a tool. You can drive a car under it; it's a good name for that purpose. But it melts outside the car, and evaporates once he reaches his own doorstep.

Kimi is famous for his reticence. Silence wasn't invented by the Finns, yet all the same they have processed it into several successful products: taciturnity, pauses, three-word sentences and half-minute silences – traps for an outsider to fall into, as they wonder what is happening now that nothing is happening. And then the Finn carries on as if the silence had never existed.

In Kimi's official job, his loudest silence is provoked by a question that's stupid enough. In the noisy and verbose media environment, silence may be the best way of attracting attention. In Kimi's case, taciturnity springs from a combination of shyness and intelligence: if the questions are platitudes, he answers with two words and by scratching his neck.

Kimi Räikkönen had no chance of getting used to the Formula 1 media climate. He plunged headlong into a hole in the ice in 2001: hundreds of reporters and TV channels attended the opening race at Melbourne, where ten micro-phones were shoved in his face. In his previous life, in the Formula Renault series, there were only occasional inter-views. Then everything changed in an instant. The young man speaking in fractured, broken, halting English was in deep shit, but positively so. A miracle had taken place: he had got into F1, a world that only a year ago loomed in the far distance.

Kimi's old friend Teemu 'Fore' Nevalainen has an interesting theory: 'If the journey to fame had been longer and he had been given more time to prepare, I bet it would have resulted in a different Kimi from the one we've got. A more boring one, I'm quite sure. He would always have given the answers people wanted to hear. Now he says more in three words than the others put together.'

**'It would be brilliant to drive in Formula 1 incognito,' he says, and I make sure the Dictaphone stored this first sentence.**

Kimi isn't the first Finnish sportsman to shun the micro-phone, or to fear it. But he's the first one whose reticence has become an international brand; *has become* – he didn't manufacture it. He hasn't constructed the brand, but only realised one day that's what he was. The strongest personal brand is always true and therefore happens by accident. The weakest one is impersonal: it's been manufactured, learnt and taught. Kimi is an organic product pulled out of icy-cold water, with deep roots in the place he was born: Karhusuo, Espoo.

I press the red 'rec' button on the Dictaphone. It's now ready to record speech. Kimi glances at the machine and doesn't let it distract him – or if he does, he doesn't show it.

He struggles to cope with celebrity; it's a bitter pill to swallow, a necessary evil. 'It would be brilliant to drive in Formula 1 incognito,' he says, and I make sure the Dictaphone stores this first sentence. And when he says it, Kimi knows that no such world exists or will ever exist. It's possible to move a razor, or drive a lawnmower incognito, but not a racing car worth €7 million.

'There weren't that many interviews in karting, perhaps the odd one if you got to the podium or during the Finnish Championships. And that was true of Formula Renault, too. It didn't feel that awkward in F1, but the interviews irritated the hell out of me. I think they're pointless, though I understand them from the team point of view. It's just the same questions day in, day out. Perhaps there aren't that many questions that can be asked about the sport. They could just replicate the answers – it'd be a lot easier all round.'

Robin is playing with at least ten cars and a track with an ascending start straight. The cars must be tuned to enable them to climb to the top of the loop, from where they accelerate to the finish straight. Kimi does the tuning, engrossed in the game, while the Dictaphone's red light blinks, demanding speech.

'I don't quite see why, with twenty races a year, they've got to ask about the previous race every Thursday and, on Friday, about the free practice. They look at the results of Friday's practice and ask why you were eighth, seventh or sixth when it's of no importance. They create headlines out of the free practice results, though the pole won't be decided until Saturday. And the actual race takes place on Sunday.'

Kimi opens the morning's third bottle of Penta, purified water recommended by Mark Arnall, his physiotherapist. It's absorbed slowly by the body and has no contaminants.

I pause to think about Kimi's relationship with the PR part of his job. Ferrari's annual budget exceeds €400 million. The sum is off the scale and carries with it sponsors' requirements and requests, sales and marketing, fantasies and figures of speech. No one sees the bigger picture; everyone views things from their own angle, through a keyhole. And all you see through that hole is two drivers.

One of them grants, reluctantly, a sentence or two, and scratches his ear.

Hublot, the Swiss manufacturer of luxury watches, contributes €40 million. Kimi's wrist is bare. I ask about it because I'm interested in the visibility of the massive investment. Kimi says he can't wear watches; they inflame his rash. I wonder what might inflame Hublot's chief executive. Kimi says he carries the watch in his rucksack if there's an event where it has to be on show. I recall the press conference of the Rolling Stones' European tour in 1995. The main sponsor of the tour was the car manufacturer Volkswagen. The reporters asked Mick Jagger what he thought of the make. Jagger said he preferred driving a Rolls-Royce.

Kimi's voice is familiar from TV. It's low, hoarse and deep. The tone is due to an accident he suffered at five years old. He fell with his bike, hitting his neck against the handlebar. As a consequence, his vocal cords were damaged and never fully recovered. It's a very distinctive voice.

Minttu comes downstairs carrying six-month-old Rianna. Kimi's eyes show he needs to spend a little time with mother and daughter. I switch off the Dictaphone and take myself elsewhere. I walk around the big house and think how he got here. The distance from Karhusuo in Espoo is 2,440 kilometres and twenty years. I reach the toilet facilities on the middle floor; the decor is familiar from the rest of the house: grey and black. My mind wanders back to the early days of his career, the moment when he signed the

Sauber contract. The young man, who had abandoned the car mechanics' course at a technical school, stared at the document while seated at a table in a luxury hotel in the small town of Rapperswil. The other people sitting round the table included his managers, Dave and Steve Robertson, Peter Sauber, the owner of the team, and a solicitor. He was being offered $500,000 a year and $50,000 for every point earned. The man doing the signing came from a house with no inside lavatory. Soon there would be. He wanted to repay his mother and father, who had initiated this and made it possible.

Minttu, Robin and Rianna go out for a walk. We carry on from where we left off. 'You're famous for not being known. You're famous for not saying a lot. Is your taciturnity prompted by the parroting of identical questions, or do you find it disagreeable to talk to strangers?' Kimi doesn't answer but, instead, comes up with an interesting view.

'Even bad memories can be good memories. Everyone thinks that if you didn't win, it was a bad race. Over the years there have been lots of races when you've started from some shitty place on the grid, say place X, and then you've been fifth or fourth, and you know full well that no one could have driven any better from that place but no one seems to get it. You've only done well if you come first. The race might have been as dull as hell but when you're number one, the reporters think you've put in a great performance. You could just as well say that it was a dull and shitty race because the others had all sorts of incidents and I, by some amazing piece of luck, got to be number one, and then they say that I was bloody good. It doesn't make any sense. That means bad memories can be good memories. People think that number one is what matters, though everybody in the team knows full well that fourth place was really good in the circumstances. But there's no point in explaining these things if people just want to see who's on the podium. The end result is all they look at. I can have good memories of races I didn't finish because everything was bloody great until the engine blew up. For example, in 2002 I suffered a hell of a lot of engine failures, but all the same, I have many pleasant memories of the year. I learnt a lot even though everything didn't go well. People watching can't possibly understand it.'

**'You could just as well say that it was a dull and shitty race because the others had all sorts of incidents and I, by some amazing piece of luck, got to be number one, and then they say that I was bloody good. It doesn't make any sense.'**

I look around the big living room and search for something that would reflect the occupant's fame, occupation, stardom. I spot a large, red book on the bottom shelf of the coffee table. It documents Kimi's World Championship year 2007, a book dedicated to him by Ferrari. It reminds me of the special quality of the man lying on the sofa in his tracksuit.

Apart from the usual media, Formula 1 is surrounded by so-called paddock celebrities: megastars, A-list names, rock stars, business gurus, peacocks, queen bees, ministers. They all want their piece, a crumb, a slice. Of what? The same as a fan from Pälkäne, Finland, or from Tokyo: a sensation, a touch, closeness, a memory. *I touched someone who shook hands with death.* The drivers do something they shouldn't do but they do it all the same. Dangerous? Yes. Exciting? Absolutely.

YouTube shows a clip in which the world-famous actor Nicole Kidman comes to Ferrari's garage to meet the drivers. Kidman stretches out her hand to Kimi and says: 'Nice to meet you.' Kimi shakes hands dutifully and looks away. The stark image says a lot. The video is popular because it contains an error: Kimi's conduct. An unspoken set of codes dictates how you should behave before a celebrity: how lovely of you to visit, I've seen many of your films; films starring your husband are also good. Instead, Kimi's expression speaks of his discomfort at getting out of the car and coming face to face with the downside of his occupation: shining stars. They should stay up in the sky; why are they hanging around here, in my workplace?

Kimi does some channel-hopping and finds motocross. His eyes focus on the giant screen. Young men drive in a circle in a hall. They're up in the air for most of the time, springing towards the ceiling, thumping onto the floor, and ride along a bumpy straight to reach the ramp again for the flight to start. Seen through an outsider's eye, the race is terrifying, and I wonder aloud if the riders' balls are ground into mincemeat. Kimi smiles. He clearly enjoys the chance to reveal some of the details of the sport to a dimwit. He explains that jockstraps aren't worn in motocross because the rider more or less stands on the bike; he hardly sits down at all.

Kimi likes to talk about motocross, because that's where it all started and he has invested in it. He owns a motocross team called Ice One Racing, which is based in Belgium and run by a former top rider, Antti Pyrhönen. Kimi is passionate about the sport, and has built a motocross track at his summer place in Porkkalanniemi.

Around thirty-five years ago, Kimi mounted a children's Italjet, a mini motocross bike, outside his home in Karhusuo, Espoo, and stepped on the gas. The bike jolted the little boy into a speed that hasn't yet slowed down. He and his brother Rami, who is two years older, ploughed the garden outside their home into an unrecognisable mess, until they graduated into the world of four-wheelers. Kimi's son Robin will soon be the age at which his dad was turning over grass and soil under his rear wheel.

What makes speed interesting? What makes it exhilarating? Why can't someone stand still? Does their body contain some throbbing virus? What brings about excess speed? This overdrive is required in many fields: art, business, dozens of sports in which success is based on quick reactions, intensity, recklessness and fearlessness. A human being who is used to going into overdrive may be appalled by the everyday, that grey strip revealed by the sun on a dusty kitchen floor. After you've experienced it, everything feels boring, like coming back to level ground after the scariest fairground ride. Matti Nykänen, Finland's most successful ski jumper, was happy for four seconds in the air, but was often lost on the ground. A master of the skies eats humble pie when he comes down to earth. Sometimes it's hard to find a compromise between the extremes.

Kimi gives some thought to the nature of speed. Perhaps he hasn't before. Perhaps he can't define it in precise words – but he can drive all right. The words elude him, while the racing line presents no problem. It's hard to put into words, but he does, all the same.

'You don't feel the speed, not until it slips away from you for a bit. Sometimes, after the summer holiday, when racing along a straight at full throttle, I feel my head has been left behind. I feel I'm going into a tunnel and, when I brake, I become conscious of the speed for four seconds, maybe. Then the feeling goes. Usually, my neck hurts after every holiday, my head won't stay up, and I ache all over.'

I'm scared, just listening.

'I've never been afraid. If I were really frightened, it would be time to give up. I like being in the car; driving is the one good thing about the whole job. You're left alone.'

I get it, though all my life car journeys have been spent in ordinary passenger vehicles.

An F1 car is the world's smallest workplace. The worker lies in a made-to-measure capsule wearing a helmet, knees slightly bent, visibility restricted. There's no contact with the employer unless you count the team radio, which connects you to the race engineer. All the other drivers are rivals; some of them want to do you out of a job at the next bend. The notice period is one second, the annual salary is disproportionate, the atmosphere is at times tense, and the benefits are immeasurable. The most intense spell of work ranges from one and a half hours to two, while the actual working hours are incalculable, and leisure time is limited. You're recognised everywhere you go, and you're forgotten fast.

I ask Kimi to illuminate the uniqueness of his exceptional job a little more. He pauses to think about it – no wonder he takes his time. There are other occupations with unique features that are hard to verbalise. And, on the other hand, why should you? Which would you prefer: to read an author's work, or to go and listen to him or her talking about it? Would you prefer to hear a composer's exposition of his composition, or the opus itself? You wouldn't be interested in hearing a plumber's report on how well he'll soon install the heat pump. I've read hundreds of books and hundreds of author interviews during the course of my life. I don't remember anything about the latter, while many books have made a lasting impression.

**'I've never been afraid. If I were really frightened, it would be time to give up. I like being in the car; driving is the one good thing about the whole job. You're left alone.'**

Kimi adjusts his position, empties the bottle of Penta and burps. He's not accustomed to thinking about what he does; he just does it. Many of the professionals I've inter-viewed in connection with Kimi repeat one word: instinct. You've either got it, or you haven't. Almost everything else can be acquired through practice.

'Driving and the decisions during driving come from somewhere automatically, subconsciously. If someone asks how you know where to brake, I can't say. The impulse just comes from somewhere. If I had to think where I'm going to brake, I wouldn't have a snowball's chance in hell. I'd be late every time. Somehow you just figure out where you've got to brake.'

Kimi looks at me to see if I get the message. I do. But I want to hear more. Many people watch the start of a race because it crystallises one of the characteristics of the sport: at full throttle towards chaos. It's virtually incomprehensible. The cars accelerate side by side towards a bend. On Malaysia's Sepang circuit, the speed at the end of the start straight is 230 km/h compared to 80 km/h at the first bend. The driver's pulse is 180 compared to 110 on the start grid a few seconds previously. His stress has reached its apex at the first bend.

'You've got to figure out where the others are. It's wheel-to-wheel driving. When you've been driving for years, you know pretty well what so-and-so will do, because you've seen it so many times. You can drive wheel to wheel with someone and you know he won't do anything stupid. You can trust him. Then you've got those you just don't know about; you can see that, with them, you've got to be more careful. It's pretty much the same everywhere. You've got to know the other fellows' weaknesses. The computer in your head whizzes through different alternatives; you just choose the best of them. Or the second best.'

The voices of his family echo in the hallway, and it

suddenly feels inappropriate to talk about a dangerous job. Robin runs into the living room and wants to pile the cushions into a tower from which it's good to jump down. Robin carries a future which is harder to fathom than racing lines. November light floods in through the wall-sized window. Kimi jumps onto the floor and starts arranging the cushions with his son. Time stops, or there's an abundance of it. He throws himself into the game. Dad's expressions and growls make Robin laugh. Kimi lets me know with a look that I can go on with the questions – he can answer from the floor.

I'm intrigued by tiny time differences. Finnish skier Juha Mieto missed out on the gold medal by one-hundredth of a second in the 15-kilometre cross-country at the 1980 Winter Olympics in Lake Placid. The small difference earned him a place in the history books. In Formula 1, you get the feeling that an additional unit of time has been squeezed from the clock. The differences look minimal on the scoreboard but they are something else on the racetrack.

'Everyone is basically within a two-second window. It's pretty easy to drive at a two-second distance from the leading car, i.e. if you are consistently two seconds behind the leader, you just carry on driving along – not much else you can do. When the differences come down to hundredths or tenths of a second and you drive at the maximum capacity, then the set-up of your car determines if you can get it to go where you want. Everything's got to be spot-on; so you'll know what's going to happen when you come to a bend, and you'll know you've got enough grip. Those things make the difference. If the car doesn't have the right set-up, you've got no chance. If you're a few tenths per lap slower than someone else, say, on the Brazilian circuit with seventy laps, you can calculate what it comes to. A small difference becomes a really big one.'

Kimi and Robin finish the tower. Robin climbs up to the top on a small stepladder and thuds down onto the carpet. Kimi cheers, Robin laughs. Time is measured in different units when you're with children: in moments.

Big brother and
little brother aged
ten and eight.

# WHITE GYPSIES

**Shortly afterwards, we're rolling** back the years in a dim room, which Kimi calls his office in a drily humorous voice. The room is around twenty square metres; the grey and dark decor is maintained here. The space is dominated by a sturdy aluminium desk carrying a large computer. One of the walls is covered with shelving filled with helmets from different years. There are two divan sofas for adaptable seating. The cosy room can be used as a cinema, with films projected onto the rear wall. We're not watching them now; we're looking back. The man is currently thirty-eight years old and has at least the same number of years ahead. He's not used to looking back; he hasn't spent much time thinking about what he has done; he has been thinking of what he's going to do.

We agree that it isn't easy to talk about yourself and what you have been doing – and quite often it's not that interesting. Fortunately, there are other people, others to interview. They come into the room via earlier recordings and give their own versions of events. The whole picture becomes more real, although the image of another person that emerges always remains imprecise, somewhat blurry.

Kimi Räikkönen has often been called enigmatic – an exaggeration but understandable perhaps in an age when people like to share everything that happens to them on social media, from when they first empty their bladders to their evening snacks. Someone who says little or nothing easily becomes mysterious, though in earlier times he would have been an ordinary, somewhat shy citizen. In a sense, we're sitting in the heart of *un*social media right now.

Kimi is drinking the day's fourth bottle of water and glances at the flashing lights of my Dictaphone. He looks worried. I assure him the machine isn't connected to the outside world. He can speak freely and be certain that it won't yet leave this room for undesirable destinations.

Kimi relaxes on the divan and starts talking. The talk jumps around but I want to stop it at the place where it all started. In the beginning was the smell of machine oil, petrol and exhaust fumes; money came much later. And before the smell of money became permanent, a great deal of it was burnt. Kimi-Matias Räikkönen was born into an impecunious home. When I write the word, I don't mean poor, but compared to motor sport, there wasn't much money around. Sami Visa has said that the best way to have an interest in motor racing is not to drive. As soon as you start driving, banknotes start flying out of the exhaust pipe.

Matti Räikkönen knew this, but is unfortunately no longer with us to answer any questions, having died in 2010 at the age of fifty-six. Matti, Kimi's father, was the engine; Paula, his mother, the petrol. Together with their two sons, they formed a family of petrol heads, who inhaled the same stinking air. Matti's job involved driving a road grader, but he spent all his free time tinkering with machines, and in stock car racing in Finland's Everyman class. Matti took the boys along to the races, allowing them to get their hands greasy, to repair, and to weld. The boys learnt quickly that if they wanted something they had to do it themselves.

'That's where we got started, outside the house. There was always some kind of competition going on with my big brother Rami – if not a wrestling match, then some sort of scrap. I remember it well when we went to watch karting for the first time. The son of Dad's workmate drove us, it might've been to Bemböle. Very soon afterwards Dad bought us this ancient microcar. Then we started driving, the two of us taking turns, because the pedals had to be adjusted for me. Rami was that much taller. The pedals were adjusted every ten minutes, so the other one could have a go. There were club races on Tuesday evenings; that's how it started. I just grew into the job, or was in the middle of it, because Dad was a mechanic in rallying and in the Everyman class, so engines and things were always there. We were around them all the time. The family was always into bikes and engines. There had to be speed, never mind what kind of equipment was underneath.'

Kimi talks about speed, not competing. He evidently sees racing as a given. First he wanted to beat his big brother, then everyone else. The competitive instinct is buried deep, out of sight.

When I asked big brother Rami to give me a picture of his little brother, this is what he remembered: 'One day we played footie outside, and held a sort of penalty kick competition. Five kicks each. If Kimi was losing, then another fifteen kicks, and if that wasn't enough, then another twenty. No matter if it took till midnight, as long as Kimi liked the result.'

Mum Paula says that she has two very different boys. 'I could put it like this: Rami stands for reason and Kimi for action. When it's Kimi, if there's the smallest gap, he'll slip past. Rami is more of a gentleman, so that if someone catches up with him, he might think, *Go on, pass.* If Kimi sees the tiniest chink, he'll exploit it.'

Rami is amused by Kimi's normal driving style, its uniqueness. 'He thinks that if the other guy can't squeeze through, then he will. He sees a space, and thinks that the best way to ease this jam is to accelerate, not to brake.'

## 'I could put it like this: Rami stands for reason and Kimi for action.'

Kimi's old mates have their own views of his usual driving style. Uffe Tägström, his long-standing helmet designer, thinks he has an incredible feel for driving. 'If he has driven somewhere, it doesn't matter in which city, he's certain to remember the route, no need for a sat-nav. He's got his own. He has complete faith in himself – no hesitation.'

Juha Hanski, who has known Kimi since early 2000, awards the driver both bouquets and brickbats. 'He's shit in traffic, totally reckless. All the same, you feel calm in his car – he's got good spatial awareness. We might try out a new motocross track, and Kimi can ride at full speed straight away; he gets the special features of the track really fast, while the rest of us need a long stint before we're able to figure out how it'll work out when we start accelerating. And that ability is particularly important in Formula racing.'

I recall the Malaysian trip and the way Kimi drove

from the hotel to the circuit. He's unlikely to remember it, unlikely to take notice of the way he drives. It's what he does routinely.

Our chat moves back to childhood. The boys played, practised sports, mucked about. They were constantly on the move: football, ice hockey, athletics. Tuesday was the only day with no sport practice. On top of all that: tinkering with everything possible. Matti had the equipment, the boys had the enthusiasm. Rami tells me that, if a bicycle didn't look good, it was cut with an angle grinder and welded into a new shape. Matti let his boys do what they wanted pretty freely, and although not all their ideas were that brilliant, they were realised.

Karting. One word, a thousand stories. One word embracing the whole family. No other hobby is likely to be as all-consuming as karting. For the Räikkönens it meant doing things together, being together; it took everything and gave even more. They didn't know, back then, how much it would give to the younger son. It was a way of life, living for the moment. There was no reaching for the stars yet; their eyes were kept on the road. Their hands were covered in oil. They lived from hand to mouth, or, to be more precise, from hand to petrol tank.

'When I was young, tinkering with things was normal. Not anymore. Many have rich dads so they don't have to do anything much. But it's not something I thought about when I was young; it was normal to wash and maintain cars yourself. Of course, these days you've got these shitheads whose dads have got millions, so they don't do anything. They get there in a helicopter, everything's been laid on.'

**Kimi and Rami Räikkönen: excited by speed from early on.**

**Kimi's voice carries a** note of irritation felt by a driver who has come a long way. He talks like a mechanic – he holds them in high regard. Getting your hands dirty and understanding the car are fundamental things. Rami comes from the same place but with the difference that he finished the car mechanics' course that Kimi abandoned. But Rami knows that, even without the course certificate, his little brother understands what goes on inside an engine.

'You've got to be able to tell engineers and mechanics what the car feels like, how it behaves; you've got to understand technology, up to a point. A car mechanic's background is useful there,' Rami comments.

Kimi is attuned to a car's message. The spadework was done in childhood, in conditions of austerity. The family's used van was full of information and emotion. Nothing comes of anything without the latter. Kimi's mother knows it and has her memories.

'Sometimes, after we'd packed and squeezed all the karting gear into the van, I used to cry out, "I'm just so happy to be here." We always showed our feelings of happiness, hugged each other, felt close. It was our family's free time. I often said we're white gypsies in the sense that we spend winters paying off debts and, when spring comes, we're back on the road.'

Karting is more a way of life than a hobby. It's not a hobby in the same way as football, skating, ice hockey or horse riding – sports that require a bit of money and parental support. No youngster can take up karting without full family support and all its money. Ville Myllyrinne, the Finnish actor-comedian, knows all about it. He's been going to the races with his sons for a few years and talks about the essence of the sport in his colourful way. He became a karting parent as a 35-year-old and was totally ignorant of engines. It was a plunge into a strange new world. I'm sure Myllyrinne benefited from his comedian's background; otherwise he might have become a nervous wreck. He had to deal with two cars, an old van and a total lack of knowledge. 'I was a technological ignoramus but there were some damned nice people, who were willing to help with everything. It's a hell of a job for a father with zero knowledge, who doesn't understand anything about adjusting the chassis or the rest. It takes years to start getting to grips with. You've got to remember that, in a way, it's not a hobby, because it means competing all the time. And because I didn't have any idea of things like gear ratios, I just thought the boy was a hopeless driver. But it wasn't just about that, but about Dad being useless.'

Kimi listens and grins. For him, this is living and familiar history. If the event is on a weekend, you get there on Thursday, or on Friday at the latest. The racing takes place on Saturday and Sunday. The cars are then washed and serviced and packed, and the same routine is repeated the following weekend. Know-how is highly rated in this community; particularly fathers who have driven themselves or are able to repair or set up a car. In Kimi's case, it was his father Matti. No one cares about the parents' backgrounds: dignitaries and labourers are interchangeable in the shrill noise. And it all moves into overdrive, with parents shouting, red-faced, by the racetrack. Subsequent chats in the sauna sometimes continue till late. Ville Myllyrinne admits that speed is contagious and gets your nerves tingling. 'I've also shouted, "Don't fucking give them any space, just go in there!"' The mental turmoil of a karting dad is a familiar story to Kimi, and so is the way the parents sometimes go over the top in the evenings. Kimi recalls the summer nights of his childhood.

Karting. A single word, a thousand tales. A single word for the whole family.

**'The races were pretty** hectic sometimes; people got drunk and shouted, their heads full of beer. If you tried to sleep in a van and there was a crowd making a noise near you, of course you were pissed off. And people shout out all sorts of weird things by the racetrack. You don't hear anything anyway when you're driving with a helmet on. It's different in ice hockey: you hear everything. Mostly it's a game for the kids but it isn't for the parents.' He wants to clarify that his parents weren't that deeply into the extreme madness. Perhaps because in their heart of hearts they weren't only thinking of victories, and certainly not of a great future. The main thing was for the family to share something.

The resourcefulness of Kimi's family, which enabled him to get started, is thrown into even sharper focus when Myllyrinne outlines the present costs of the business. 'There's no average budget; it tends to grow all the time. In a main class, the engine costs a couple of thousand and the chassis a similar amount; in addition, you've got to buy a van and a trailer. Thousands disappear in no time at all. And then you enter a different realm altogether if you start driving abroad in earnest. A weekend costs between €5,000 and €15,000 – the difference depends on how much you're prepared to do yourself. If you pay €15,000 to some karting factory, then you get a mechanic, a data engineer and everything else. It's obvious no normal human being can go down that road.'

Kimi has understood, throughout his F1 career, what an enormous job his parents did. And he also realises that, without external finance, he would never have been able to get on in the sport. Many things have fallen into place. He has needed some luck, while one thing has been clear from the start: Kimi is extremely fast. Karting hints at something which is then crystallised in Formula 1: the differences are so minimal that you have to be, for that fleeting moment, more brazen and audacious than the others. A driver's nerve is tested in places where it should be impossible to pass – and yet someone does.

Myllyrinne talks about the wretched side of the coin. 'From the very beginning, people believe that their own son will become the new Räikkönen, or someone like that, and some are prepared to invest ridiculous sums of money, even though the facts clearly advise against it. It's an addictive sport because the difference between a top driver and someone almost at the top is so tiny. I know that there are lots of people doing the rounds of European races. They've taken out big bank loans and mortgaged their homes. And I know it'll come to nothing. When it gets just too big and you don't find a sponsor, it's so much better to walk away and put an end to the whole business.'

Rami continued in karting with Kimi for a long time before giving up and becoming a mechanic. 'I was about fifteen when I gave up; I lost my motivation. Also, I was 4–5 kilos too heavy. It's really good that all the work put in by Mum and Dad, plus luck, took Kimi to places where someone spotted his talent. And you've got to hand it to him: he just doesn't give up. Nothing else matters when he's got to overtake.' He currently looks after Kimi's real estate and day-to-day affairs, jobs he took over following their father Matti's sudden death.

At some point, Kimi became so quick that everyday life felt slow. School in particular: sitting, reading, swotting. Learning was made more difficult by his dyslexia, which he inherited from his mother. Paula thought that the boy should have received help for the condition straight away, from year one. 'Rami always got on well at school, but it was more challenging for Kimi because of the dyslexia. We had to fight till he reached the third year.'

'When Kimi had the patience to concentrate, things went well. When he had to repeat year five, it was really tough on him, but it was the right decision. It was better to repeat a year in the small school at Karhusuo, where his old mates still remained close by. The experience of going to the big school at Karakallio would have been a lot harder. Reading was never Kimi's thing; he was into doing things with his hands, and into sports and driving.'

The world has always been and will always be full of restless boys and girls who keep glancing around or picking their noses when they should be pondering mathematical formulae or the word order of the German language, but few of them end up in Formula 1. Kimi couldn't see that far ahead either, when, at the age of ten, he drove his first race in the Mini Raket class.

Karting was racing, though it didn't yet entail clenched teeth or white knuckles. Toni Vilander, a year younger, stepped on the gas next to Kimi and became a lifelong friend. Toni recalls that they weren't best mates straight away but, by and by, doing fun things outside the track welded the boys together. They were at the dizzying age of eleven when their spirits were high and they had no worries about tomorrow. Being friends came naturally. They could try to grab each other's hamburgers but not the other's place in the team. Toni remembers Kimi first visiting his home in Kankaanpää in 1993. Toni and Kimi have stayed in contact ever since, though their busy lives make it hard to arrange get-togethers. Toni Vilander has been driving sports cars for Ferrari for years.

The pace soon picked up. The Räikkönens were

surrounded by the smell of petrol and plagued by a shortage of funds. Racing required more and more money, and it wasn't easy to acquire sponsors. 'We needed more money all the time; it was never enough. My mum gave us some now and then. We had an account with Racing Jaatinen and settled it in winter,' Paula says.

Racing Service Jaatinen continues operating in the Konala district of Helsinki. Lasse Jaatinen, a qualified engineer and former racing driver, has followed the story of the Räikkönen family with lively interest. According to him, the family embodies the old ethos of the sport: doing things together. 'We still see that sort of father-son system among our customers. Masa [Matti] was a warm-hearted and loving father; there was a good atmosphere in that family. These days, there are more teams and there's less commitment in the business.'

Toni Saarinen, Jaatinen's right-hand man, agrees. He has won Finnish championships and is a car technician with over thirty years' experience in the field. The Räikkönens came to Jaatinen's shop in the early 1990s. 'We could get the stuff at good prices – it was a step forward. And they wouldn't have been able to go to European races if we hadn't leased the equipment. We did charge something for it; we used the same system with Toni Vilander's family,' says Jaatinen.

Tyres represented a major item of expenditure. One set costs €200, and one race uses up three sets. It was hard to extract that kind of money repeatedly from the parents' modest monthly pay packets.

Jaatinen recalls how Kimi's speed gradually got noticed.

'At the European Championship race in Lake Garda, Peter de Bruijn came to me and said: "Now I've seen it!" – and he was talking about Kimi.'

Kimi couldn't be bothered to read books but he made up for it with his ability to read the racetrack. Toni Saarinen remarks that a good driver is able to anticipate, to see as far ahead as possible, and to avoid collisions. And he's able to be aggressive at the right place. Kimi gained the upper hand within the team – something felt by his good mate and racing partner Osku Heikkinen, who almost always reached the finishing line as a solid number two. And Kimi, from Espoo, didn't fail to remind his Savonian friend of the position. Saarinen stresses that if you don't have a bottomless purse, you have no choice but to cut loose. The situation today is even more impossible: if you want to race for a factory team in Europe, you've got to find €150,000. We're no longer talking about a hobby for ordinary people. In Finland, though, you can still practise the sport with family support.

What made Kimi stand out? One factor was his age. He was challenging drivers who were four or five years older than him. It was something that stuck in people's minds – lots of people's minds. And the word got around, sometimes faster than a car.

Chance is even more effective than word of mouth. The reputation of the Räikkönen family as a knowledgeable bunch spread in the right directions. One day, the white gypsies met a group of marketing and sales professionals who had caught the speed bug and appeared at the karting track. They felt they had to get away from the conference room for a bit and inhale petrol fumes, becoming the so-called senior class, in which managing directors and marketing executives let off steam. It didn't take long for the class to be called the 'senile class'. It was in this context that the Räikkönens met, for the first time, Petri Korpivaara, Sami Visa and Riku Kuvaja. The last two would play major roles in Kimi's life later on. Kuvaja was Kimi's affairs manager from 2005 to 2015; Sami Visa has been doing the job since then.

But at that time they were successful businessmen, who needed all the help they could get in servicing, tuning or cleaning engines. 'There was no choice – we had to get a mechanic because we didn't know any more about the business than a pig knows about flying. Jukka Soimetsä suggested the Räikkönens,' Sami recalls. Rami was Kimi's mechanic at the time but received a substantial additional income from keeping the businessmen's cars shipshape. In turn, the financiers of the senior class were able to procure significant sponsors for Kimi, who helped the big, clumsy boys alongside his brother. This way, the Räikkönen family got a bit of oxygen for their hobby. Sokos Hotels, Carrols and Koff proved good partners, which guaranteed better equipment and more tyre sets.

Toni and Kimi advanced side by side in karting towards Europe. To get there, you needed to have money; and to be competitive there, you had to have speed. At the beginning, both appeared to be in short supply. Wind blew through the Räikkönens' wallet, and without outside help, they would have been stuck driving round in circles in Finland. Racing at European Championships would have remained a dream.

The help that made the difference arrived from within the extended family. Jussi Rapala, the husband of Paula Räikkönen's sister Valpuri, came from a line of well-known fishing lure manufacturers and was a keen motor sport fan. He opened his wallet – and with it the window to Europe. 'But we paid every euro back to Jussi later,' Paula points out.

Kimi takes a swig of water and drifts far away. He's trying to recapture his young self, a restless boy messing around in the technical school on a car mechanics' course. His eyes stray from books but start glinting and focusing as soon as they alight on an accelerator or a drive shaft. If I'm competitive in Finland, will I be all right in Europe? If I concentrate now, will I pass the next maths exam? What will I do if all the money spent on my hobby turns out to be wasted? What if I make a mess of big races? Nothing comes about without some pressure, but if the pressures get too heavy, it'll be white-knuckle time.

The young man, still at school and ignorant of his future occupation, was already mulling over its central questions.

# A SODDEN BALE OF HAY

**We've finished for the** day. I can sense that all that talking has been exhausting. Kimi jumps up from the divan and strides down the long hallway towards Minttu, Robin and Rianna. Before he leaves, we have agreed to go to the sauna and have a swim in the evening. But first, Kimi wants to be with his family, and I take myself to the gym ahead of him. We have also decided that, in the morning, we will move on to his recollections of Europe, a continent that looked like a big, frightening lump when he viewed it through the eyes of a seventeen-year-old with very little knowledge of languages other than his native Finnish.

The gym of the house features the full range of equipment designed to make you sweat. Here, Kimi has tortured himself for years in order to prepare for almost two hours of inhumane pummelling in a cramped car. Nothing will work unless your body is in perfect condition, including your neck, the back of your neck, shoulders and midriff. Motor sport entails many variables; therefore, the concept is worth splitting into two words: motor and sport. The driver can't influence the durability of the car, but he can work on his own body. There's a strange machine at the back of the gym – it turns out to be the seat of a Formula car. A helmet is connected, on both sides, to the chassis by cables, and the steering wheel is fastened to weights. The machine starts, the torture begins. My head is subjected to roughly the same g-forces as in a race, the steering wheel vibrates. I estimate I last one and a half minutes in the device.

The sauna is circular with a continuously heated Harvia stove in the middle. Kimi wasn't happy with the feel of the previous sauna, and wanted to engage a Finnish carpenter to make everything to as high a standard as possible. If you don't spend a lot of time at home, you want to enjoy it a lot when you do.

Kimi and Robin arrive for a swim. The energy of the two-and-a-half-year-old raises waves and lifts the atmosphere. Dad goes along with everything Robin fancies doing. He's teaching the boy to become a champion swimmer – something he already is himself. Kimi swims a few lengths; his freestyle technique is virtually faultless. Robin imitates him straight away. Imitation is necessary for the continuation of the human race, but it can, on the other hand, lead to habits that divide opinions. In Minttu's view, urinating outside is no longer acceptable behaviour, while Kimi has already got round to teaching the habit to Robin. Minttu knows that it dates back to a distant childhood. Kimi and Rami, brothers without an indoor loo, used to pee outside, and Kimi sees no reason to change now, since he's got the land to do it on.

Robin wants to show Dad and the visitor that he has learnt to hold his head underwater. The boy is praised for his first steps towards diving, and redoubles his efforts. Water splashes; some of it gets into his lungs. The scared boy coughs and his dad comforts him.

It's getting dark in the Swiss home. I go to the downstairs guest room. On the door it says: 'Regiment Räikkönen', a humorous sign from a man who abhors authority. The compulsory stint in the army wasn't easy for him, but the bitter memories have gradually morphed into sly humour. Before falling asleep, I recall a story told by Toni Vilander which is an even better example of Kimi's kind of humour. When the driver made his surprise comeback to Formula 1 in 2012, he called Toni and asked for the telephone number of J. Parkkonen, commander of Lahti sport troops. 'Kimi wanted to call him with the news of his comeback, explaining that it didn't matter that ten years had elapsed since his army days. Parkkonen took good care of us and was, in that sense, our team boss.'

There's no sign of the driver first thing in the morning.

Minttu is preparing a smoothie in the kitchen and says Kimi is still asleep. No news there. He sleeps whenever it's possible, anywhere. Sleep is for him as peaceful a place as a racing car. No one asks stupid questions, for one.

Eventually Kimi turns up on the middle floor. His voice is low, his hair sticks out, his lopsided smile comes easily. The porridge, berries and smoothie in front of him vanish quickly.

Robin wants to play before we move on to Europe. The games are boisterous, high-speed and loud. Small cars whiz across the living room. Robin crawls after them and chatters away in his own language, a mixture of Finnish, toddler talk and English. Kimi's expressions show that he's well into his son's play. He gets the hang of any action – he's always keen on action. He bends to tune Robin's toy cars to make them even faster.

Robin goes out with Minttu; we move into Kimi's room. Europe awaits.

By the mid-1990s, Finland had become old hat; it was time to try something bigger.

The Finnish climate can be a hell in four parts: a mild winter, a cold spring, a rainy summer and a muddy autumn. It's possible to race in a small car under a clear, blue sky for a few months at the most. In Italy, France and Spain you can burn rubber almost all year, so it's no wonder that Kimi Räikkönen and Toni Vilander went to their first race as underdogs. Their European rivals had been able to practise considerably more, their equipment was more expensive and they had traditions. Kimi, Toni and the other Finns had only two products on offer: speed and primeval fury. They can go a long way. Or you can end up pissed off, in a battered van, eating tinned tuna.

Kimi scratches his calf, returning to painful memories, though enough time has passed to gild them. You can still glimpse rust under the surface, however.

'Rami was my mechanic. We drove to the races in an old van, mainly on the family's own money, which was enough at the beginning. Jussi Rapala helped a lot, we wouldn't have got there otherwise; we went on borrowed money. Most of the big races were in Italy, and I figured out quite early that, damn it, Mum and Dad have thrown all their money at it, and then when we got there, I had the feeling that I'm not going anywhere. We had the van and a tent; once or twice we slept in some run-down hotel. That was quite normal then; now it feels strange with all the motor homes and stuff.'

Money was in short supply, but inventiveness made up for it. Matti, Kimi's dad, would sit down, his peaked cap pushed back, and ponder what he could design himself next. One day, the familiar crackle of the welding torch sounded in the garage. Matti was welding something. He came out and showed Paula lengths of pipe and a tarpaulin. He called the contraption a 'rain-repellent temple', and assembled it alongside the van to protect the karting equipment.

Kimi tested his speed for the first time in legendary Monaco in 1995. His Monaco Cup race ended in a sodden bale of hay. His future mechanic, Kalle Jokinen, accompanied the Räikkönens for the first time and retains a photographic memory of the incident. 'Kimi was doing great in that Monaco race and started the last lap in fourth place, a huge achievement. He didn't come to the finishing line when expected. I wondered what part of the car had failed. Kimi then arrived in a Transit van and cried bitterly. I asked what had happened. "I hit a bale of hay." He had swerved a little at this chicane made of bales of hay. He thought that the hay would fly out of the way but it had rained during the night and the bales weighed a ton, and that was the end of his first international race.'

In 1996, the following year, they went to the European Championships. It was a hard lesson, demonstrating that you don't succeed in karting by talent alone. This is how Kimi remembers it: 'It was a washout. I think Toni Vilander and I came last and second last. It was miserable, getting stuck. The car seizes up if you drive too slowly. There was a hell of a lot of rubber on that track. We felt that we'd never make it. There were lots of races when we didn't even get to the final. Then we changed tyres. First we had Vegas and then we got Bridgestones, and things were going better towards the end of the year.'

Kimi's success was also hampered by things other than a sodden bale of hay: a non-existent knowledge of languages, lack of money, and shyness. More often than not, this combination means you end up washing dishes or cleaning cheap hotels. How did Kimi succeed where many others didn't? If you prise success apart, a large quantity of small parts, like the components of a Swiss watch, pours out. In addition to a protagonist, a success story invariably includes several minor characters, who fall off the pages of history like breadcrumbs. Kimi's story is that of the whole gang. It required a father, a mother, a brother, Finnish sponsors, a mechanic, as well as messengers to spread the word about the fast boy to the right people, who in turn would pass it on to even more important decision-makers and risk-takers. Before you know it, out of the blue, he's there: in the heart of speed. More happened to him in three years than to many people in their lifetimes. The penniless boy suddenly finds himself in Formula 1, at the pinnacle of the sport.

**Kimi's success was also hampered by things other than a sodden bale of hay: a non-existent knowledge of languages, lack of money, and shyness. More often than not, this combination means you end up washing dishes or cleaning cheap hotels.**

In motor sport, opinions and preferences are of no importance in the presence of two great deciding factors: the chequered flag and the clock. In many other walks of life and occupations, there are viewpoints and assessments, which vary according to who is doing the talking. But when the chequered flag is waved, there is no point in explaining. And it's difficult in any case if you don't know English. On the other hand, there is no need for languages if your driving pleases the clock. Kimi's did, though eventually someone had to speak English.

At that time, Kalle Jokinen was Kimmo Liimatainen's trainer and mechanic but became free just at the right moment. Kalle had a crucial role over the next couple of years, when it was vital to demonstrate speed. He went to the Räikkönens' aid, accompanying the family as they toured European racetracks. There were successes – and large expenses. Somehow, they had to get hold of better equipment.

It was the year 1997. At this stage, Kalle's knowledge of languages and his experience proved beneficial to Kimi. Kalle had left a career in karting and minor Formulas and he knew a lot of people. And, of course, it's not necessary to know everyone: one is enough.

Kalle went to have a word with Peter de Bruijn, a Belgian, who was at that time engine tuner for CRG Racing Team. Peter knew Kalle as a karting driver and good mechanic. Twenty-one years later, de Bruijn has a clear memory of his encounter with Kimi: 'I first met Kimi in Lonato in Italy at the beginning of 1997. His mechanic, Kalle Jokinen, who had been a driver with us a few years earlier, came to ask if I could help his driver to get better engines because they had quite a small budget. I remember Manetti, one of our top drivers, losing to this unknown boy in red overalls. After the race, Kalle came to me and asked if I had seen his driver's performance. I asked which one of them he was. Well, the one in the red overalls. At that time, I worked for CRG, tuning engines for CRG Racing Team's drivers. I decided to let Kimi and Kalle have the spare engines no longer required by the top drivers.'

Peter also remembers a detail, which has become Kimi's trademark. 'Kimi once came to us with his parents, to talk over some practicalities. After a short time, we noticed that he had disappeared. His father Matti stated calmly that Kimi was bound to be asleep somewhere. I was a bit surprised when a little later on we found him asleep in a carton of Bridgestone tyres. I should have taken a photo. In any case, we then decided that Kimi would continue receiving support from me and CRG. I saw him improving all the time, but he was also a little lazy. We talked about it and I tried to influence his attitude.'

A year later, Peter de Bruijn set up his own team together with his wife, Lotta Hellberg, who drove in the same class as Kimi. The Finn was engaged by PDB Racing Team, and he and his mechanic began travelling to races. Kimi assembled microcars, which were for sale, and helped with practicalities. He got a bit of pocket money but the most important thing was to get to drive decent cars.

Kimi remembers an interesting detail about de Bruijn. 'Peter himself drove Formula cars for a bit but gave up because he got so bloody stressed by having to use seat belts. In one test, he was so pissed off that he undid the seat belt as soon as he left the garage. He drove off hanging out of the car. That made him see it wasn't his thing.' Sounds like a sensible decision.

Kimi shifts his gaze to look at a shelf that carries helmets from the past eighteen years – significant mementoes and handsome objects. When you look at them, you don't immediately associate the owner of the helmets with a youngster taking off in a Lada in October 1997. He had received the Soviet-made car suitable for wintry conditions from his mother's colleague Anne. Kimi and his mates replaced its engine with a better one at the technical school, and as soon as the driver got his driving licence, the tailgate of the Lada creaked open and in went the tool kit.

'I totally lost it with the school. I stuck the kit into the boot and headed for Holland. My mate Fore was in the school yard to see me off. Or he just had to see it.'

Kimi moved to Holland and lived with PDB Racing Team's mechanic in the town of Vlaardingen, close to Rotterdam. After a short while, Kalle moved to the same place and joined Kimi. And from there they drove in a van to races all over Europe. The equipment was almost as good as Kimi's ability to sleep. Peter de Bruijn bears witness to it: 'The name "Iceman" was invented later but we got a foretaste of what it meant. Kimi really didn't get stressed. I remember a European Championship race in France. He was always late when we left for a racetrack. I told him the night before that we wouldn't wait for him in the morning. In the morning Kimi rang and asked where I was. I told him I'd left as there had been no sign of him. The circuit was forty-five kilometres away and I was certain he wouldn't be on time for the practice session. He appeared half an hour after our arrival, smiling and relaxed, and said he had got a lift in another team's car. No problem.'

A hint of laziness, an outstanding ability to sleep, a relaxed mind, and high speed – Kimi had made an impression. Everything was possible – and impossible. Kimi's memories jump from good races to bad ones, and he doesn't once forget to mention Kalle, who understood engines and English.

Kimi's room suddenly feels large enough to accommodate a post-war house in Tampere. Kalle Jokinen, mechanic and trainer, sits on the ground floor of the house. He's a 45-year-old veteran of motor sport who travelled with Kimi in fluctuating circumstances all over Europe. Kalle's eyes light up when his mind goes back to those colourful times. He hasn't yet completely abandoned karting, though he currently makes his living in the district heating business.

'Peter promised me a job as a mechanic with his team, and Kimi a bit of pocket money for assembling the odd chassis and for welding work. Kimi was bloody good at working on engines, possibly the only one in F1 who can repair an engine single-handedly. He's a technologically competent bloke. We shook hands with Peter, and then we headed for Holland. We were on the move all the time but we were based in Holland. Kimi's speed was so breathtaking that Bridgestone invited us to a tyre test. Kimi and I started touring on our own. Peter handed over some guilders* and a credit card and we were off. Go on: go and do some racing. We even did all the tyre work together, while the others had separate men for those jobs. Kimi always made his own carburettor; no one else was allowed to touch it. Now that I've toured with small boys, I've noticed that it's all going in the wrong direction. They don't touch anything; they've got physiotherapists and managers from the age of ten. They don't really know anything about technology. That's bad. Kimi can develop a car.'

Kalle talks about the nomadic life of the two young people before and after Kimi had obtained his driving

---

* Dutch currency before the euro.

licence, before a race and after a race, before being drunk and after being drunk. The goings-on only differed from ordinary young people's lives in one respect: in the middle of it all, they were involved in racing in a small car. Speed was exciting, everyday life was austere, and sometimes reason fell by the wayside.

It was necessary to get a feel for traffic, even without a driving licence. According to Kimi, his first longish stretch without a licence was from Lahti to Helsinki. Kalle acted as a benign map reader and irresponsible adult. The van didn't swerve off the straight road; chicanes are few and far between on the Lahti route.

Kimi recalls driving without a licence at some point in Sweden, too. The trip to the race was a long one; the entourage included Anette Latva-Piikkilä, a karting driver; and Kimi's dad Matti, who was then also Anette's mechanic. They were travelling in her family's Hiace. 'The droning of the Hiace started making Dad drowsy and he wanted to have a break. I said we're not going to stop – I can drive. Dad said to wake him up when we were near Stockholm. I woke him at the harbour. I was fifteen.'

Kalle also remembers letting the underage driver get away with it. 'I was young and stupid and said: "OK, step on it." We often swapped seats without stopping. Kimi drove just as much as I did on German autobahns. We were at Imola at one point in some sort of underpowered hire banger. Kimi pleaded with me to let him drive to the hotel. I let him. He went round a roundabout lots of times with the car skidding nonstop. I watched his hands and feet and tried to work out how he got the car to go like that. Then I had a go myself – I had done some racing in my time. I couldn't make the car move like that. We then had a really good go of the roundabout. When we returned, the car still had its wheel rims – just about.'

Kimi recalls his longest trip with no breaks. They left Helsinki to drive to Ugento in Italy to take part in Bridgestone's tyre tests. The distance was 3,359 kilometres. 'The situation was good in one respect: I had a driving licence by then. We stayed in the car for three days, and nearly had a collision when I couldn't see properly anymore on the motorways. We had to stop at Rimini and got pissed. We stayed for two nights, one in a hotel and the other in the van because we were broke.'

As Kalle and Kimi drove round Europe, word spread in England. Peter Collins, an influential figure in the karting world, told David and Steve Robertson that there was a Finn on the move who was at least as fast as Jenson Button, whom they managed. They had recently got a contract for Button with the Williams team. Father (David) and son (Steve) didn't drag their feet. They found out about the duo's movements. And they weren't the only ones: Harald Huisman, the Norwegian talent scout, had also heard about the fast driver. And again, luck was on Kimi's side. They were at the Nordic Championship race in Mosse,

Norway, when Kimi's phone rang. He heard a strange language and passed the phone to Kalle, who listened and said they had to drop by and see someone called Huisman.

Harald Huisman was a former racing driver with an indoor karting track. Kalle relates an incident that played a part in us now sitting on Kimi's divan in a big house above the town of Baar. 'Huisman asked us to come round. He would feed us, and it would be good to meet. We sat there, busied ourselves somehow. We ate something. Then I asked Huisman if he wanted a new record for his track. He said the track was dusty and seconds slower in that state. I said that's not what I was talking about; I had asked if he wanted a new record. Kimi went on the track; it took a quarter of an hour for him to smash the old record.'

Huisman didn't waste any time in telling David Robertson about the incident, and Robertson didn't waste any time either.

# 'NO, I KNOW SO'

**The phone rang in** Holland. An unfamiliar number. Kimi has learnt to be cautious. He doesn't pick up. A foreign language, English, lies in wait on the receiver. Kalle answers. At the other end, far away in England, a gentleman speaks good, clear English, and he's got something to say. He asks them to come and visit. The purpose of the meeting is to discuss the young driver's future. Kimi is scared, Kalle is excited. David Robertson is a manager, whose protégé, Jenson Button, has just got a contract with the famous Williams team and now he wants to talk to them. But how do they put it to Peter de Bruijn, whose men they are?

Kalle and Kimi decide to try the truth, which had been the way forward up until now. Peter got angry and went as far as to say to Kalle, 'If you take away my top driver, you can take yourself out the door at the same time.' Kimi and Kalle took it to be a threat, which it was. Kimi consoled Kalle: 'I'll drive so fast that we're bound to make it.'

In the end, Peter met them halfway. He even lent them his wife's Renault Clio, and they set off in it. The meeting was due to take place in the Thistle Hotel in Brands Hatch. They reached the French border and slammed two Finnish passports on the desk. The immigration officer examined the passports, looked at the Clio and asked if the Finns had the necessary paperwork, i.e. permission to drive a car registered in Holland across the border. There were no papers, so there was to be no border crossing.

They returned to the car, humbled but seriously pissed off and some deep thinking followed. They had to get to the meeting; they had to find a gap in the border. Kalle shoved the map at Kimi and ordered him to find a smaller place where the officials wouldn't check. A possible spot was discovered fifty kilometres away, and the Finns in their Dutch-French car were allowed to cross. It was late by the time they arrived at Brands Hatch and they parked outside the hotel. The car seats were cranked into optimum positions, though going to sleep was easier for one of the duo.

In the morning, Kimi was nervous. He asked Kalle to do the talking; he himself would sit to one side, a silent, hang-around member of the club. Kalle liked the proposed arrangement, though he kept repeating a sentence for Kimi to say: 'My name is Kimi Räikkönen, nice to meet you.'

They entered the foyer of the luxury hotel and peered into

the restaurant. A gentleman of around fifty was seated at a table. Kalle knew immediately it was David Robertson, the manager. They shook hands, Kimi said his sentence, and Kalle assumed his speaking role. David asked if they would like something to eat or drink. The newcomers were too nervous to accept, even though their stomachs were crying out for toast, bacon, fried eggs, fruit juice and coffee after the long journey and bad night's sleep.

David put the questions, Kalle did the answering, and Kimi remained quiet. The atmosphere soon became warmer, talking got easier. Then David paused and asked Kalle to give his view of the situation.

Kalle said: 'If you give this boy a chance, he'll win the Formula 1 World Championship one day.'

David took a swig from his glass and asked:

'Do you think so?'

'No, I know so,' Kalle replied.

David looked at Kalle, then at Kimi, and promised to explore, with experts, the possibility of a test and other follow-up activities. A silence ensued. Then David asked what role Kalle the mechanic might play in the matter – was he part of the package? Kalle answered that he was simply a mechanic and a friend of Kimi's. Kalle said later that, had he answered any other way, David might have thought there were too many cooks in the kitchen. What he thought of at the time was the agreement he and Kimi had made: we'll drive so fast that we're bound to succeed;

no point in saying anything more at this point. David said he understood the situation and handed Kimi a thick wad of papers. It was a draft agreement. Kalle knew that, by signing the agreement, Kimi would write his mechanic out of his everyday working life. Later events would prove that Kimi never forgot him.

Kalle and Kimi shook hands with David, walked out to the Renault Clio and drove back to Holland. At home in the small room, they spread the contract documents on the floor and began studying them. Kalle led the examination. There were lots of words, some of them extremely difficult. Kalle had good reason to be suspicious; he'd had bad experiences of written agreements. During his own racing career, he had been in a bad collision. The resulting neck injury put paid to his career and the promised compensation money never arrived. The legal language of the current contract was pretty convoluted and the papers lay on the floor for a week. Then they were sent to Sami Visa in Finland. He checked the text with Tommi Mäkinen, the rally driver, who had experience of contracts of this nature. Everything was fine, the document was credible. After that, it was time to decide.

The agreement was for fifteen years. Kimi was terrified, Kimi was excited, Kimi went into overdrive. He was at a crossroads. From now on, driving would cost nothing: he'd always have the equipment, and no one close to him – Mum, Dad or any other relative – would have to line up the banknotes.

The contract contained exciting figures, which the young man, a drop-out from technical school, viewed in astonishment. He would be paid £1,000 a month, equivalent to 10,000 marks – meaning 120,000 marks per year. It was an enormous amount for a boy who, until now, had only handled crumpled 10-mark notes and the odd smooth 100-mark note.

Kimi had only ever wanted to drive. Now he would get paid for it. There might not be a second chance. A race-track offers several alternatives; the piece of paper gave him only one option: he had to sign it, stick out his foot, step on the gas and look into the horizon.

Before signing the final contract, the Robertsons wanted to ascertain their driver's speed. David announced that Kimi should come and show them what he could do on the Snetterton track in December. Fine. There was only one snag: Kimi had never driven a single metre in a Formula car, which is totally different from a karting car. Kalle and Kimi faced a pressing problem: Kimi *had* to try out the car before Snetterton. 'Marko Koiranen promised to lend a car, and we went to Alastaro to test it. And straight away, there was a new track record,' Kalle recalls.

'A slippery thing. That's what it felt like. No wings. No grip. It looked like a toy car.' Now, the memory makes Kimi laugh, but it wasn't much fun inside the car at the time. A lot was at stake on the first few laps. His nerves jangled, his knuckles were white.

## He had to sign it, stick out his foot, step on the gas and look into the horizon.

'On the fifth lap I nearly drove into the wall. I just about managed to stay on the track. If I hadn't, I bet the contract wouldn't have come to anything. A few days later, at Donington, I was just as fast as their own drivers.'

And Kimi didn't know that Steve, David Robertson's son, was one of the people by the trackside. Steve had a career in the British F3 series behind him, and he understood the sport; he had raced with Mika Häkkinen and Mika Salo several times. His father had asked him to go and take a good look at this boy. Steve has a vivid recollection of Kimi's first few laps: 'I observed the way that he drove at the bends. I was stunned by the way he handled the car and kept it under control. He could go to the limit without crashing it. That's something you remember. And when he got out, I was surprised how young he looked, no more than fourteen.'

Kimi got out of the car and signed the piece of paper that sealed his future. Initially, the contract was for fifteen years, but the Robertsons asked him if he wanted to make it shorter. The eventual decision was for twelve years. Even after that, however, and following David's death, Steve has taken care of Kimi's contracts.

The memory, going back eighteen years, floats in Kimi's room and is weighty enough to create a silence. 'Dave and Steve have been like a father and a brother to me, decent blokes. They have always been on the lookout for the best alternative for me,' says Kimi.

The contract meant a move to England. Kimi, who knew practically no English, packed his red suitcase and had no idea of the journey that awaited him. If he had known, he might have stayed in Karhusuo. And Kimi wasn't the only one who left. His elder brother Rami departed in January 1999 to do his national service and silence descended on Kuru Road in Karhusuo. The almost simultaneous departure of both boys was a bitter pill for Masa and Paula to swallow. The garage was empty of boys; Masa was shaken.

KOEAJO: LEGENDS FORD

VERTAILU: KANSANKILPURIT

BMW kauden yllättäjä **F1**

Jouhki tyrmää kierrätyksen **WRC**

Casey Stonerin muodonmuutos **RR**

Luunmurskaaja Vehviläinen **MX**

# VM

vauhdinmaailma.fi

12·2007 6,95 €

## Isä oli sankari
MARCUS GRÖNHOLM PALASI
LAPSUUDEN MAISEMIIN

## Mika Salon
### hurjat ideat
NASCAR, A1 GP, AVARUUS...

# Uskomaton
# tie mestariksi

KIMI RÄIKKÖSEN ALBUMIKUVAT
JA SAO PAULON IHMEEN TAUSTAT

KISAT
Fuji
Shanghai
Brasilia
Katalonia
Korsika
Japani

V-M SAARELAINEN     MIKA KALLIO     HENRI HIMMANEN

Cover of the December 2007 issue
of *World of Speed* magazine.

# THE BIG WORLD AND THE SMALL WORLD

**A fax whooshes out** of a machine in Kuru Road in Espoo in January 1999. In it, David Robertson explains where in London Kimi has to come on a certain date. Masa and Paula see Kimi off to the airport with his red suitcase. At the last moment, Masa asks if Kimi needs any money for the trip. Father and son agree on a round figure of 100 marks. (A bit of information for younger readers: the sum would be equivalent to €17.)

Kimi boards the plane and wonders what he will say at the other end in three hours' time. His head contains a couple of hundred grams of English. A bit more would be good – say, a kilo. He's nervous.

He arrives at Heathrow airport. There's no sign of Steve Robertson, or Dave. They promised to come and meet him. Or then he has got it wrong. He panics, takes the fax with the hard facts from his bag and sees the name of a station, train timetables and addresses. The place is Rugeley, which isn't in London but somewhere further out. It's a small town. He's close to panic-stricken but calms himself. He'll be all right, somehow, though this is a hundred times harder than driving. Peace reigns inside a car; outside, it's chaos.

Kimi finds himself in London, at Piccadilly Circus tube station. He stands there, looking lost. All of a sudden, Steve Robertson pops up, gives Kimi a large Nokia mobile and instructions, and leaves. Kimi had thought Steve would take him to the house of the man from Haywood Racing Team, or at least to the right train. It doesn't happen. The words 'what the fuck' show up on Kimi's forehead in invisible letters. Steve's instructions appear to say that he needs to use a train, a taxi, a bus and another taxi. Or just a train. It's as clear as mud.

Meanwhile, back home, Kimi's mum Paula sits at work in an office of Kela, the Finnish government benefits agency, in central Espoo. She's a nervous wreck, afraid that Kimi won't get to his destination with the instructions he's been given.

On the train, Kimi shows his ticket and the directions to some passengers but communications fail. He thinks he's on the wrong train. It's getting dark. He takes the Nokia mobile out of his bag and tries to figure out how it works. He can't.

He shows his ticket to another passenger and tries to stammer something but the English language gets stuck in his throat. Judging from the fellow passenger's expressions, he may well be on the right train. He starts re-examining the mobile, and keys in the numbers. He lifts the phone to his ear, hoping that the area codes are right.

His mum answers and exhales. It's the boy's voice from the big, wide world. Kimi says he may be on the right train. *May* be; it's not certain, but he hopes so. Paula asks him to call as soon as he's got to where he should be.

**There's nobody to meet him. It's late; it's eleven o'clock by now. Kimi sits on the red suitcase. No one comes. It'll all come to nothing. He'll never get there. He'll never get into a car.**

Kimi gets off the train at Rugeley station. Again, there's nobody to meet him. It's late; it's eleven o'clock by now. Kimi sits on the red suitcase. No one comes. It'll all come to nothing. He'll never get there. He'll never get into a car.

Eventually, a stranger turns up and says hello. His name is Jim Warren, the team boss of Haywood Racing. Kimi tries out his scant vocabulary; the words stumble.

The main thing is that he has found his way to the small town of Rugeley, which is around 200 kilometres from London. Kimi gets to race, makes tea for the mechanics and starts learning the language. By and by, everything falls into place.

Children are the best thing in the world, small children in particular. Jim Warren, the team boss, has two boys, neither of whom knows his mother tongue yet. Kimi begins to learn English with them. All three are on the same starting line. Kimi goes driving, and when he gets home, he speaks English with the children. With children, you don't have to worry about making mistakes.

A treasure turns up in Warren's home: a large collection of video tapes full of races in Formula Ford and Formula Renault classes. Kimi watches them two or three times. You can always learn something: about tactics, bends, overtaking – and the commentator's language.

After a while, Steve Robertson asks Kimi to relocate to their place at Chigwell in Essex, and the Finn moves into a large upstairs flat in the Robertsons' house. The flat would later be used in the filming of the drama series *Footballers' Wives*. The upstairs represents a unique world. Before Kimi, the space was occupied by an ageing porno king, whose taste in interior decoration was not minimalistic in the Nordic way. The apartment contains several groups of sofas covered with leopard print, there are pictures of naked women on the walls, and ceilings clad with mirrors. Kimi finds the place a tad nauseating, particularly as he himself hails from a small, modest house.

Scott, one of Steve's two brothers, is a keep-fit fanatic and a bundle of muscles, and trains with Kimi. Sweat knows no language barriers. Kimi goes to races with Steve. The events go well and badly at the same time: the driver does well, but the car goes badly. Haywood Racing isn't able to offer a competitive car. The driver does his utmost but fails to win. The first car is a French Mygale, which is slow and ugly – a poor combination. Kimi comes third and second, and in the third race, he crashes the car. After that, Dave Robertson announces that there will be no more driving during that season.

Bloody hell.

Tail between legs.

In all, a shitty trip.

In his mind's eye, Kimi can already see the mocking headlines of the Finnish magazine *World of Speed*. 'Is this, once more, the end of a Finnish racing driver's international career?' Nothing for it but to step on the gas in Finnish karting, and from there move into some Teboil grease pit for the annual servicing of Toyotas and Opels.

Kimi travels back to Finland and fails to grasp Dave Robertson's thoughts or plans. His head is filled with the words of his mechanic friend Kalle Jokinen, tales of the precariousness of the sector. Dave assures Kimi that the decision was due to the poor car, and a decent team would be found for the next season.

*Yeah, yeah. I'll believe it when I see it.*

Kimi returns to Finland, unsure of his future. He doesn't hear from the manager for a long time. He goes karting using Peter de Bruijn's equipment in Finland and in Europe. Money is in short supply.

One weekend Kimi is at the Down by the Laituri rock festival in Turku with his mates. His pockets are empty, his head throbs with a hangover he can only blame himself for. He walks to a cash machine, certain that it will display a balance of zero.

*What the hell?*

There are over 20,000 marks in his account. Kimi finds it hard to believe that the amount is real, because he doesn't, at that moment, remember what the contract says: 'We'll pay you £1,000 per month irrespective of whether you get to drive or not.'

The party in Turku continues, of course, with Kimi harbouring nice thoughts about his reliable manager. Soon afterwards, Dave calls from England to tell Kimi that he will be able to drive with the better equipment of Manor Motorsport during the winter series starting in the autumn.

In the autumn, Kimi's world is split in two: the big world, or England; and the small world, or the army. The worlds stand for 'open' and 'shut'; opportunity and duty. Race engineers give you tips, army officers give you orders.

Kimi becomes a citizen of two countries. He gets to taste something that he will experience more and more in the coming years: a nomadic existence. He moves from a cramped car into an aeroplane, from there into the army's fragrant quarters, and soon he's back on a plane, heading for a race again.

Kimi-Matias Räikkönen enters the Finnish Defence Forces' Sports School in Lahti on 4 September. It's a tough place for someone who is not used to taking orders from anyone. A silver lining is provided by Toni Vilander, a good mate and rival, donning the grey uniform at the same time.

Kimi's mother Paula later revealed she was afraid the boy wouldn't be able to cope with the army. Her concern was well-founded, because Kimi and discipline was a bad combination. And when the demands of constant trips to foreign races were added, the young man began to think of putting an end to the whole army business. Luckily for Mum, he dropped the idea.

**Kimi's mother Paula later revealed she was afraid the boy wouldn't cope with the army. Her concern was well-founded, because Kimi and discipline was a bad combination.**

**The physical exertions of** army life weren't a problem for a superbly fit young man, but the timetables were. For a super sleeper, getting up at six in the morning is toxic, particularly when the commands start immediately. Kimi tries to apply reason, with varying success. His sensitive nose scents any whiff of freedom. Every time there's the smallest opportunity to prolong leave at the other end, he seizes it. The army personnel aren't familiar with the race schedules, and Kimi informs the military staff of his own flexible version. If a race ends on Sunday, he says it won't end till Monday. He doesn't go back to Lahti from the airport but takes a day off. Sometimes he spends it at home, sometimes with his cousins in Vääksy.

Manor Motorsport's car, the Italian Status, is much faster than the equivalent provided by Haywood Racing. Kimi wins all four races of the winter season. Dave and Steve Robertson realise that they have made a contract with an exceptional talent.

Victories have to be celebrated, of course. Moderate alcohol consumption hadn't yet arrived in Finland, where a bucketful was preferable to a goblet. But when you're in a state of joyous intoxication, you forget to keep an eye on the watch. It gets late whether you do or don't. One night, the army's clock showed a distinctly different time from the watches of Kimi and his mates. There was no way of closing the gap – they had to creep back in somehow without anyone noticing.

Now the grown-up Kimi talks in his own words about the events of the long night, which earned him the unofficial record for the length of time anyone had ever been gated at the barracks:

'I was having a drinking session with my cousins at the Rapalas' house. If I remember rightly, Toni Vilander was due to take me and Osku Heikkinen back. We said to Toni that we couldn't go in through the gate while pissed out of our minds. He should drop us by Lahti Road; we'll go over the fence, so no one will see us.

'As luck would have it, a military policeman stopped nearby when we were standing by the ditch. He wondered why on earth those guys were there in army gear. I dived into the ditch. Osku Heikkinen froze. I heard the policeman ask, "Where is your mate? We saw there were two of you." Osku said that he didn't know anything. They threw him into the back of the van. I had already thrown my jacket over the fence when I heard they had sent dogs to the area. There was a bloody big field and I ran like hell across the grass. I rushed into our place and said to the sentry: "Make sure you don't tell anyone that I've come." I ran upstairs and threw the blanket over myself.

'Ten minutes must have passed. It's hard to measusre time when you're pie-eyed. Then an officer came in, switched on the light and called my name. I shouted, "Why the fuck are you making that racket? Some of us are trying to sleep!" Two minutes passed before he came back and said: "You bloody well come here, Räikkönen. Now." I was lying in the bunk, covered in grass after crawling in that ditch. Osku Heikkinen had confessed everything. He had broken down under pressure; otherwise he would have ended up in prison. They knew full well there were two guys. I got up and swayed and zigzagged from wall to wall. I was breathalysed. The result was around 1.5 per mil. Then they ordered me to go to bed.

'In the morning I remembered that I had a weekend race in England in two weeks' time. I was fucked if I didn't get there. Then I thought that I'd better scarper first thing in the morning because I'd be gated whatever happens and wouldn't make it to the race. I thought, *I'll run across that same field.* I met the captain on the stairs and saluted. He didn't yet know about the previous night's events. I walked over the grass, ordered a taxi back to the Rapalas' at the nearby petrol station and switched off my phone.

**'The sergeant major shouted, red-faced, and asked how the hell I had managed to escape the dogs. I replied that it's exactly what you teach us here. We're Scouts after all.'**

'Then the phones went mad. The lines were hot: I hadn't just got drunk and been late, but I had also run away. Someone from AKK Motorsport, the national motor sports federation, phoned my cousin, but we just lay by the river drinking beer. Everyone was shouting that "you bloody well better get back to the barracks". I then phoned the captain and I said I wasn't coming because I wouldn't be allowed to go to the race whatever I did. I struck a deal with him: I would come if he let me go to the race. My cousin gave me a lift to the service station where the captain came to get me.

'I was tipsy at that stage, too, and that's why the unravelling of the situation didn't start till next day. The sergeant major shouted, red-faced, and asked how the hell I had managed to escape the dogs. I replied that it's exactly what you teach us here. We're Scouts after all. As far as I remember, I was gated for something like twenty days.

'I stayed put the following weekend; the race was the weekend after. Though I was gated, I didn't have to do anything as long as I went to report regularly. The captain asked me to come along when they did some skeet shooting in the forest. They shot at disks, and grilled sausages. It was really relaxing.

'But then they said the following week that I wasn't allowed to go to the race after all. I said, "That's it then, I'm finished with the army." Then they phoned from AKK and my managers Steve and Dave got in touch, but the situation was unchanged. I said to the captain: "Fucking dickhead. You bullshitted me."

'They made me ladle out some soup from the back of a lorry in Lahti Road. They were doing an exercise on bicycles. Suddenly a military police vehicle stopped by the lorry. They came to get me and I was allowed to go to the race. They asked when the race would finish and I said I thought it was on Tuesday though I knew it was Monday. I spent the extra day at home.

'I won the race.'

# MIDWIFE TO A RACING DRIVER

**What does a penniless** Finnish driver aged twenty-one need in order to drive in Formula 1? How many midwives are required for the birth of one Formula 1 driver? And why is it so quiet in the maternity ward? Is the pinnacle of motor sport a team sport after all? Kimi Räikkönen's career was made possible by a number of people who believed that he, of all people, could drive faster than his contemporaries on an enclosed track.

I think of these things as I open door D of the Helsinki Deaconess Institute in February 2018. I'm met by a bearded man of around sixty with a ponytail. He has tied a colourful scarf around his head and is wearing ancient tracksuit bottoms, a sports shirt and a waistcoat with pockets. He looks like a man for whom comfort is more important than outward appearance. He's one of the midwives who assisted at the birth of a new F1 driver over twenty years ago.

The man's name is Jukka Viitasaari, and he is a nurse and physiotherapist by profession. He resembles a shaman and his nickname is Viita. He leads me into a large basement room with an armchair, a rocking chair, books, posters, photos, sports clothes, and mountain and touring bikes.

We shake hands. Viita has done a long stint of working with top sportsmen; in recent times, he has concentrated on looking after the elderly. He's one of the people who trained Kimi to withstand vibration, wobbling, loud noise and landscapes that change in the blink of an eye.

Viita invites me to sit in the rocking chair and serves tea from a Thermos flask. Time stands still; the conversation meanders. His list of clients is long and impressive: Arto Bryggare, hurdler; Valentin Kononen and Sari Essayah, race walkers; Juha Salminen, enduro driver; Pekka Vehkonen, motocross driver; Janne Lahtela, mogul skier. And Kimi.

Viita recalls his journey with Kimi. AKK Motorsport asked him to take a look at a karting group in Vierumäki. They knew at AKK that he had already worked with Mika Salo, the F1 driver. At Vierumäki, he encountered an exceptionally talented generation: Markku Palttala, Toni Vilander and Kimi Räikkönen.

'Kimi is a cat. Lively and bouncy. A cat does what she wants, a dog does as he's told. You can't order Kimi about.'

Viita says Kimi wanted to improve himself because the next classes of cars demanded even greater levels of fitness. The driver first came to him in 1996, and they kept in touch until the first F1 race in spring 2001.

**'I noticed straight away that Kimi improved at a terrific pace, because he had a genuine desire to improve. Then one day we got a request from Sauber Team that Kimi should run the Cooper test. Matti Väisänen, the talent scout helping Jari Kurri, was a witness. Kimi ran 3,300 metres.'**

'Kimi was highly competitive. I recall Heikki Kovalainen taking part in skiing races, and Kimi wasn't far behind. We went cycling, swimming, worked on his neck and did a lot of balancing exercises. We got the proper toys: mountain and racing bikes. We placed a plank on a ball to improve balance. I noticed straight away that Kimi improved at a terrific pace because he had a genuine desire to improve. Then one day we got a request from Sauber Team that Kimi should run the Cooper test. Matti Väisänen, the talent scout helping Jari Kurri, was a witness. Kimi ran 3,300 metres.'

Suddenly, Viitasaari gets up from his battered armchair and asks me to take a look at a framed picture on the wall. It shows two smiling men with shorn heads, Kimi's father Matti and Viitasaari. It was taken in the Melbourne sun after Kimi's first F1 race. 'We promised to crop each other's heads if Kimi got into the points. He drove well – so it was off with the hair. The toilet was nearly blocked with it all.'

Viita takes swigs of tea and mulls over my question: 'What was needed for the young driver to succeed in Sauber's first F1 tests?' There are many answers – the way a cat has many lives.

'Kimi sees incredibly quickly. Eyes convey information. It's a talent to be able to perceive shape and movement. We also practised handstands and headstands – it helped him to get the measure of a space when it was upside down. In this, he was just as phenomenal as Juha Salminen, the enduro driver. And you can't forget low-impact exercise. Kimi understood it. He didn't use a heart-rate monitor. We practised swimming techniques; he learnt quickly, understood the resistance of water, gliding along it. And once you've learnt, you want to repeat what you've learnt.

Repetition is the basis for everything. I said to artist Osmo Rauhala that I'd like to learn to draw. Osmo said it was perfectly possible. Around 10,000 hours would be enough.'

Viita chuckles softly. 'But Kimi liked repetition – he didn't have to force himself.' He pours more tea from the flask and talks about his long career with sportsmen. In the next four years, his last at work, he'll be occupied with older people. Viita is interested in movement – from cradle to grave. 'When someone gets out of bed, it's a miracle and cause for celebration. We're as young as our spines. Practical stuff – that means the front line – is my thing. That's why I'll work with people till the end.'

Viita points out that our teacups are empty. It's time to take a look at the gym and the swimming pool. We walk in the depths of the labyrinthine building, formerly the premises of Hotel Aurora. The modest gym is located at the end of a long corridor and contains only basic equipment – weights, bars, fitness balls and benches.

Viita takes out a plank; you put a tube or a ball underneath. The device is called a rola-bola.

'This is a brilliant piece of equipment for balance training. Kimi used a bowling ball – not many can do that.'

Viita throws two thick, lumpy cushions onto the floor and asks me to stand on them. He calls them pads. It's hard to keep my balance, my body wobbles. Viita gives me a stick for support. I shift my centre of gravity forward and stare at the wall. I sway. And now I have to crouch – slowly.

Viita smiles. 'It gets to your ankles, activates them. This simple exercise strengthens the small muscles of your ankles.' I move onto the floor from the pads; my ankles are aching.

Viita takes me to the swimming pool and we stand on the edge, silent. He studied in America, at Tulsa University, Oklahoma, in his younger days. There he saw something that opened his eyes. After difficult knee operations, as soon as the stitches had been removed, patients were taken to the swimming pool and started treading water. It was gentle and painless exercise. Viita brought the concept of water running to Finland.

We talk about life. Viita says he is a believer and lifts his eyes to the basement ceiling. 'God called me to go among the elderly during the last few years of my working life. I also run a keep-fit group for older men in my own time. I expect I'm trying to be some kind of pastor, who says that it's time to crucify your baser passions and desires if you, by any chance, have led a dissolute life.'

We talk about the driver. 'Kimi has got a big heart. He watches and listens; he doesn't speak immediately. While you're talking, you're not receptive. "Observe" was the advice of an old monk. Kimi doesn't like to talk to total strangers. Idle conversation makes the battery run low, and the battery must be fully charged. Then, when he comes out with a statement, it's often something considered.'

We talk about old people and how they should be

physically lifted up. Suddenly, Viita comes very close and demonstrates. 'I went to a wrestling ring to observe the movements and holds of the sport. In wrestling, you get close, under the ribs.' Viita pushes his hands under my armpits and onto my back, and lifts me up – strongly and safely. I feel I'm a young oldie and remember what Kimi said to me about this man: 'Viita is sort of a bit different.'

Kimi in Sauber uniform.
**PHOTO © SUTTON IMAGES**

# THE BIRTH OF A DRIVER

**Kuru Road, Espoo, summer** of 2000. Kimi is drinking beer outside with his cousin Jouni Forström. The phone rings. The long row of numbers on the display means that the call comes from abroad. It's his manager, Dave Robertson. Kimi puts the beer can down and pricks up his ears. Dave says that Kimi gets to test Sauber's F1 car in September.

It can't be true.

It is true.

Dave says he'll go over the details later. Kimi announces to his cousin Jouni that one more celebratory can is called for. But before that, he has to make a call.

A forest in central Finland on the same day: Masa and Paula are watching their elder son Rami's rallying event when Masa's phone rings. It's Kimi. The boy's message is brief but so sharp it pierces his dad's heart. Matti has to sit down, away from the others.

Paula notices that Masa has gone to sit behind the family's old van. That's nothing new. He often sits, his cap pushed back, planning something new. Paula thinks he was born old; he appears older than his years, always thinking of things. But now he looks different, as if he's had a shock. Paula asks: 'What is it?' Masa tells her that their boy gets to test Sauber's F1 car in September. Paula nearly faints; he takes hold of her.

A little later, Kimi's assistant Kikka Kuosmanen rings to say that Dave Robertson thinks Paula and Masa ought to come along to watch the tests. They hesitate. They can't afford a trip like that. It would cost 12,000 marks, or around €2,000 in current money.

Once in a lifetime.

There won't be another opportunity.

They'll take a loan.

On 12 September, they're at Mugello in Italy. Everything seems unreal. All that's known is that Peter Sauber is looking for a new driver to replace Mika Salo, who is moving to Toyota.

The slight young man lowers himself into Sauber's C19 car. He faces his first test lap in a real F1 car. The young man is scared – not of driving, but of failing. He's got to drive fast, stay on the track. He's got to meet the expectations, which are so high they're almost out of sight.

He starts the car. A terrible, ear-splitting noise follows. The first straight isn't important; anyone can drive on a straight with their foot down. It's the bends that decide everything, including the fractions of a second. The young man turns the wheel; his neck hurts, his hands tremble. Every instance of braking and every bend pummels his body.

**The slight young man lowers himself into Sauber's C19 car. He faces his first test lap in a real F1 car. The young man is scared – not of driving, but of failing.**

'At the beginning, I could do two laps at a time. Mugello is one of the most taxing circuits. In those days, Sauber didn't even have power steering. I couldn't hold my head upright.'

Kimi drove twenty-nine laps on the first day, and as many as forty on the next. The times improved as he got the feel of the car. He examined the telemetry data with Sauber's engineer, finding new braking spots and driving angles for the bends. The results were so convincing that Peter Sauber, who had arrived at the scene for one day only, was convinced about the young man's ability.

'He was walking on air. His feet must have been at least a metre off the ground. And even Schumi [Michael Schumacher] had asked who this young and fast driver was,' Paula recalls.

Peter Sauber wanted Kimi in his team, though he didn't yet say so to the driver. Another test was arranged for 28 September. After that, the way forward was clear: F1 driver Kimi Räikkönen was born.

Only he wasn't. He still needed a superlicence, a prerequisite for driving in F1. It was uncertain before the 2001 season whether Kimi would obtain one. They were granted by the FIA, the international motor sport federation, and the conditions include having racing experience in certain smaller Formula classes. The Renault series Kimi had driven in was so small that experience gained in it wasn't deemed adequate.

The driver wrote a letter to the top brass. His managers, Steve and Dave, composed the actual text but Kimi copied it in block letters on a piece of paper. The letter argued convincingly why he should be allowed to drive in F1. Max Mosley, FIA president at the time, was the only one to vote against. It has to be said that many influential figures in the sport had doubts about Kimi's ability to cope in the elite class, considering his scant experience to be a safety risk.

Eventually, though, the licence was granted and the road was clear.

'Masa looked cool as a cucumber but he was on fire inside. Of course he was proud. Masa said to Anne, a good friend of mine, "Tug my sleeve if this goes to my head." And it did, naturally enough, and no one wanted to tell him; he was that proud of his boy. We never imagined that Kimi would get there. I thought that the boys might become international enough to get jobs as mechanics at some good team. A hobby could become a job,' Paula says.

Kimi was accepted as a talented and fast driver, but he wasn't yet fit enough for sixty-lap F1 races. He began training under the guidance of Josef Leberer, Ayrton Senna's former trainer, in order to acquire the fitness level required for racing.

Kimi Räikkönen drove his first F1 race in Australia on 4 March 2001 and was sixth straight away. Dave and Steve Robertson saw that the risk had been worth taking. They thought that Kimi's strong character was a result of having to do things unaided, without a big budget. During that season, Kimi came fourth twice.

His first-year wages were $500,000 plus $50,000 for every point. At that time, the average Finnish pay was around 140,000 marks per year (about $27,000).

Money could be discussed now; previously the only talk had been about the lack of it.

With McLaren 2002–2006.
PHOTO © SUTTON IMAGES

# FINISHING SCHOOL

**Kimi Räikkönen drove so** fast during his maiden season that he was given the chance to drive even faster: McLaren wanted to buy him from Sauber in the middle of his contract period. Peter Sauber didn't want to end the contract. Often, when money talks, all you see is numbers on a piece of paper. This time you saw lots more: McLaren acquired Räikkönen by providing the Swiss team with splendid trucks and a very expensive wind tunnel. Years later, members of the Sauber staff joked about the tunnel and how Kimi got it for them.

McLaren signifies a dramatic turning point in Kimi's life. Now he's in a big team, surrounded by eminent sponsors, scrutinised by a strict boss, blinded by the media spotlight. Yesterday he showed promise; now he gets results. He has been noticed.

The young man in his early twenties got what he ordered:

speed. And he also got a freebie that comes with speed: disproportionate attention. He wasn't left alone anywhere; his private life became fertile ground for gossip, which sometimes produced thistles and at other times spring flowers.

**The beginning was brilliant; the omens were good. But what happened at the very next race in Malaysia was a sign of what would become the curse of his whole time with McLaren: the engine fell apart.**

One year earlier, Kimi had met a nineteen-year-old model called Jenni Dahlman. They were engaged soon afterwards, and once their relationship was official, they became big celebrities in a small country.

Kimi was third in his first race in Australia and drove the fastest lap. The beginning was brilliant; the omens were good. But what happened at the very next race in Malaysia was a sign of what would become the curse of his whole time with McLaren: the engine fell apart.

In no other sport does success depend on the tools as much as it does in Formula 1.

During his time with McLaren, 2002–06, Kimi experienced twelve engine failures in the middle of races. Points that should have been secure were scattered onto the asphalt. Without technical glitches, he would have won two championships. Equipment failures aren't unknown in other sports, of course, but it's hard to imagine that the consequences would be quite as dire as in F1. In cross-country skiing, lubrication may fail, but it's impossible to imagine a skier blaming his back-up team throughout his career. And we can't imagine Roger Federer blaming his defeat on a poor racket or a ball with a wobbly flight path.

Formula 1 folk like to talk in the conditional: 'If the engine had lasted ... If that driver hadn't hit me at that corner ... If the safety car hadn't been introduced ... If the sun were the moon and pigs could fly ...' Speculation of that nature is the favourite hobby in the paddock; gossip comes as a solid number two.

One thing was plain sailing for Kimi: in 2002, he helped finance the modernisation of his childhood home, including the addition of an inside toilet. Most likely, the other top drivers had sat on warm toilet seats from the very start of their lives.

McLaren was a tough school. It was overseen by a strict headmaster, team boss Ron Dennis. The pit garage was filled with easy-going, down-to-earth blokes: race engineer Mark Slade and mechanics Marc 'Elvis' Priestley, 'Gearbox-Philly', Marcus Prosser and many other characters with their feet on the asphalt. And, of course, there was Mark Arnall, the physiotherapist who remains with Kimi to this day. Arnall also functioned as Ron Dennis's grapevine. Every time Kimi did something inappropriate, Ron phoned Mark to ask what had actually happened.

In joining the McLaren team, Kimi entered an unpredictable world, where the quickest of the day could become the slowest in the blink of an eye when the tyres or the car fell apart. It tested the driver's character, which in Kimi's case proved strong. A team spirit was cultivated outside the paddock, too, and there were times when the spirit smelt of liquor.

Kimi sits on the grey divan and recalls his time with McLaren and Ron Dennis with equanimity, though it wasn't always calm in those days. Distance evens things out.

'I thought Ron Dennis was a control freak. I suppose he's that in everything he does. He doesn't watch you on purpose, it's just him. Everything has to be straight, papers and things. These days I like things to be in order at home, so it doesn't look like a bombsite. I'm sure that dates back to Ron. And he didn't stress me out that much; maybe he was more stressed by what I did, for example by a newspaper report of my partying. I didn't really give a flying fuck but I expect it was harder for him.'

Fire and water, two opposites with a common passion:

the will to win. But they had totally different ideas of leisure pursuits and public relations. It was enough that one was a 23-old rascal from a working-class family and the other a 55-year-old team boss with heavy responsibilities. Ron had polished manners and a sense of style; Kimi was a country boy dependent on his instincts.

McLaren's sponsors included two luxury brands: Swiss watchmaker TAG Heuer and German fashion house Hugo Boss. The latter naturally wanted to clothe his drivers.

'How you dressed was really important during the McLaren period. The Boss suits were really awful; black and shiny. Terrible to wear. But Ron thought that everything had to be just so.'

*Iceman.* Ron Dennis gave this name to Kimi. It amounts to no more than half of what Kimi is, but defines his professional identity accurately: he comes from a cold climate, drives fast and talks little; he doesn't explain anything, does his job to the best of his ability, and then moves on to the next race. A little later, the role will entail wearing dark glasses everywhere except in the shower.

Professional boxers and freestyle wrestlers almost all have nicknames, which they can hide behind while getting on with punching and blood-letting without their real names being tarnished. 'Iceman' is of no use in everyday life – the same applies to the 'Executioner of Käpylä', title of Jukka Järvinen, a professional boxer. Also, you might not think much of the nickname 'Idi' given to Amin

Asikainen, another boxer. What works on a racetrack and in a boxing ring doesn't work in a living room or a supermarket queue. 'Iceman' has worked exceptionally well on the racetrack and its immediate vicinity but melts away in its ineptness in the middle of a young family's everyday life.

## *Iceman.* Ron Dennis gave this name to Kimi. It amounts to no more than half of what Kimi is.

The five years at McLaren taught Kimi everything and a bit more. While he was at Sauber, he only just got by with minimal English. Now he learnt to speak with greater versatility but still selectively: he talked to the team but didn't give anything to the press. Above all, Kimi acquired a good group of people, a racing home. Physio Mark Arnall and race engineer Mark Slade were at the heart of it. The latter had been in the team since Mika Häkkinen's time.

'I got on really well with Slade. I asked him to come to Ferrari with me, but it was hard because he had a family and would have to move to Italy. When, later, after the rallying period, I was negotiating with Lotus, I said I wanted to pick my own engineer. You've got to have a good engineer, or nothing works. I knew that Slade was in fact available, because he was doing a totally different job at Mercedes. He already knew some of the Lotus staff and, if you take that into account, he was the best choice. My present engineer Dave Greenwood [since replaced by Carlo Santi after Greenwood moved to Manor] and Mark Slade are, without doubt, the best engineers that I've had. They're very similar, they could almost be brothers.'

Mark Slade proved a really strict man who didn't put up with any pointless remarks. When angry, he was in the habit of hurling his pen.

'Once we tied his pen to a string, so it couldn't fly terribly far.'

The group was welded together because, in those days, you could test the car as much as you wanted, sometimes for six days on the trot and even between races. The sponsors were after their pound of flesh, too. Mercedes, West, TAG Heuer and Hugo Boss all wanted their share of the driver.

The McLaren years had their ups and downs, as years tend to do. Looking back, the smooth asphalt feels like a rollercoaster. Kimi's engines kept falling apart or he just had a lot of bad luck right from the start. In the French GP on the Magny-Cours circuit, Kimi was still leading on the penultimate lap and close to the first race win of his career, when it was all ruined by an oil spill left by Allan McNish's Toyota at one of the last corners of the track.

'I had to brake and slow down, and Schumi was gifted with a chance to pass. It pissed me off for a long time. It would have been my first win.'

The following year, Kimi won his first Grand Prix in Malaysia, but it wasn't much of a consolation when the year came to an end. Schumi won the championship with a two-point difference. And here we go again: if technology hadn't let him down in such and such race . . .

In 2005, Kimi could have won the championship again, but the engines coughed and the drive shafts clanged. In the German Grand Prix, wheel suspensions fell apart. Engines had to be replaced, which meant a ten-place grid penalty. And even then, coming from so far behind, Kimi often reached the podium.

In the same year, he showed in the Japanese Grand Prix the meaning of the word tenacity. He started the race way back in seventeenth place on the grid. He passed car after car until, on the last lap, only Giancarlo Fisichella was in front of him.

'And then I managed to overtake Fisichella, too. It was cool. I remember that. And, of course, my first Grand Prix win in Malaysia.'

What else did Kimi gain from the five McLaren years? What did he learn in that time? He learnt to put up with pain and bad luck, and to get the drift of a mechanic from half a word, with two words from the team boss sufficing. What changed in five years? What sort of a graduate emerged from the British school? Is it really a coincidence that one of his helmets bears the name of James Hunt?

The redtops have written about Kimi's leisure pursuits in large, black letters – with and without reason. Sometimes his partying has been so colourful that the lurid headlines are understandable. At other times, the karaoke antics of a young man in his twenties have hit the headlines pointlessly. Perhaps Kimi has really led a completely normal life for a racing driver but at the wrong time? And what is normal, and from whose perspective?

It's hard to have an insight into another time from the viewpoint of where we are now. Or is it? In Kimi's room, that other era is half a metre away. A helmet bearing James Hunt's name has pride of place on the shelf covered with helmets. Kimi wore it at the Monaco Grand Prix in 2012. And he registered for a snowmobile race under Hunt's name.

Why James Hunt, specifically? And what is special about the McLaren team? The answer is England, where the magic of the enclosed track has a long, sodden and blood-drenched tradition. James Hunt is one of the best-known British drivers, a hothead who lived recklessly and was nicknamed 'Hunt the Shunt' after repeated collisions. Hunt won the Formula 1 World Championship in 1976, but he's remembered even more for his way of life, which seems immoderate by today's standards. What was standard back then is an abomination today.

What does Kimi admire about that past?

'In Hunt's days, drivers respected each other much more. If you bumped into someone, it could mean death, because the petrol tanks were on both sides of the car. Now that everything is much safer, you can do stupid things. You couldn't then. They respected each other so much because they knew their lives were on a knife's edge. It's nothing these days if you cut in on another car. In those days, the drivers spent more time with each other and went out together. The fellow feeling was bound to spring from a fear of death,' Kimi says. James Hunt said the same thing. According to him, it was better to let his hair down at night because it might be his last one. His philosophy is summed up in the biography by Gerald Donaldson.

The combination of having fun and the proximity of death feels bizarre now but it was a reality then. Eleven drivers died in Formula races in the period 1970–82. And another one should have died in all probability, but this badly burnt man continues attending races, walking from one microphone to another, commenting on the sport and its rules. Niki Lauda's experience, combined with his burnt skin, holds the reporters' interest.

In 1976, Lauda was involved in a serious accident at the Nürburgring. He nearly lost his life and suffered severe burns. A Catholic priest had already given him the last rites, but in just over a month Lauda was back behind the wheel of his Ferrari. At that time, the chassis of the cars were made of aluminium. Carbon-fibre chassis only came in the 1980s.

The world of Formula 1 in the 1970s and 1980s was different from how it is today. The drivers smoked and burnt in their cars. They lived like there was no tomorrow and sometimes that was the case. Beer was measured in buckets and cigarettes in cartons.

Kimi doesn't hanker after insecurity or beer, but a relaxed, carefree and informal atmosphere. And maybe a touch of that sort of thing was to be found in McLaren's paddock.

'No way! I am not wearing a blazer. You guys are wrong to make people conform like that. It's not what appeals to the younger generation. They don't want to see people all dressed up like Jackie Stewart! ... Life is too short to be bound by regulations when it isn't absolutely essential.' (Gerald Donaldson, *James Hunt: The Biography*, Virgin Books 2009, p. 148) This is what James Hunt said; this is what Kimi Räikkönen could have said.

Hunt was a chain-smoker who got through forty cigarettes on a bad day. Kimi is an occasional smoker.

'I smoked for a couple of years when I was a kid but I haven't smoked habitually during my career. Except I've gone through quite a few fags when pissed, and I've been pissed pretty often. And during the Lotus period, I had the odd fag both in the paddock and when I went out for a beer with the Lotus boss. After that I haven't had many cigarettes. I've got asthma, so I gave up regular smoking. I did even have a go at the green North States, the ones without filters; they made me cough in the morning. And everyone knows I take snuff now and then, but no one has said anything about it.'

Boozing is a time-honoured tradition in English motor racing circles, one that was vigorously upheld among McLaren's staff. Kimi valued the tradition and was supported by colleagues close to him. Mechanics and tyre changers were naturally pleased that the driver joined them in drinking sessions.

'I've got to say that I've drunk a hell of a lot considering that I'm a racing driver. I must have drunk on behalf of all of them many times over. But I no longer wait for the season to end in order for me to start boozing. I don't think that the end of my career will present an opportunity to take up drinking. I've had my fill; I don't need to carry on.'

James Hunt's idea of a cosy evening was this: shooting the breeze with his mates in front of the TV, with take-away dishes on their laps, a few beers, and maybe a cannabis joint. Kimi's current idea of a nice evening is very different from this scenario, but it's clear that booking a table at a Michelin-starred restaurant wasn't his thing either during his years of partying.

James Hunt was only a metre away when he witnessed the death throes of his rival Ronnie Peterson in 1978.

Hunt was the first to rush to the burning car to try to help. Because of this and many other fatal collisions, Hunt became more and more frightened.

'The thought of dying frightens the hell out of me. I think about what it's like being dead and if there's life after death. I want to retire when the time comes. Voluntarily. To do that I have to survive and to survive in motor racing means not exposing yourself to the risks for too long. Motor racing makes me come alive. But it also scares me to death.' (Donaldson, p. 198)

Kimi isn't frightened because the cars are vastly safer than in Hunt's day. Instead, he has always loathed the extracurricular activities of the sport, just like Hunt, who hated big parties full of strangers at which he was the centre of attention. Both men also share a highly developed competitive streak. Hunt opined as a young man that if he didn't reach the top in F1, he would do so in another field. Kimi thinks that driving fast is the safest way. Hunt agreed, thinking that fast driving improved his concentration and reduced errors.

Hunt was a nervous wreck before every race. He walked back and forth in the paddock, chain-smoking, putting his helmet on, taking it off, and throwing up. Kimi has only one ritual before a race: 'I always go into the car from the right-hand side.'

We find out from Donaldson's biography of Hunt that the driver loved birds and animals. And he loved his dog

Oscar best of all; he was totally devoted to him. This sensitive side of Hunt was never generally made known. Kimi loves children, and, unlike Hunt, this side of him has become public knowledge.

James Hunt announced his retirement on 8 July 1979. Driving had ruled his life for twelve years. For Kimi, it's been eighteen years. And the end is not in sight.

Hunt was deeply depressed. In the end, he found peace of mind, gave up smoking and heavy drinking. He met Helen Dixon and proposed to her on the phone. Two days after the successful proposal, Hunt died of a massive heart attack, in 1993. He was only forty-two. Kimi fell in love with Minttu Virtanen in 2013 and abandoned binge-drinking. He's now a 38-year-old father of two children. When his career has come to an end, he'll get a dog.

World champion 2007.
PHOTO © SUTTON IMAGES

# ONE POINT

**Someone else's defeat is** always buried inside a victory; it's like a hard stone grown inside an avocado. Kimi Räikkönen wouldn't have won the World Championship without Lewis Hamilton's failures at two successive Grand Prix. This fact doesn't take away from the value of the championship. Kimi deserved it; he gained the necessary one-point advantage. The sweetness of the achievement was made even sweeter by the fact that the championship came in his first year with Ferrari. It had been a close call twice in his time at McLaren.

Moreover, winning the championship shouldn't even have been possible. Kimi won six of the seventeen races. At the lowest point, he was twenty-six points behind the leader, Hamilton. Before the last race, three drivers were in with a chance of winning the world title: Lewis Hamilton had 107 points, Fernando Alonso 103 and Kimi Räikkönen 100.

Everything was possible at the Interlagos circuit on 21 October 2007 at 9pm Finnish time.

**Kimi's red car leaves from third place on the grid. Kimi drives confidently, Hamilton badly. Kimi has to win; Hamilton must be seventh. One man's good fortune requires another one's misfortune.**

The gate is closed at Porkkalanniemi in Kirkkonummi. Only Paula and Masa and their good friends Ani and Kari are in. Paula has banned the press from her home. Reporters would have liked to watch the decisive race together with Kimi's parents, but Paula stood firm. Masa would have enjoyed the publicity. She promised that the reporters could come in if Kimi won the championship.

Paula is on edge, as she always is when Kimi drives. Kari and Masa leave the room to watch the upstairs television; Ani and Paula stay downstairs. They switch off the lights.

Kimi's red car leaves from third place on the grid. Kimi drives confidently, Hamilton badly. Kimi has to win; Hamilton must be seventh. One man's good fortune requires another one's misfortune.

Paula Räikkönen usually drinks brandy during a race but she has forgotten to stock up with the calming drink. All she and Ani have got in front of them is a row of bottles of Vichy water and champagne flutes. They drink the plain fizzy drink as if it were a special treat. Upstairs, Masa and Kari have got something to drink but the women won't move right now. Kimi is in the lead.

During the last five laps, Paula stands in a corner holding a sick bucket. Kimi drives the last laps confidently and with style. He crosses the finish line – the winner but not yet the world champion. He has to hear on his radio where Hamilton is. After half a lap past the finish line, he gets a message to say that Hamilton has been lapped. Kimi wins the World Championship by a point.

Masa picks up a pair of scissors and cuts off his hair. He embraces his son's championship with a shorn head. Paula dabs her eyes and goes to find smarter clothes to replace the holiday gear. Ani starts making coffee. Jussi Rapala, Paula's brother-in-law, announces that he is at the gate. He turns up outside the house with the reporters and says that they came in with him through the gate. The start of a commotion.

Kimi sprays the bubbly and dedicates his championship to Ferrari and his family. He has won what he could have won twice at McLaren if the engines had not broken down.

The 'if only' talk is finished; now he wants to go and celebrate with the team, with his tribe, away from the public gaze. The son of a close-knit family wants to be with his red family.

Paula and Masa try to call Kimi. Finally they get hold of him. They cry and shout into the phone. They can't find the words; they are beside themselves. There is no defeat inside their victory – only an enormous amount of shared experiences: tears, laughter, disintegrating drive shafts, the smell of chain grease, thousands of kilometres in an old van, empty words of vague sponsors, handshakes of reliable people, fear, excitement, penny-pinching. Words are hard to come by when there are so many actions behind them.

Kimi is in the hotel with the team. Celebrations are put on hold. They have to wait for an obvious decision on a pathetic protest that has been mounted about the amounts of petrol in the cars of Nico Rosberg, Nick Heidfeld and Robert Kubica. The protest fails. The World Championship is confirmed. Bottles open, drinks flow, boozing goes on till the morning.

Paula and Masa wake up; it's a great morning for a small nation. The press wants everything and it gets a lot, too. The parents make statements, go over their emotions and search for words.

Kimi has one more working day. He travels to Mugello in Italy, the place where it all started on 12 September

2000 with Sauber's tests. Both the Finnish and the foreign press are present. The circle has closed.

Bläk, the Helsinki nightclub, opens its doors. Family and friends are there, all waiting for Kimi. Finally he appears. Night changes into morning; it's barely noticeable and takes place in no time at all.

The decision-makers of Espoo are faced with a dilemma. They wonder how the town might commemorate the great son of Karhusuo. It's customary to award cross-country skiers and javelin throwers a scenic plot or a house, but how do you reward a racing driver who is already unnaturally rich?

The town has designated an area for a new motocross track but the whole project is still up in the air. The track is due to be near the Ämmänsuo dump. The decision-makers notice that there's a road behind the dump. An idea is born. What if we call the road 'Kimi Räikkönen Way'? It would be a splendid tribute to the new world champion. The matter is put to Räikkönen, who doesn't warm to the idea. For some reason, having this road named after him doesn't excite him. It leads nowhere and, on it, you see only seagulls flying to a dump. The matter is buried, as is the whole motocross project. The official name of the road is Kulmakorventie.

PHOTO: ILARI SUHONEN

# RALLY MAN

**When Ferrari announced at** the end of September 2009 that they were letting Kimi Räikkönen go a year before his contract was up, no one knew exactly what would happen. Would Kimi end his racing career? Would he move to another team? What would he do? Something became clear: Kimi was fed up with the by-products of the Formula 1 circus – namely, the shit-mongering and the politics.

Kimi's choice of rallying was a surprise move only to those who didn't know him. He was already drawn to the world of rally driving, which is completely different from the glitter and razzmatazz of Formula. He admired the daredevils who hurtled along narrow, tree-lined roads at breakneck speeds.

'He's a rally man to the core,' says Kimi's affairs manager Sami Visa, who has followed the sport all his life and knows many Finnish rally drivers.

He uses the word *ralli-ukko*, a very Finnish expression which means this: The country's best rally drivers are almost without exception daredevils who come from the backwoods, ordinary men of the people. They're approachable. They're not prima donnas, but a bit like the boys next door. Does this sound familiar? Kimi's appearance and his way of speaking make him more of a *ralli-ukko* than a peacock of the paddocks.

Simo Lampinen, Timo Mäkinen, Hannu Mikkola, Timo Salonen, Henri Toivonen, Markku Alén, Juha Kankkunen, Tommi Mäkinen, Marcus Grönholm . . . the list of Finnish rally drivers is long. Many youngsters, intoxicated by speed, have emerged from farmyards and gravel roads.

Sami Visa personally knew Henri Toivonen (1956–86), who died in the Corsica rally, and he's also a friend of Tommi Mäkinen. According to Sami, Kimi and the men mentioned above share an incredible will to win. 'And they can all act like arseholes on race weekends. They aren't very good company during those days; they shut you out completely.'

Taking up rallying wasn't a sudden whim for Kimi but a logical extension. He had always followed the sport and was interested in it. He had earlier even bought a rally car from Fiat, an Abarth Grande Punto S2000, which was maintained in race condition by Tommi Mäkinen Racing. That was the car Kimi drove in his first attempt at rallying in the 2009 Arctic Lapland Rally.

The Räikkönen family
and the thrill of speed.

**Practising for the Formula 1 World Championship.**

Masa deep in thought.

Mother and son at Kimi and Minttu's wedding.

Brothers.

PHOTO: JUHA HANSKI

Kimi's stag do. Enduro safari and boats. It's easy to celebrate holding the Wheelmonkey award.

In Matti Nykänen's footsteps in Levi, 2003.

PHOTOS: ILARI SUHONEN

PHOTOS: ILARI SUHONEN

'Kimi was three years old when he first mounted a children's Italjet Motocross bike. The sound of a bike revving carries on.'

He speaks to his beloved.

She listens to her beloved.

Sami Visa, Rami Räikkönen, Robin and Kimi.

Paula and Robin at the Barcelona tests in spring 2018. PHOTO: SAMI VISA

Mark Arnall with his fans, and Sami Visa in Shanghai, 2018.

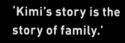

'Kimi's story is the story of family.'

'I went to watch Rally Finland in Jyväskylä in 2005. I went to the sauna with Tommi and Kaitsu Lindström. Way back then I said to Kaitsu that, if I start driving, you'll become my map reader. Kaitsu and Tommi have been a bloody great help to me.'

Tommi Mäkinen has a wealth of experience as a driver; these days he works as team principal of TOYOTA GAZOO Racing. He recognises a real driver when he sees one.

'It was easy to see that Kimi has driven a lot – his handling of the car was good straight away. It didn't take him long to get the hang of it. It's not easy to swap a Formula 1 car for a rally car. I had a little go in a Formula 1 car myself. It's a totally different piece of equipment,' says Mäkinen.

Kimi's older brother Rami has done a lot of rallying, and wasn't surprised by Kimi's choice. He thinks that a rally driver needs a good eye for the road. Also, he needs to drive along the route a couple of times at race pace before he can assume that he can challenge the top drivers.

**The wheel was turned by a relaxed man, the paddock was made up of the forest edge, and his mates were covered in snow, sweat or grease.**

'I knew that Kimi was capable of driving the special stages on public roads really fast, because you can drive using your eyes and don't need to plunge into darkness,' says Rami, who was second in the junior series of the Finnish Championship.

Kimi drove a Citroën C4 WRC in the World Championship series for Citroën's number two team. Kaj ('Kaitsu') Lindström was his map reader. The results were up and down but the men had fun. The wheel was turned by a relaxed man, the paddock was made up of the forest edge, and his mates were covered in snow, sweat or grease. There was no glamour but there was atmosphere. There was no media circus, just a few reporters. He was up against the forest and the clock, flanked by fields and trees. The clock is cold; it has no opinions – it just tells the truth. The harsh, tough and crude feel of rallying suited Kimi, and he has fond memories of the freezing cold and the bleak conditions.

'When my managers Steve and David got there, they were like, "What the hell? It's minus twenty and there aren't any warm places." They were used to totally different conditions in Formula 1. In rallying, you're just told to go and stand over there by the roadside, the cars will be here soon.'

Kimi's natural speed was demonstrated at the Arctic Lapland Rally. He drove off the road at the second special stage, but at the finishing line, it was calculated that he had been an average one second per kilometre slower than the winner, Dani Sordo. Only one second per kilometre – and it was his first event.

In the third rally of the season in Jordan, Kimi was eighth, and came fifth in Turkey. He amassed twenty-five points during the season and won the Newcomer of the Year award. More important than the points was the fact that he was one *ralli-ukko* among others. The only stars were in the sky.

'The mechanics are a special tribe. They dig and delve in the freezing cold and take care of everything. When you've overturned the car and limp to the tent and it's all got to be done in an hour, they attack the bodywork with an angle grinder, hammer the thing into shape, and you're back on the road. You can crash into the bushes pretty badly and they still make the wreck look like a car. I've thought lots of times that the car is a goner but then they start swinging some sledgehammer, and in an hour's time they say, "That's it, hit the road, off you go."'

During the whole of his previous career, Kimi drove on his own in a cramped space on an enclosed track, whereas now he sat side by side with a map reader facing an open road, driving to the tune fed into his ear. Someone else told him what was coming; his own eyes weren't enough. Only a seamless feat of coordination would keep the car on the road and the speed as fast as possible.

'I wasn't used to listening to another person. It's the confidence you have in the map reader's instructions that

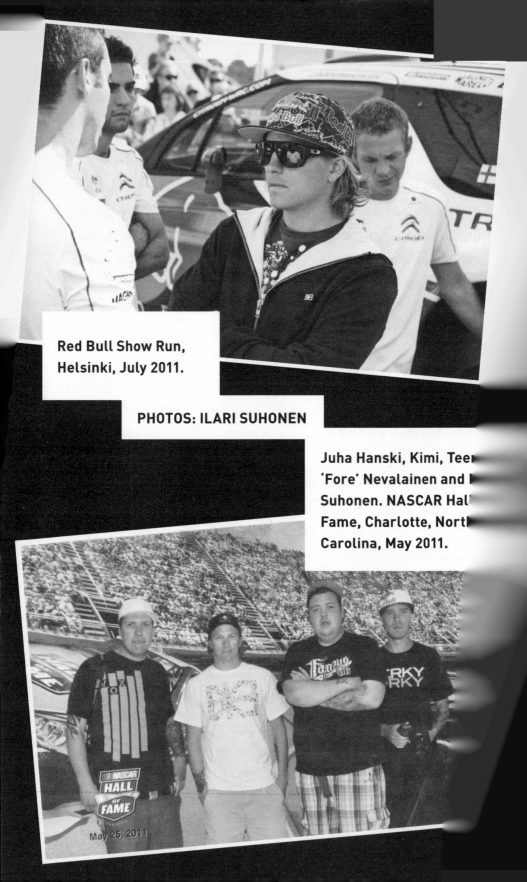

Red Bull Show Run,
Helsinki, July 2011.

PHOTOS: ILARI SUHONEN

Juha Hanski, Kimi, Tee◼
'Fore' Nevalainen and ◼
Suhonen. NASCAR Hal◼
Fame, Charlotte, Nort◼
Carolina, May 2011.

NASCAR
HALL
OF
FAME

May 25, 2011

makes the difference between rallying and Formula 1. The second year was easier because I knew the routes.'

Kimi funded his second year of rallying himself. He founded Ice One Racing and hired a car from Citroën for it. The season was patchy and Kimi didn't take part in all the individual rallies. In the end, his team was excluded from the Manufacturers' World Championship series.

Kimi was left with good memories and an increased respect for the sport. Apart from the mechanics, he remembers Kaj Lindström's job.

'I learnt to admire the map reader's job. The amount of work is insane. They write the pace notes and take care of all the transfers and timetables. And then they've got to transcribe all the pieces of paper.'

Apart from rallying, Kimi also tried out the NASCAR series in the US – something totally different. The cars go round an oval track close to each other at horrendous speeds. The spectators never lose sight of any of the vehicles, which are filled up manually. Their tyres are changed with a jack. The audience hears the conversations between the drivers and the teams. At best, the number of spectators can reach 160,000, and every race is watched by ten million people on TV. After American football, NASCAR is the most popular sport in the US.

NASCAR combines the same qualities as rallying: it's informal and casual, with the added ingredient of the inimitable American style.

'It was an easy-going business. And they were beautifully made cars. When I started in Formula 1, everything was much more relaxed. These days, all the sports have become more serious. Much of the fun has disappeared.

There's more money, and less play. Initially, snowboarding was easy-going and fun; now it, too, has become a serious business.'

Kimi drove two NASCAR races for Kyle Busch Motorsports, one in the Trucks series and the other in the Nationwide series.

Kimi's placements in rallying and in NASCAR aren't particularly memorable; the main thing was to get away from the world of Formula 1 and its tight schedules. It's revealing that, during this period, Kimi didn't follow his main sport at all; instead, he followed his instinct, which took him into the heart of clubbing and having fun. Also away from home, which no longer felt like home.

# MASA

**Porkkalanniemi, 21 December 2010.** Matti and Paula are in their cottage. It's evening.

Masa is downing spirits. He's not in a good mood. Paula tells him that Kimi and Jenni have asked them to visit. Masa doesn't feel like it, and she says that she'll go on her own. Kimi's summer cottage is a couple of hundred metres away, and Paula would like him to come, too; the boy is in Finland and, for once, has time. She phones Masa from Kimi's to persuade him, but her bad-tempered husband still doesn't want to come.

Masa is pissed off. This is pure guesswork, of course, because I can't ask him about it anymore. Let's put it this way: it's fairly certain that Masa is pissed off because he has quarrelled with Kimi. His son thinks Dad drinks too much and the last straw was Masa shooting at clay discs, drunk, with his mates. Kimi was furious enough to come and take the guns away. Now Masa is ashamed and peeved, perhaps in that order. His head isn't as it used to be; it hurts. It generates bad feelings. He injured it badly a couple of years ago when he fell off a quad bike. He was left with a neurological problem. Dark forces started gnawing inside the sunny man's head, and he couldn't do some of the things that he had been good at before the accident. A digger no longer obeys his hands like before. Masa fills his glass and stares out of the window.

Paula is enjoying her visit to Kimi and Jenni, though Masa is on her mind. Her beloved husband has become a stranger. She gets back to the cottage late. Masa is dozing on the wooden settee. She asks him to come upstairs to bed but has no success. She decides that the settee is a warm enough place for sleeping on, and goes upstairs. She watches a bit of television.

When she gets up in the morning, Paula finds her husband has fallen and hit the back of his head against the floor. She can't wake him up. Alarmed, she runs to Kimi's place to get help. When Kimi, Jenni and Paula rush back, Masa is still lying on the floor; he has hurt his head badly. They call for an air ambulance but it won't pick Masa up because his condition is too bad. Kimi props his father up, who then throws up. At last an ambulance arrives to take the patient away. The family watch its rear lights, their Christmas lights.

Masa is taken to Töölö Hospital in Helsinki. They say

that there's nothing they can do; the brain haemorrhage is too severe. The next day, the hospital informs the family that they will switch off the life support machine because nothing can be done. Paula and Kimi head for the hospital. Rami joins them. The family are at Masa's bedside during his last moments.

Matti Paavo Ilmari Räikkönen dies on Wednesday, 22 December 2010.

Back in Baar, Switzerland, in Kimi's room, November 2017. A quiet moment. I approach the subject with caution. Kimi hasn't yet had a long life, though it's been a fast one. The days spent on travelling outnumber those spent at home. It's a succession of roads, aeroplanes, hotels and circuits, with cars in front, cars alongside and cars behind. There's no time to think when you're on the move and, when the speed stops, it takes time for the mind to catch up.

The death of a parent reveals the last hurdle to the child, and even if the hurdle is made of concrete, he sees through it: his own turn will come. Kimi was thirty-one when he lost his father. Matti was fifty-six when he died, a middle-aged man. He wasn't ready to go. Normally, parents wait a bit longer before they leave you.

Kimi has a drink of water and glances at me and the Dictaphone lying between us. I almost think that I can read the question in his eyes: can Masa fit into such a small gadget?

'At first, I just lay around at home, crying and sleeping. But then we went to Tahko for the New Year celebrations. To start with, I didn't want to go, didn't want to see anybody, but we went all the same. I had no plans for what to do next – would I be rallying or what? It all happened around then. And in the end I decided I'd take up rally driving. It must be one of the best decisions I ever made, because if I had stayed in that state, I'd have fucked up my life. It meant that there was at least something to do. I wasn't just moping around.'

A pause. Kimi gathers together the thoughts and memories of that one day. I know from experience that they can be hard to capture: they fly around like leaves and bits of rubbish in the wind. What did I feel then, what do I feel now? Are my memories accurate or do I want them to be false – that means, more pleasant? And who does it benefit if I temper my memories? No one, so I won't. Kimi tells it as it is, picking up a memory as if it were a fresh fish he has caught in a trap.

'You should always settle a quarrel before death. But it didn't happen then, just like it doesn't in lots of films. It was such a shitty business because of the row. I was mainly pissed off by his boozing. I was pissed off because he couldn't stop it. And the row was caused by his shooting at clay discs with some mates of his. They were drinking and shooting. I lost it because of that. I went to take all his guns away and he was angry. He did later make a joke of it on the phone, calling me a bloody weapons snatcher in a sort of good-natured way. And he said he loved me.'

A pause. A swig of water. Kimi carries on in a calmer voice. The quad bike accident was a turning point – Masa wasn't his former self after it. Kimi got a call from his mother when he was in the middle of testing: Masa is in a coma. Instead of returning to Switzerland, he flew straight to Finland and phoned Toni Vilander to ask his mate to come to the hospital with him. Toni was only let in after Kimi introduced him as his brother.

'He was never 100 per cent after that. Something went missing. He gave up smoking and he gave up booze as well – for a year or so. Then he took up fags again and had the odd beer.'

Kimi sighs and changes positions. No position feels good right now.

'It gets easier with time, though it will never go away. I'm sure all this was at the back of my mind during times when I didn't care a flying fuck or when I was partying. I decided to take up rallying. Without it, booze could have gained the upper hand but the sport helped me feel better.'

A pause. A large swig of water.

'It was really strange when there was no more Masa. If only I had anticipated his death a little. These days I wake up with a more-or-less-clear idea of the bloody events. And then the row. It's still bothering me, and I expect it always will.'

Kimi's eyes glaze over and shift to the helmets on the shelf. There is no refuge from memories.

We're in Karhusuo, Espoo, in the Konehalli machine shop in February 2018. Kimi had the shop built, and its upstairs incorporates a sauna, a living area and a small bar. Paula Räikkönen sits in an armchair. I'm on the sofa.

Paula says that these things have never been talked about outside the family. For a moment, it seems it won't happen now, either. I make it clear that she doesn't have to but it would be useful. Kimi's story is the story of the family. Without Matti, the story is one person short. Paula is quiet. Then she turns her head slightly to one side and goes back to December 2010. It's a long journey, but emotion speeds her along.

'I had been expecting it for a couple of years, but still . . . Kimi and Rami didn't quite realise that the situation had been bad for a long time. We had lived in Porkkala for something like six years. Kimi bought the cottage for us in 2004. We got married in 1976, so we'd been married for thirty-four years.'

We go outside for a smoke. Paula pushes fresh snow around with her foot and looks at the small, green house. She tells me that the boys had been happy to live in a space of thirty-three square metres before the family moved to the house next door, built by Masa's father.

'We were poor in money terms, but we led a rich life in other ways. I've had a good life. Masa and I shared an easy and lovely time apart from the last couple of years – they were hell.'

We go back upstairs. In the shop itself, a McLaren F1 car hangs from the ceiling. The interior of the upstairs living room reflects Kimi's career: helmets, photos, overalls, prizes. We sit in the middle of fulfilled dreams, and one of the people who made the dreams come true is absent. At one stage, Masa had three jobs in order to amass enough banknotes to enable the boys to continue driving. And when Kimi succeeded beyond all expectations, his dad didn't want to hide his joy. Paula tells it straight. She has every right to; she's talking about her loved one.

'Masa always said that we should let him know if he got a swollen head and it did happen at some point. He had to have lots of things, all sorts of stuff, and he had free time, too, though he always did work hard on all sorts of jobs. Then he got pancreatitis and diabetes. He didn't drink for a long time. In 2007, Masa was in good health, coping with his diabetes. I liked to drink white wine on weekends, and I noticed at some stage that he had started tippling secretly. Then it was the quad bike accident in 2008. I took him to neuropsychological therapy at the Orton clinic for six months but he pulled the wool over the expert's eyes. He needed a tougher approach. After that, his psyche changed: something went missing from his emotional centre. He became abusive when he spoke to me; he got angry. Then he added vodka to the mix – it made him feel better. Masa looked after all of our properties. After his long leave of absence, he would no longer work for an outsider. When Rami, after his father's death, started taking care of all these assets, he said he finally understood why Dad was always in a hurry. There were always adaptations and repairs underway somewhere.'

A long silence. Paula looks away. The trophies in the glass case shine to rival her eyes. Paula knows the true meaning of the wedding vows: 'to have and to hold from this day forward, for better, for worse, for richer, for poorer, in sickness and in health . . .' She has done it uphill, downhill, at corners and on the long straight that ends in the horizon.

We're back in Kimi's room in Baar, Switzerland. It's November 2017. Grief has no specific landing time. It arrives unannounced; it comes when it feels like it. With Kimi, grief took some time to land – it circled over Zürich, homeless. But before long, grief comes and performs a crash-landing inside your head. It does it anytime, anywhere, here and now.

'I wonder often what Masa would say to this or that. I don't suppose I've really dealt with his death properly.'

I switch off the Dictaphone.

# MONEY AND TRUST

**Kimi spoke about money** when he didn't have any, but after he had plenty, he didn't say a word about it. When you've got enough money, there is no point in talking about the amounts. In Kimi's line of work, wages are not public knowledge, and for that reason there's constant speculation about them. It's enough to say that the top drivers get paid disproportionate sums.

If you've been penniless, you appreciate money considerably more than someone born wealthy. In that sense, Kimi is the right person to talk about the opportunities afforded by money in an appreciative voice. Apart from real estate, he has bought time – a luxury item in his line of work.

'I've spent a lot on hiring planes to have more time at home. I can leave for Italy in the morning and come back the same evening. It wouldn't be possible on scheduled flights; it would take two days. I value my time highly. And I get home from races much more quickly on a hired jet.'

Kimi's houses represent his largest investments. He comes from a small house, and that's why it's not surprising that he treasures both his Swiss and his Finnish homes.

'I didn't get into this because of the money but, of course, it's good not to have to worry. I've been able to help Mum and Dad and provide them with the indoor toilet which fell by the wayside because of the microcars. I've put quite a bit of money into these properties. I've always wanted to have a good place to live in. They're there, ready and waiting when my career ends. I never had the sort of things that I can offer my own children.'

A pause.

It's not easy for a wealthy man to talk about his wealth. When a man has lots, he talks little. Expansive gestures go with little money. The silence hides Kimi's trials and tribulations over the past few years. They are crystallised in one word: trust.

A beautiful sloping green field rises outside Kimi's windows. The sound of a tractor comes from somewhere nearby; we see the vehicle approaching from the left. It stops at a distance of around 100 metres. The farmer gets down and goes to check a hosepipe attached to the back. Then he climbs back into his cabin and starts moving. A stream of shit rushes out of the hose in a wide arc. The smell penetrates the whole residence through the open kitchen door on the side and nearly knocks me unconscious. The comforting thing here is that the shit flies for a reason; it has a purpose: fertilising the soil. Shit flies when your trust is betrayed but it doesn't smell and it doesn't knock you out. It breaks your heart.

Money never moves alone – other things come with it. People attach themselves to banknotes, though the money doesn't belong to them; they smell it. A small amount of money causes as big a quarrel as a large amount. Quarrels over paltry sums are noisy, while disagreements over large sums are kept quiet. They are discussed in confidence – after all confidence has gone.

Kimi Räikkönen is a person who keeps his word. He's loyal. That's why betrayals of his trust are not pleasant spectacles. His affairs manager Sami Visa has witnessed them at close quarters and thinks that a nice and good-hearted man has been let down badly.

The journey from good-heartedness to credulity is short and easily travelled, as easily as keying in internet banking codes. A nice man doesn't suspect a trusted person; he reserves his suspicions for a strange passer-by. Kimi finds it hard to talk about, but says that he believes in the law of karma. According to theosophy, karma is the sum total of the consequences of the actions and choices made in an individual's life.

'I've thought that karma will take care of that side of things. They will come to light and be cleared up.'

Unfortunately, district courts don't apply the law of karma. When I ask for the details of the case, Kimi's voice becomes tense. According to Ludwig Wittgenstein, the Austrian engineer and philosopher, it's best to be silent about things that you can't talk about. Wittgenstein clearly didn't live in the age of the internet and social media, but I do understand Kimi's reluctance to say anything more.

We resort to a fable. Fables are about us, though we talk about pigs, cats, dogs, sheep and foxes. I apologise to the fox in advance for the following story:

Once upon a time there was a dog who did very well in running races – so well that he was invited to compete abroad. The dog's home was short of money, but when all of it was put in one basket, and cat relatives lent a bit, there was enough for the dog to travel. And so he could take part in a GP for four-wheel drives – all the dogs of the world attended. He won almost all the races and got lots of money. The dog was an ordinary mongrel but he had two exceptional qualities: a big heart and a sincere soul. It was both a good and a bad combination: good because all his best mates could experience his generosity; bad because he was also sought out by some who pretended to be his friends but had a hidden agenda. The dog didn't realise that not all of his new animal mates liked him; they liked his banknotes. The dog signed papers, paid off other creatures' debts, and even gave a leather card to some for them to buy unlimited amounts of dog food.

He ran and ran, travelled from one country to another with his paws pounding new asphalts. Until, one day, he examined his piles of notes and papers and saw strange things. The dog was horrified. He had been deceived, his tail had been twisted, he had been outfoxed and a hole had been gnawed in his generous heart. The dog confided in an old acquaintance, an older hare, asking him to look into it. The hare did so and discovered muddles. The dog hired the hare to look after his affairs and everything has gone well ever since.

The end. Except it isn't. The story is still open-ended because, at some point, the fairy tale became reality.

In this fable, the dog is Kimi Räikkönen and the hare is Sami Visa, Kimi's current affairs manager.

I have interviewed several people for the purposes of this book, and almost everyone has mentioned Kimi's loyalty. That's why it's so bizarre that he, of all people, was so badly deceived in Formula 1. It was 2010. Lotus got in touch because they were interested in Kimi joining the team. Via his manager Steve Robertson, Kimi told them that the matter was not yet a done deal and emphasised that there should be no publicity. But the story was immediately leaked the story to the media. Trust was betrayed, and Kimi didn't pull his punches in an interview in which he slated Lotus to Heikki Kulta, a reporter.

The following year Kimi drove a couple of NASCAR races in the US and the experience reignited his interest in racing against other lone drivers. In rallying, the driver is up against the clock, while on the racetrack it's one man against another. Kimi phoned Steve, asking him to explore vacancies in Formula 1 teams. Initially, Williams was under consideration, but the agreement with Lotus was made public at the end of 2011. Kimi met the man he had slated.

## Trust was betrayed, and Kimi didn't pull his punches in the interview in which he slated Lotus to Heikki Kulta, a reporter.

'Gérard López, the owner of Lotus, remembered the article. He yelled that I'd given them a bloody good roasting. I answered that I had been given a good reason. All in all, it was a nice first meeting.'

Everything began swimmingly at Lotus. Kimi drove fast, the atmosphere within the team was great, and everyone worked well together. It was fun to drive, particularly when the race engineer was Mark Slade, a trusted figure from Kimi's McLaren period.

The emphasis of Kimi's contract was on bonuses – that is, he was promised a substantial amount for points and podium places. He drove so well that the bonuses were well in excess of his basic pay. But it became apparent quite quickly that the team wasn't paying the promised money on time. Kimi waited patiently. The owners of Lotus swore that the wages issue would be sorted out. It didn't happen and, when the chips were down, the euros didn't show up.

The pay dispute became public, and not least because, with his brilliant driving, Kimi lifted the team towards the top; he was eventually third in the World Championship.

He could have made the firm suffer financially, but didn't want to, because the whole staff would have got into difficulties through no fault of their own. He's annoyed by the pay thing because the team was good and was well able to exploit his reputation.

'In the end, I got tired of fighting them.'

Kimi sighs and gulps down half a bottle of water in one go.

We've spent a couple of hours talking about money and trust. That's one hour too long. We leave the room to rejoin the family. Robin runs to meet us and suggests hide-and-seek. The dog goes along with the game.

# YOU'LL NEVER
# WALK ALONE

**Malaysia, October 2017. The** same hotel foyer. 'You'll Never Walk Alone' is the signature song of Liverpool Football Club. Many people have walked by Kimi Räikkönen's side during his career, but one has done it longer than anyone else. He's Mark Arnall, the 46-year-old English trainer who caters for the driver's every need during a race weekend. Mark accompanies Kimi everywhere, from the hotel foyer to the circuit, from the racetrack to the small room in the paddock, and from there to the start straight. He stands by the car holding a bottle of water and understands from the smallest of gestures what Kimi wants or needs.

This morning in the foyer, Mark passes Kimi a concoction containing ginger and lemon. Or something else.

Kimi doesn't need to ask about the separate ingredients of the beverage – he knows that Mark has found just the right blend for the temperature.

We're in the paddock, in Ferrari's facilities. Mark Arnall guides me along the narrow corridors. There are people in red everywhere: mechanics, engineers, tyre changers, the team boss, press officers. They give me long looks. For a moment I wonder what is wrong with my outfit, then it dawns on me: the colour. Everyone else is in red. I'm saved by the pass hanging round my neck, showing I'm a guest of Kimi's. Even so, some of the reds glance at me suspiciously: what are you doing in the heart of it all? It's been made clear to me that I'm not allowed to take photos. I understand their concern when we pass the room with four men bending over a heap of steel. It's the engine of SF70, the crux of it all. I assure the engineers that I won't take a photo, which I could use as a basis for building my own engine.

We come to a white door which says 'Kimi Räikkönen'. Mark opens it and says straight away that he can talk about everything else apart from the small, white pots. They are business secrets. The idea of doping doesn't cross my mind, because there's no one more careful about these things. Kimi can't even take a cold preparation before Mark has checked the product twice over.

'Basically, my job is to make sure that everything's ready for the race.'

The laconic statement contains an enormous amount of invisible, behind-the-scenes preparation.

Mark goes through all the essential details of the small room; each aspect must be in order. He explains things with the precision of a surgeon: 'There are three different helmets. Kimi picks one to fit the weather. If something goes wrong – for example, if a stone damages the helmet during the formation lap – there's an identical spare one available.'

There have to be three sets of earphones and three pairs of driving gloves. Each back-up item is backed up. Mark keeps one pair for the drive, and the two spare ones are needed if the gloves split or develop a hole. The gloves are never changed during the drive unless there's pouring rain and the race is interrupted. The same applies to the balaclava: if Kimi comes into the garage for one reason or another, a dry balaclava awaits him. The driving shoes are protected against rain. Mark has also got an extra pair in case the shoes get wet. Damp soles can slide on the pedals.

To be on the safe side, Arnall takes some medicines for the pit lane. For example, a nasal spray, some kind of antihistamine and anti-inflammatory drugs. There must be two drink bottles in case Kimi leaves one in the toilet by accident or gives it to a fan.

Mark Arnall's checklist is breathtaking. I've been following his actions while writing this book and have reached the conclusion that the title of 'personal trainer' isn't adequate in his case. He's also a nutritionist, a psychologist, a masseur, and a trusted friend.

He doesn't leave anything to chance. He follows the latest research tirelessly to keep up with everything that can enhance a driver's performance. In Malaysia and Singapore, the biggest problem is dehydration. The driver must be kept cool. Mark takes a thin, light-coloured shirt packed tightly inside a plastic bag out of a drawer. For a moment, I think I'm in the laboratory of a James Bond film with Q, who is responsible for equipping the espionage service, introducing his latest innovations.

'This product here is liquid ice.'

Mark spreads the shirt out onto the table. He pours some of the bluish liquid that he's just introduced over the shirt, evens it out and packs the shirt back into the bag. He closes the bag as tightly as possible. The liquid freezes the shirt in no time at all.

'This is a way of trying to delay dehydration. The shirt functions as a cooling mechanism, or keeps Kimi cool for thirty-five to forty minutes. I always prepare three of these shirts. We have to wait for the start of the race in the pit lane, and the shirt keeps Kimi cool. Then he gets out of the car, listens to the national anthem and chats to the mechanics. When he goes to the toilet, we replace the shirt. This way, he remains cool for around thirty minutes after the start of the race when dehydration and the warming-up of the body has already started for the other drivers. For Kimi, it only starts around lap twenty. Dehydration weakens the muscles, slows down reactions and impairs concentration. That's why we do everything possible to prevent it.'

Mark notices my incredulous expression when I listen to all this but carries on talking with his unwavering expertise. Before the race, Kimi gets a special drink – Mark doesn't want to say more about the ingredients.

'We've given Kimi blood and urine tests. They have yielded us more information about hormones. I try to enhance his adrenaline and testosterone levels and other associated factors. I use amino acids for the adjustments. We can enhance these levels one and a half hours before the race.'

Kimi doesn't know the contents of the drinks but he trusts Mark 100 per cent. Trust – the word crops up constantly when we talk about the most important people in Kimi's life. It's typical that he hasn't read his managers' contracts; things have been agreed with a handshake. This is the way he has dealt with Mark.

When Kimi descends into his car, he has been fed and watered. Mark has done his bit, for the time being. The formation lap is about to start. At this point, Mark has already run across the track.

The red lights go off, the cars accelerate on the start straight. Mark always feels tense. The tension hasn't diminished over the years. He watches the race, wishing Kimi every success. But if the red flag is raised and the race is interrupted, all hell breaks loose. Mark has got to be ready with the spare helmets and other equipment. The interruption of a race is like a shit storm. The mechanics rush to the scene, the cars are covered up; it's chaos. Mark's job is to walk to Kimi and calm the driver with his presence. If he is stressed, part of his anxiety could transfer to Kimi, and that can't be allowed to happen.

Mark sighs deeply. He recalls the pile-up of the previous race on the start straight.

'Everything is geared to that one start and then it all goes wrong, like in Singapore. You get to drive 100 metres before a collision, and that's it. That's when I think that we travelled a hell of a long way for this. Kimi is very good at this. He forgets quickly and moves on. And he never blames the team or the other drivers.'

We're about to leave the room when my attention is caught by a small basin resembling a plastic bathtub.

'When Kimi gets out of the car, he steps into the basin for three to seven minutes. I put some ice in it about ten minutes before he comes in. It beats all the other cooling methods.'

**The interruption of a race is like a shit storm. The mechanics rush to the scene, the cars are covered up; it's chaos. Mark's job is to walk to Kimi and calm the driver with his presence.**

The lecture is over. Mark checks that everything's in its place. He walks back in to put Kimi's driving shoes in their correct position.

We've been talking about technology; now it's the turn of emotions. What is it like to be so totally in someone else's service? Mark is silent for a moment and suggests a quiet chat in the hotel foyer.

Two hours later, the same man arrives in the foyer. In some ways, he's a completely different man. He has showered and changed out of the red clothes into his own. He orders a glass of red wine and sits down. His working day has been twelve hours long. He has been thinking my questions over.

'Kimi is Mr Text Message. He sends short, clear messages with no superfluous words. If he's in a bad mood, he's in a bad mood. I don't take it personally. He is what he is. It makes things easy. But when something really big happens, he's the first one to call.'

Mark.
PHOTO: SAMI VISA

Mark recalls his mother's death a year ago.

'Kimi rang and said I didn't need to come to the next Grand Prix if I didn't feel up to it.'

A pause.

'When we first met, I would never have believed that he would one day have a family. But now, when you think about it, it seems perfectly natural. Of course, he has got Minttu and the children. When he was about to leave McLaren, he asked me to come with him. It was an easy decision. We were like a small family: managers Dave and Steve, Kimi and me.'

Trust and family. Certain words keep being repeated, giving solidity to this book. Their true meanings are inside people's heads, not on paper.

The wineglass is empty; it's time to go to bed. Mark gets up and walks to the lift. Then he remembers that I had asked him to sum up some feature of the man whose energy drinks will again be his first task in the morning.

'A massive heart.'

PHOTO: TEEMU NEVALAINEN –
UPPIE DIGITAL

# STUFF HAPPENS

**Kimi Räikkönen has, in** the course of his life, put into practice the kind of ideas most people abandon at the planning stage. The rationality of both the ideas and their realisation can be disputed, and many do. Kimi has had the means of carrying out his whims. A mechanic buys his beer in a supermarket and dreams of a free ticket for an Iron Maiden gig; a Formula 1 driver orders a private jet and heads for Iceland to look at the moonscape. It's worth noting that Kimi is still keen on supermarket beer in good company. Because his work is tightly scheduled and controlled, it's logical that boundaries have become blurred during his leisure time. Sometimes the boundaries have disappeared. It's all got out of hand, or, to put it another way: the car has run off the road.

Kimi has driven for his dear life: into a wall, over a finish line, into a crash barrier. He's been first, second and the last but one. His life has been a little random, which means that not everything has gone according to the script. In life everything adds up, while in a race it's just the points.

This chapter visits memories as if they were a dimly lit cellar. Memories can be dark and mouldy as well as golden. Dust, drink stains and ashes collect over them. Some people clean and polish the past to make it look good, something that isn't going to happen here. Maybe not every little detail took place exactly as described here, but no coloured pencils have been deployed. It's more accurate to say that the rubber of oblivion has erased and blurred some bits.

Those who have been close to Kimi also get their say. This detached narrator has recorded the stories as they were told to him – not necessarily as they really happened.

———

It's 2005, a moped race. For six years, Kimi and his mates used to go to Mikkeli, to the summer cabin of someone called Ville to race on so-called children's mopeds. The race took place in August, and the participants also went to the sauna on a couple of days. On one occasion, they decided to build a ramp on top of their trailer and use it to ride into the lake. Kimi attempted a backflip on his moped but failed. He abandoned the bike mid-flight and flopped into the lake. 'You won't do that on my moped,' said many of his mates. At least ten discarded mopeds were found at the scene.

Sepi, Ville's father, was in the habit of visiting that same cabin every summer to go to the sauna and to have a swim. He happened to be there at the same time. When he got into the sauna, he found a young man sitting on a bench. The two of them sat there having a chat. When Sepi said he was going for a swim, the young man (Kimi) was alarmed: 'Don't for God's sake jump in – it's full of mopeds!' In the morning, the lads borrowed an anchor from next door to pull the mopeds out of the water. 'Be quiet, we're fishing Kawas,' Kimi said. All the mopeds were Kawasakis.

Later, Sepi told his son Ville that he had met a totally unhinged chap in the sauna. The chap had been drinking, claiming that he was a Formula 1 driver.

———

It's 2008 in Singapore. After the race, Kimi plans to fly to Thailand, where he has bought a holiday home. He is in the private area of Singapore airport, when he thinks he's got a great idea. In security control, he puts his baggage on the conveyor belt, and the officials expect him to walk through the security gate. Instead, Kimi dives onto the belt after his belongings. The officials are enraged. The driver says that he only wanted to get an image of the precise details of his body, his bone structure in particular.

He wanted the image as a souvenir. The officials didn't grant his wish, suggesting leg irons and a tough interrogation instead.

———

Kimi's circle of mates has its own ice hockey team, which organises the so-called Ham Tournament every year in December. The group of around fifteen members plays the tournament in one of the following places: Helsinki, Espoo, Tampere, Mikkeli or Zürich. It was organised for the eleventh time in 2017. Lahti Pulicans have secured one win; in all other tournaments, Kimi's gang has walked away with the cup. Traditionally, only the worst performances are rewarded. The worst goalkeeper is awarded the Golden Vacuum Cleaner award, while the slowest skater receives the brake drum of a lorry with skates filled with concrete welded to it. The most excitable player gets the Iron Bar trophy, while the lousiest defender is awarded the back door of an old Nissan Sunny. Teemu 'Fore' Nevalainen belonged to the team at the start, but was kicked out after moving to Turku and joining a team called Kaarina Wankers.

———

It's 2013 at Helsinki airport. The private plane hired by Kimi takes off; its destination Zürich and his home. Other passengers on the plane include Illu Suhonen, Fore and Seba Koronoff. In the middle of the flight, Kimi has an idea: it would be nice to see the moon. You can't fly there, so the alternative is a moonscape. The nearest is located in Iceland and he asks the captain to fly to that country. The captain says that the plane hasn't got enough fuel, so he's got to refuel at Oslo. That's clear enough; the men's heads are far from clear. The stopover, refuelling and the purchase of a Norwegian jumper follow. The group heads for Iceland. When the jet lands in Reykjavík, Kimi sees the moonscape and is satisfied with what he has witnessed. The men stay there for a couple of days and spend time at the Blue Lagoon spa. Then it's time to fly home to Switzerland.

———

Juha Hanski: 'When Kimi sets out to have fun, something happens every minute. And he talks nonstop. If he likes a bar, he likes to stay a long time. It can be a bit funny to discover later that we've been sitting in the same place for fifteen hours.'

———

It's 2007 and Kimi's first press conference for Ferrari. It's nearly ten; there's no sign of the driver. Sami Visa knocks on the door of his hotel room. No reply. Sami has arranged with Mark Arnall that Kimi will appear before the press on time. Sami gets a spare key from the reception and goes into the hotel room. It's empty. The driver's watch is in the hotel sauna but the man isn't. Sami remembers that Kimi spent the entire night boozing with a Finnish actor friend of his. Next, he knocks on the actor's door. Ferrari's media chief looks at his watch and is getting hot under the collar. The international press is already seated. In the end, the actor's door opens and Kimi is found inside in a state of undress. He's asleep, curled up, covered only by his jacket. He resists being woken up and doesn't feel like going anywhere. Sami drills some sense into him and applies Visine drops to his eyes. Kimi smells of strong alcoholic fumes. Eventually, Ferrari's new driver steps in front of the press and says: *'Buongiorno a tutti!'* That went quite well, he commented afterwards.

———

Steve Robertson: 'I'll never forget the drive with Kimi and my dad from Maranello to Switzerland, where we all lived at the time. It was late and pouring with rain, and it had by then been raining hard for some time. Kimi always wanted to drive himself, while I didn't like to be a passenger either. To be honest, I don't think Kimi believes that other people can drive. We had a four-wheel drive under us on this trip.

The road was covered by ripples of water but there weren't many other cars. The windscreen wipers were working at the maximum setting, because the water was really coming down hard. Kimi had a strange driving position; he had adjusted the seat into an almost horizontal plane. It looked much like the driving position in Formula 1. In fact, the person sitting in the back didn't have much room. Kimi drove at around 200 km/h, far too fast in light of the driving conditions. I was dead tired but I couldn't sleep; I just held onto whatever I could, scared. My dad was the same. Suddenly, the car started swerving violently and I realised that it was rotating 180 degrees. I saw the crash barrier approaching. We would smash into it any moment now. I was shitting myself, thinking this is the end. Kimi saved the situation by sliding the car while in that odd driving position of his. Dad and I were in a state of shock, while he just laughed and went on at the same speed. The feeling of relief when we finally got home in one piece! But the incident also says something about a God-given talent and a way of living on the edge. A loveable chap.'

Folk singer Irwin Goodman died in a lay-by in Virolahti on 14 January 1991 while returning from a gig in Vyborg. Kimi is a great fan of Irwin. He has seen the film *A Ruffian's Rose* (*Rentun Ruusu*) dozens of times. He got into

Irwin's music at home. Paula and Masa were in the habit of listening to his records, and Masa often asked Paula for a dance when 'The Ruffian's Rose' was playing. Kimi was nine when the hit song came out. In order to pay tribute to the great singer's memory, Kimi and his mates are in the habit of making the pilgrimage to the Virolahti lay-by. The commemorative ceremony can't really be called solemn – a word that hardly describes the atmosphere. They always light a candle next to the wooden memorial plaque, and Kimi recalls that once the big candles were too near the wood and the plaque came close to catching fire. The programme also includes a visit to a local mate's summer cabin and the small village pub, where Kimi and co. play billiards with the locals. The stake consists of a tractor-load of firewood. If Kimi and his mates lose, they pay double the price for the wood; if they win, they get the wood for nothing. High stakes to get the mate's cabin heated.

---

Kimi often forgets that he's Kimi. A good example: Uffe Tägström, the helmet designer, and Kimi stopped at traffic lights in Zürich. The driver wondered why the hell everyone was gaping and gawking. 'I expect it's because this car is an Enzo Ferrari and you are Kimi Räikkönen.'

Paula Räikkönen: 'Sometimes people have asked me why I don't go and watch a race more often. My answer has been: how many mothers sit in their sons' workplaces watching them work?'

Kimi's worst incident of driving off the track may have been during the morning practice session at Monza in 2007. He drove at tremendous speed into a pile of tyres. According to those close to him, he downplayed his aches and pains to get to drive in the race itself. In the Grand Prix, his neck was in such poor condition that he was unable to hold his head up during braking. His neck muscles weren't up to it. Kimi came third in the race and gained some vital points – something that became clear in retrospect. He won the championship that year by one point.

It's Baar in Switzerland in February 2006. Fore, Toni, Sami and Kimi get it into their heads to go and support Finland's national ice hockey team at the Turin

Olympics. Dr Aki Hintsa manages to book them one hotel room, which is not, after all, required by Tarja Halonen, President of Finland at the time. McLaren has received a brand-new multipurpose vehicle with a four-wheel drive from Mercedes-Benz for testing. The MPV, part of the R-Class, has not yet been launched and has been lent to Kimi for a short time. The men set off. Toni has a bout of travel sickness and throws up over the bonnet in a lay-by.

The match has a great atmosphere – not least because Kimi's group has donned suitable match outfits. The Finland look is complemented by clown glasses that make the supporters unrecognisable. Kimi supports the Finnish team with gusto and accidentally spills some beer over a large Czech man sitting lower down. A scrap is narrowly avoided. The group visits the Finnish changing rooms to show support. Trainer Erkka Westerlund considers one visit to be quite enough.

The group starts back towards Switzerland. Because of a dense snowstorm, the motorway is closed. Kimi and his mates explain to the authorities that they've got a four-wheel drive and winter tyres. They get permission to go on the motorway. Some lorry drivers are asleep in the car park of a lay-by. Kimi wakes them up by throwing snowballs at the windows. His group flees. He sits at the back of the car chatting nonstop to the men at the front. He considers that the middle console is a nuisance and in the way, so he tears it off and flings it out of the window.

At the next lay-by, the men's attention is drawn to the letters on the rear bumper. They are removed and put in a different order. The car gets a strange name. Kimi gets home and is woken up in the morning by men from Mercedes coming to get the car. He hides and peers from behind the curtains to see how the removal crew react to the pimped-up car – even the iconic star has been twisted into a new position. Kimi hears nothing more of it.

Finland reach the final. They've got to get back to Turin; this time, they hire a plane. The atmosphere in the aircraft is great. The previous customer has left behind some powder for treating children's skin conditions. The tourists have an idea and decide to act on it. Because the flight is from a non-Schengen country to an EU country, the group is faced with customs at Turin. The customs official takes a long look at the passengers covered in white powder from top to toe. He asks where they have come from. Kimi replies: 'From Colombia.'

Sweden beat Finland 3–2 in the final. Kimi's gang first pays a visit to the Finnish changing room. The atmosphere is melancholy – 'really poor feng shui,' Kimi opines. The group moves to the Swedish facilities. There's a chap at the door, and Kimi tells him to get Forsberg, one of the Swedish players. The Finnish driver has an Iroquois haircut and sports the official fan scarf of the Finnish team round his head, so the doorman gives him a slightly suspicious look. Still, he goes and gets Forsberg. 'Foppa' welcomes Kimi's group to Sweden's party and straight away gets them a few Budweisers. Someone takes a photo of the party-goers and the matter causes a mild hullabaloo in Finland: How can Kimi celebrate Sweden's success? 'It's not my problem that Finland didn't win.'

———

Montreal in 2006. After the Montreal race, Kimi's group flies to Miami because the next one will be in Indianapolis, USA. It's possible to have a bit of fun in between. The group includes Osku, Uffe and Toni. They're up in the air, above the Bermuda Triangle. Kimi has an idea: how about freefall at this point? He suggests it to the captain, who agrees. Uffe has gone to sleep, his laptop on his knees. The aeroplane dives into freefall, down and up; it takes about ten seconds. Uffe turns upside down and wakes up on the ceiling.

The men hire a boat in Miami and go out to sea. They spot Peter Nygård's island. Kimi met the businessman at a Grand Prix and contacts the island. It turns out that the owner is away and his son also recently left for New York. Kimi calls Nygård, who insists on being hospitable. He promises to send his son back to the island to entertain the surprise visitors. The son comes and joins the group. The island is an extraordinary holiday resort with plenty to marvel at. One of the walls in the sauna section is made completely of glass. All you see through it is water; the wall is shared by the swimming pool on the other side. The rest of the group sits in the sauna sipping drinks when Kimi suddenly appears behind the glass and knocks.

Paula Räikkönen: 'As far as I know, our boys missed the stage of swilling supermarket beer. Perhaps Kimi reached it later; it's got to come at some point.'

It's Spa-Francorchamps in 2002 and the qualifying session for the Belgian GP. The car of Olivier Panis, the BAR-Honda driver, breaks down on top of the steep Eau Rouge section. The car emits a massive cloud of smoke which blocks visibility. Kimi, coming from behind, drives through the cloud of smoke at full pelt and gains the first front-row place of his career. Later it's discovered that Kimi had asked on the radio for the location of Panis' car, so that he was able to choose the other side. He trusted the team to tell him the correct side.

Motocross in July 2007. Kimi and Juha 'Juspek' Vierimaa.

A kebab party. New Year 2012.

Dallas, March 2010. Kaj Lindström and Kimi on their way to Miami.

Before Monaco GP 2010. Kimi and Ilari Suhonen.

Marc 'Elvis' Priestley: 'We were just a bunch of mechanics and tyre changers, and suddenly we were travelling on private planes. We had amazing experiences and, above all, we were part of Kimi's personal life. It was great to get to know his Finnish mates and get away from the stresses and strains of the pit lane for a while. We felt privileged, because we knew that Kimi only trusted a handful of people in the F1 circles.'

———

Uffe Tägström: 'He'll never be able to kowtow to anybody. Ever.'

———

Steve Robertson: 'Sauber wanted Kimi to spend half a day on making sure that he knew all the functions of the steering wheel before the decisive test drive. If you don't master them totally, you can break the engine and that's the end of the test. It took Kimi half an hour to take in all the buttons of the wheel and their functions.'

———

Juha Hanski: 'Getting that pick-up truck is a story in its own right. If I remember rightly, I told Kimi that there was a fantastic car for sale on the net. And Kimi had looked at the same vehicle. *What the hell?* we thought. *Maybe we should go for it?* The price was somewhere around €10,000. We had no cash and it was a Saturday. I phoned a friend, Laamanen, who owned a scrap yard and always had cash. I asked if he could lend us some. He had the money and he lent it. I haggled like hell and rang the vendor of the truck loads of times, saying that we had no more money, the price had to come down. I think I got €4,000 off the cost. When we got out of the car and the vendor saw Kimi, his expression spoke volumes: are you saying that you've got no more money?'

---

Kaskisaari in Helsinki in 2006. It's night time. Kimi's friend Sami Visa is asleep in the driver's home in the city. It has been agreed that Sami can use the place temporarily because of his exceptional situation. Sami is woken by loud clattering and gets up to investigate. A bunch of unfamiliar, unkempt, long-haired men has arrived in an advanced state of drunkenness. One of them is wearing Kimi's helmet. Luckily, Sami also spots the owner of the house downstairs. It turns out that the rockers are Guns N' Roses, minus Axl Rose, who's spending the night at Hotel Kämp. Sami calms down when Kimi says that he has invited the band for a late-night snack because the men have another gig the next day and need to relax. Kimi got to know Axl Rose when the Guns N' Roses singer came to say hello to him at the British GP at Silverstone. Tonight 'Akseli' doesn't come to Kaskisaari because he isn't feeling great. The other rockers stay till the following afternoon, when they leave to prepare for the evening's gig.

———

Levi in Finnish Lapland in 2003. The scene is the cabin of Jukka Jalonen, a mate of Kimi's. The driver has flown the English mechanics and tyre changers of McLaren, as well as an engineer and his personal trainer, to Finland to take a look at the winter. Those present include Marc 'Elvis' Priestley, 'Gearbox-Philly', Long-John, Marcus Prosser (all mechanics), Chris Thompson (engineer), Mark Arnall (trainer), Toni Vilander and Uffe Tägström. The men go to the sauna, drink and practise sledding. There's a drinking competition, and the teams are distinct: Finland vs England. The Brits are careless in the sauna and in the cold. One of them stumbles against the stove, scorching his buttocks. Mark Arnall finds some cream for his backside. Then they realise that they can't see Chris Thompson anywhere. They search high and low and eventually find him in the snow, frozen stiff. He's carried in and warmed up and recovers well enough to start drinking again. It remains unclear where Thompson was heading, whether he was going to take a leak or jump into the nearby river, Ounasjoki.

At some point in the evening, Kimi spots a familiar ski-jumping suit in a glass case on the wall. It's the Calgary suit of Matti Nykänen, winner of several ski-jumping contests in the Winter Olympics. He takes the suit down and puts it on. It seems the right size; the mood in the room brightens. All he needs is a ski jump to take off. It only takes a little organisation. He gathers together all the cushions and arranges them carefully into a landing slope. He climbs onto the gallery, concentrates and takes off. The flight of the first jump leaves something to be desired but the landing is practically faultless. He does it again. Uffe takes out his camera and records the jumps. The spectators are satisfied with the performances. All parts of the ski-jumping package hold together; Kimi's flight is calm and perfectly executed. He decides to keep the suit on for the rest of the evening.

The next morning Kimi is not to be found anywhere. The men ring the owner of the cabin and search around but to no avail. Finally, someone happens to open the door of the large drying cupboard in the hall. Kimi stands in the cupboard, fast asleep. When he wakes up, he explains that he managed to get the suit wet during the course of the evening and had to dry it. He set the temperature control of the cupboard at 45°C for ten hours and fell asleep. This way, both the man and the suit got thoroughly dry, and the garment could be returned to the glass case.

# SIXTEEN DAYS

**This is the story** of a period of time which now seems far away, though it was only a few years ago. Kimi no longer lives like this, though he once did.

If this were a film, it would be introduced in the following way. The stars: Kimi Räikkönen, F1 driver, and Kimmo 'Piki' Pikkarainen, ice hockey player. Supporting actors: the Prince of Bahrain, assorted Finnish chaps. The plot: Muddled. The genre: Unidentifiable. Cinematography: Hand-held camera. Production: The Kingdom of Bahrain, and self-financing or Backpocket plc. The action takes place in Italy, Bahrain, Switzerland and Finland.

It all starts in Milan, where Piki Pikkarainen plays his last match in the Milano Rossoblu team. Piki sends a text message to Kimi in Switzerland, suggesting he could come and visit the driver because the matches are over. That's fine by Kimi. Piki travels to Switzerland. The host himself is still on his way back from the Chinese Grand Prix, but Jenni is there. When Piki wakes up in the morning, the driver has arrived and says that he swiped some snuff off his guest during the night. Jenni leaves for the riding stables. The marriage has already broken down.

The Bahrain GP awaits but there's still time for some relaxation. In the early part of the week, Kimi and Piki play badminton, go to the sauna and bake pizzas. There is nothing to foreshadow the future events.

Piki says that he will next fly to Finland – the season is over and it would be nice to see old acquaintances. Kimi suggests that Piki comes with him to Bahrain. His mate hesitates but agrees; he can always go to Finland a little later. Gérard López, the owner of the Lotus team, picks up the young men and they fly to Bahrain together. At their destination, on the way to the hotel, they see burning tyres. Someone says that the current unrest could cause problems for the Grand Prix; the protesters demand the abdication of the country's Sunni king. The problems don't materialise.

Gérard López promises that, if the team finally gets onto the podium, he will instantly employ Piki as the team's official mascot. Qualifying is a disaster. Kimi is eleventh, but dismisses the matter by saying that he was among the first twenty, he spared the tyres, and he has a good plan for the race itself.

On the day of the race, Kimi drives brilliantly and comes

second. His team-mate Romain Grosjean comes third. At the final stages, Kimi nearly catches Sebastian Vettel, but there aren't enough laps left for him to win. It was a fine result for the team in any case, a cause for celebration. Kimi and Piki get off to a good start drinking at the hotel, clinking glasses, topping them up. David Coulthard happens to walk past and asks if the two of them are going to the Prince of Bahrain's party. Kimi hesitates; he thinks the party might be a bit of a damp squib. David thinks they should definitely go, and so they do.

The Prince of Bahrain's banqueting rooms and the feast on offer are splendid: swimming pools, good food, refreshing alcohol. Piki gets chatting to some stranger. He asks what the man does for a living and where he comes from. The stranger spreads his hands and says this is where he comes from and this is his palace. The prince has swapped his official clothes for jeans and a T-shirt. Piki is embarrassed but only for a second because he's enjoying his drink so much.

**The Prince of Bahrain's banqueting rooms and the feast on offer are splendid: swimming pools, good food, refreshing alcohol.**

Kimi and Piki come across a few people they know. The atmosphere fizzes. Security is taken care of by men who have served in the French Foreign Legion. Kimi's head is buzzing with the good result of the race and the points earned by the team. It's worth raising a glass or two of bubbly, perhaps having a bit of snuff.

At some stage, Kimi and Piki plan to get back to the hotel because they're due to fly in the morning to Qatar's capital Doha with López, and from there home to Switzerland. Kimi says he's going to take a leak; the toilet is behind the swimming pool. Piki receives the message and raises his glass. There's no sign of Kimi coming back. Piki is beginning to feel awkward; he feels out of place at the posh party. He goes in search of his friend but can't see him. Suddenly, Piki hears a splash nearby. He's surprised: surely no one at such a high-profile banquet would dream of plunging into the swimming pool? He walks to the edge to have a look, but there's no one there. All he can do is go back to the table and wait.

In the end Kimi comes back, saturated, and slams his soaking-wet mobile on the table. Piki asks what happened. Kimi mutters vague words about some chap pushing him into the pool after an argument.

The Prince of Bahrain, known as a staunch Kimi fan, arrives at the scene. Kimi tells his own version of the damp episode. The prince clicks his fingers and trusted men appear before him. He asks them to find the culprit and, soon enough, suspects are being brought before him. Every one of them denies pushing the racing driver into the pool. A few minutes pass. Then someone turns up and confesses, and the prince ejects the man from the party. The prince's son, aged around twenty, pleads with his father not to throw out his friend. The prince tells his son to go as well. And, finally, to show his appreciation of Kimi, he jumps, fully clothed, into the nearby swimming pool, then climbs out and slams his own soaked mobile onto the table next to Kimi's. They're quits.

The happy ending to the swimming excursion needs to be celebrated with a few exotic drinks. Then Kimi and Piki are brought down to earth. It's five o'clock in the morning and the flight to Doha leaves at eight. The prince is dumbfounded and of the opinion that there's no good reason for anyone to rush off in the middle of a good party. He says he'll despatch his private plane to the airport for two in the afternoon. 'You'll fly to Switzerland on it and you'll carry on partying in the palace.' Kimi and Piki look at each other and approve of the arrangement. The prince clicks his fingers and asks the subordinate responding to the click to make sure that the plane and the crew will be at the airport.

The men raise their glasses to the successful change of aeroplanes. Kimi and Piki get back to the hotel at nine, take a nap then head for the airport. The private twelve-seater promised by the prince has taxied to the scene, and the tired men climb in. The journey back home to Switzerland can begin. Kimi falls asleep instantly.

The plane leaves the men at Zürich airport and turns back, empty. Kimi and Piki wonder if that might be called wasteful and take a taxi home. It's a good place for carrying on with the tippling and the chatting. Piki isn't in a hurry to go anywhere – no one is calling him, particularly now that his mobile, too, is kaput.

Days follow each other: one, two, three. Warm, beautiful days, one much like the other, blending with the nights. On one of these days – the men no longer recall the exact point in time – they watch a video clip of footballer Diego Maradona's warm-up routine. It was a feast for their eyes. How can someone make a ball part of their body? How come that the ball and the man form such a beautiful alliance? The friends have an idea.

They get a ball, deciding to imitate Maradona. When you're tipsy, it's possible to imitate anybody. Piki, an attacker, tries to chip the ball in past Kimi, the goalkeeper. Kimi snatches the ball and falls onto his side, just like the versatile actor Vesa-Matti Loiri, whom he admires a great deal. Something hurts. Piki isn't immediately convinced by the moan and accuses his friend of acting for the cameras. Kimi isn't: he has twisted his ankle; it's starting to swell. The tests, due to start in a few days at Lotus, begin to look improbable. And he couldn't tell Lotus the whole truth about the manner in which he sustained the injury.

Kimi phones F1 doctor Aki Hintsa, who advises the driver to come to his private clinic. Jerry, a car dealer and a friend, is called and he takes Kimi to be examined by Hintsa. The driver returns home after a short time with walking sticks, blood-thinning preparations and painkillers. He has asked Hintsa to call Lotus to make sure that the team believes his story.

His ankle is jet black but his spirits are high: no need to attend the Lotus tests, so he can carry on drinking despite a slight physical impediment. Kimi remembers that, somewhere in the house, he's got a baggage trolley of the sort used by bellboys in hotels. It's suitable, in this case, for transporting a person. Piki pushes Kimi around in the gold-coloured trolley.

The swelling of the ankle goes down, but the drunkenness doesn't fade. It occurs to Kimi to visit Finland, that cold and distant land. People he loves live there and the spring celebrations of 1 May are coming up. Let's go then.

**His ankle is jet black but his spirits are high: no need to attend the Lotus tests, so he can carry on drinking despite a slight physical impediment.**

Kimi and Piki arrive in Helsinki and go straight to a restaurant called Karaoke Bar Restroom, where their friends welcome them with open arms. It's good to see old mates.

The friends say that they've tried to contact the pair without success. Kimi and Piki throw light on the reasons for their silence: one mobile is wet and the other one broken.

They have a few drinks in honour of spring and friendship. They have a few more, and realise at one point that the whole weekend has rolled into one long night. Then it's May Day Eve, the real day of celebrations. Kimi and Piki and friends have evolved into a larger group, which has moved to the machine shop in Kuru Road in Espoo. The upstairs houses Kimi's sauna and bar areas, where they can do what they like – goodbye cruel world. For May Day itself, they head for Kimi's summer cottage in Porkkalanniemi.

The days swing and sway; the nights crawl along.

The talk gets stale, ideas dry up.

A change of scenery is required. They hit on the idea of going to the good old Kannunkulma, a bar in the centre of Espoo. Jukka Poika provides the entertainment. It's 3 May. 'Day number twelve,' someone says. Kimi and Piki are jolted: they've now been drinking for twelve days. It isn't worth thinking about; they've got to look ahead. Jukka Poika's music is in the style of reggae; catchy, swinging. It resembles the foggy world inside their heads, a world that's starting to lose its rhythm.

At one point, on an unspecified day, they're upstairs in the machine shop. Piki is woken up by a strange sight: Kimi is drinking from a tiny goblet. It's not a goblet: it's a candle holder removed from the large chandelier. Kimi has filled the holder with red wine. All well and good. Let's carry on. Let's go to the sauna in Porkkalanniemi in the evening. Monday dawns. Time for some talking; this is it. Sixteen days have gone by. The group disperses like dandelion seeds swept away in the wind.

Kimi points out that it will be Wednesday the day after tomorrow. The Barcelona Grand Prix will start on Thursday, so he has got to leave for Barcelona on Wednesday. That's in two days' time; alcohol disappears from your system in two days, doesn't it? A three-week break from driving doesn't mean anything, does it?

On Wednesday, Kimi is seen off to the airport by his mates. He swaps the bottle for the steering wheel, which fits into his hand like an old habit. The track is familiar, speed is his second nature. Kimi comes third in the Barcelona Grand Prix.

'I just want to wish a happy Mother's Day to all mothers,' Kimi says at the press conference.

# PLEASING TO THE EYE, RESTFUL TO THE MIND

**Midsummer 2013, Porkkalanniemi. Kimi's** summer cottage is full of revellers: young adults, friends and acquaintances of acquaintances.

Kimi and Minttu's eyes meet. They're aware of each other but they don't know each other. They first met two years ago at a similar party. Minttu was then in a relationship; Kimi was married. Now Kimi is separated and Minttu is single.

All the doors are open – and shut. Minttu can't imagine falling in love with a man with a reputation for being imprudent, particularly not now that she lives in her own place, certain that she doesn't want any kind of steady relationship for a while. But Minttu comes to see that she enjoys being with Kimi a great deal; he would make a good friend. Not a lover, though, because she's convinced that falling in love with such a reckless man would only end in tears.

The party goes on. Kimi and Minttu are left with the imprint of a memory.

After midsummer, it's the turn of the Silverstone race. Heavy drinking makes the driver's body tremble; his mind is fragile. Kimi and Sami Visa fly to England. Visa has joint interests in a baseball cap business with Lotus and also plans to ask the team about Kimi's missing wages. They don't materialise.

It's been agreed that Kimi will drive Lotus's sports cars at a promotional event in an old airfield next to the factory. It's an ideal arrangement for the racing driver suffering from a hangover. Kimi drives and sweats the old alcohol deposits out of his body. The soaking-wet driver gets out of the car, satisfied: he's back in the swing of it, all the alcohol has disappeared without a trace. Sami is both amused and appalled.

Kimi is seventh in the race. The next Grand Prix takes place at the Nürburgring circuit in Germany. Kimi is fourth. A basically good race; no particular memories. And there's no room for anything else in his mind because it's occupied by Minttu, an air hostess with Flybe, who has her own life with a job and a home in Mannerheim Road in the centre of Helsinki.

A three-week break follows. The next race would take place in Hungary on 28 July.

Kimi comes back to Finland in a restless mood; he has been like that for some time.

Friends and acquaintances are worried about his situation. Something is out of joint, even though his work inside the car is going well.

Minttu's phone rings in mid-July. Kimi invites her to his cottage in Porkkalanniemi. She's taken aback and asks if there are other people around. She's used to seeing Kimi surrounded by revellers. There's no one else here, that's the reply. She hesitates, he cajoles her. Minttu gives in, though she's a little anxious.

On 18 July, Kimi texts his friend Piki: 'I'll risk it and take Minttu to the cottage.'

And Minttu goes to the cottage with fateful and beautiful consequences.

## Kimi is fragile and frightened. He feels panicky and asks Minttu to come and support him in Hungary.

The summer parties continue but something has come to an end: aimlessness, searching, uncertainty. Everything is certain now, or almost certain.

'I'm in the cottage. Swilling spirits.' The text message to Piki dated 23 July expresses both restlessness and something of the carefree nature of summer. The message is written five days before the Hungarian Grand Prix. Kimi is fragile and frightened. He feels panicky and asks Minttu to come and support him in Hungary. She agrees and takes a couple of friends along. Wednesday is the last drinking day; the press conference is on Thursday.

The hungover driver comes second, something to celebrate. Negotiations are underway with Ferrari at the same time, and he's with Minttu. They aren't yet an item but something has happened. Kimi asks her to stay a bit longer. At this stage he doesn't know that this will be his last extended binge-drinking session.

The group returns from Hungary in a party mood and they pick up where they left off: they get on with the drinking. Kimi and Minttu's crowd plays mini golf and gets a mention in a gossip column. The image is blurry, as these photos tend to be. Minttu is wearing the hoodie of Piki's son; she has suddenly felt the cold. Kimi is holding a can. The future couple is captured with a long lens from behind a bush.

They go on partying as if that summer were their last. Kimi should have signed the Ferrari contract by now but some detail has yet to be ironed out. They decide to go to Hanko, to the Poker Run event. Kimi wants Minttu to come along though the company is loud and dominated by men. She agrees. They borrow Teemu Selänne's boat, but there's something else that has got to be sorted out: a bodyguard. Some acquaintances are called and come up with a burly man for a couple of thousand euros. Then they can sail.

Kimi's phone rings while he's in the archipelago. It's about the Ferrari contract. He has a brief chat and announces to the group that the contract has been finalised; no need to worry about it anymore. He throws the phone into the sea.

November 2017 in Baar, Switzerland. Robin, under three, messes about with his dad in the living room; Rianna, aged six months, is asleep. Minttu and I sit in the silence of a side room. She recalls the summer of 2013, one of the turning points of her life. It was a strange, disjointed summer, which turned into a calm autumn.

'I'm glad that I met Kimi when I did, not when he was around twenty. That he's past that stage. I've done stupid things in my life, too; done my share of partying and drinking. And we can still party, but not like before. If you haven't done or experienced anything, you can lose the plot when you're forty or fifty. I've spent enough time in bars; I know what it's like.'

Minttu's picture of Kimi was grainy and messy; it's a picture that most people share. The image isn't false but so black and white that it makes your eyes hurt.

'Of course, at first my opinion was coloured by the fact

that I only knew Kimi from press reports. Then I began to see what he was like with his nearest and dearest. And the first thing that struck me was his sense of humour. I spent days laughing at his stories. And the other thing was the way he treated people close to him. There were many occasions when he helped his friends.'

November 2017 in Kraphovi, a restaurant in Tuusula. I sit opposite Kimmo Virtanen, a retired financier of sixty-three. He's Minttu's father and Kimi's father-in-law. His daughter's choice of husband was as big a surprise to him as it was to everyone else. At first, Minttu was cagey, describing Kimi as a friend. That was what he believed for a long time until she admitted to dating the driver.

'At first I felt conflicting emotions, naturally enough. Particularly as I've been following F1, and I know a fair amount about the sport and about Kimi. But the public image soon crumbled when I met the man.'

Kimmo remembers vividly his first encounter with the racing driver: 'They came to my home in Tuusula in autumn 2013. Minttu had a small Fiat and it needed winter tyres. I told them to bring the tyres along. Kimi wasn't very talkative but he was extremely polite. Then we got chatting properly, thanks to him. He said, after coffee, let's go and change those tyres. I said it was raining; I can take them to Teboil. Kimi said no, we'll go and change them together.'

November 2017 in Baar, Switzerland. Minttu has gone

to Rianna, who has woken up from her nap. Kimi is lying on the divan, trying to answer the question that has been put to married couples a billion times all over the world during the course of history. 'What was so attractive about her?'

**'I can't really say what single thing is at the bottom of the attraction. We've always liked each other and found it easy to talk. And, of course, she's pleasing to the eye.'**

Kimi hums and haws, hesitates, shifts his position, and looks for the right words.

'I can't really say what single thing is at the bottom of the attraction. We've always liked each other and found it easy to talk. And, of course, she's pleasing to the eye. When I first saw Minttu, she wore tight denim shorts. I said "some arse". It became a sort of standing joke and I still use that expression, made into one word: somearse.'

Kimi is amused but it's possible that not all readers will feel the same. I sense from his expression that he could have said something else at the first meeting.

His face becomes serious.

'In the previous relationship, I was always afraid of being caught at something or other. When will the gossip magazine *Seiska* turn up? What will it say next? I would lie and try to remember in a week's time what I had said. I said to Minttu that if we get together, I won't bullshit or cheat on you. I'll never want the hell or the anxiety that lying causes.'

We're in the same room the following day. Minttu carries on reminiscing and recalls the rapid progress of their relationship in the autumn of 2013.

'After that summer, it got more serious. No point in fighting it. And then it all happened really fast. I don't need my own space all of the time, and Kimi doesn't either. We do a lot of things together; we do everything together. Neither of us feels that the other should go away for a bit. He always makes me feel that it's lovely that I'm there. I was impressed by that. If I compare Kimi to all my previous relationships, this is what makes him different from every man I know. I mean the way Kimi pays attention. I didn't feel after a few months that I was taken for granted. He shows every day that we belong together.'

In the summer, everything was unclear; by the autumn it was clear. Minttu moved to Kaskisaari and continued working as normal. She lived on her own during the times Kimi was away doing his job, touring the world. He wanted Minttu to stop working, so that they could spend more time together.

'At first I was adamant: there was no way I'd give up; I had always worked and supported myself. I said that if this thing doesn't pan out, I can't ring up work and say that I want to come back. I had to be quite certain. It was no easy decision. Of course, we missed each other all the time. That made the decision easier in the end. All the same, it was hard to give up my independence. I did my last shift in May 2014, around May Day, and then I moved here. And then Robin came along quite quickly.'

And then it was Rianna. A lot was crammed into four years. And something was lost, too: Minttu's mother died in 2006, Kimi's father in 2010. The couple encountered death and created life. And they are alike in many respects. Minttu's father Kimmo has noticed it, too: 'Minttu is decisive and competitive; she always wanted to be in the winning team. She has inherited her will to win from me. She and Kimi like similar things.'

Kimi lies on the sofa, thinking of Minttu:

'Something's wrong if there's never a cross word. She's pigheaded, too, and if there's a quarrel, there are two of us who are the same. It's good that she's strict, not bossy but strict; she's no doormat. You've got to be a bit strict with me, it's the only way. A fiery character is good. It's attractive. Life's not worth living if nothing matters.'

Those are the words of a man who at one time led the kind of life in which nothing much mattered.

# IN OVERDRIVE

**'My pulse is my** property. It doesn't belong to FIA.'

A sensor designed for the FIA (Fédération Internationale de l'Automobile), the sport's governing body, is incorporated into the little finger of Kimi's left-hand driving glove. The sensor measures the oxygen level, the pulse and other important data about the driver's body. The FIA wanted the pulses of all drivers to be displayed to the spectators during the whole of the race but the drivers didn't agree. The pulse is the driver's property; his heart belongs to him.

The sensor wasn't originally developed as a source of entertainment for the spectators but to help in crisis situations. If a car is squashed in a collision or on leaving the track, the driver is inaccessible and can't be contacted by radio. The doctors can then, via the sensor, check the driver's condition and decide whether the car must be lifted up immediately.

Kimi says that he has never measured his pulse during a race but it has been monitored during training. In the intensive training carried out with physiotherapist Mark Arnall in the early part of the year, his average pulse over twenty minutes was 173. At times it was 192.

'It doesn't get that high for a veteran but it may well have been 200 when I was younger,' Kimi says with a grin. 'I don't think it gets terribly high during a race.'

Kimi's dry-as-dust humour defuses the dramatic elements of the sport, but it's a fact that a driver's pulse fluctuates wildly. But what about the pulse of his ardent fans, or of his beloved or his mother?

Hearts go into overdrive all round the world when Formula 1 starts its race weekend. In 2017, the sport was followed by some 350 million people via TV and other platforms in addition to the over four million fans actually attending the races. In Finland, every Grand Prix is watched by around 300,000 people. The spectrum of fans ranges from fanatics to analytical observers, who follow each practice, qualifying and race and are aware of sector times and strategies.

Petri Vaulamo, the 48-year-old sales manager of Toyota Kaivoksela, is an analytical fan. In his case, being analytical doesn't signify calmness; on the contrary: he experiences every race weekend through Kimi whether the driver wins or loses. Vaulamo differs from an ardent fan in that he follows the sport with engineer-like precision. The family of four has adapted itself to the man's absence during race weekends, even though he's seated in front of a 55-inch television in his dining room in Klaukkala. His body is present but his mind is somewhere over there, at the corner of sector three or on the main straight, in Kimi's car.

'If a race weekend is on the horizon, I already change in the early part of the week. My thoughts drift to the forthcoming Grand Prix. I often follow it with my brother Mika. I attend a race a couple of times in a season, not more than that because the trips easily take four or five days.'

I meet up with Vaulamo after the unlucky Bahrain Grand Prix. The catastrophic race ended in Francesco Cigarini, Ferrari's tyre changer, being run over by Kimi's left-hand rear wheel during a failed pit stop. The man was rushed to hospital. His operation went well; he's making a good recovery.

Petri Vaulamo is also making a recovery because the Shanghai Grand Prix is in a week's time. He's already looking forward to it. That's how he always tries to deal with every bad race.

'I felt bad for the whole of Sunday evening. But life goes on. My wife had to tell me off – I came out with a few swearwords. I get het up and calm down again pretty quickly. That's my personality: up and down. It was an evening race for us, between nine and ten. If it had finished at three in the afternoon, the period of mourning would have been much longer.'

A sense of proportion – it's what reason suggests. But after an unlucky Grand Prix, reason flies out of the window and emotions rage in a fan's head like an open fire. Experience smooths things over a bit: Vaulamo has been a fan for many years. He was already into the sport when Keijo 'Keke' Rosberg won the World Championship in 1982; he became a fanatic in the 1990s, and Kimi Räikkönen's arrival on the scene triggered the final explosion. Kimi seemed special straight away because he always looked forward – he didn't remain aggrieved or chew things over or malign his competitors or make superfluous comments. His demeanour, body language and driving style continue to appeal to Vaulamo, who also follows the entire sport.

'I follow lots of details closely: sector times, tyre compounds, lap times, tenths of a second, certain corners, driving errors. I also try to spot if a driver is able to handle the same place better on the next lap. Recent technological developments enable me to see many things simultaneously.'

Vaulamo's workplace contains other Formula 1 fans. 'Yes, we celebrate here if there's been a win. It has a big impact. It's a bit of a joke but I'm telling you it's worth coming in to buy a car on a Monday after a successful race weekend.'

He agrees to switch on the heartbeat monitor for the duration of the Chinese Grand Prix. I'm interested in emotion measured by technological means.

It's the Shanghai International Circuit on 14 April 2018. The time is 9.10. Kimi is second on the grid and his car number is seven.

The green lights come on; I estimate Kimi's pulse at around 130. Then it's the first corner, and his pulse rises to 170–80. Instinct takes over from thinking and translates into movement. The wheels of the cars nearly touch; the tiniest of errors pushes the driver off the track. His body takes over from his mind, and his pulse shoots up to 180 during the rush to the first corner. Kimi gets off to a better start, Sebastian Vettel blocks the driving line, and Kimi has to give way. Valtteri Bottas and Max Verstappen are able to pass. We have no accurate data on Kimi's pulse, or on how pissed off he feels.

We're in Klaukkala, Finland, looking at Vaulamo's heart rate. Only half an hour ago, his normal pulse was 70. At the first corner, it rises to almost 100. Vaulamo becomes distracted, depression takes over. Kimi is now fourth. His qualifying was brilliant; all through the early season, he has been faster than Sebastian Vettel. Even so, he's now fourth. The question is: will the race become a procession? Surely the team doesn't expect Kimi to do the dirty work on behalf of Vettel? The cars settle into a queue. Is everything lost?

In Baar in Switzerland, Minttu Räikkönen's pulse reaches the maximum value for a fit person; her brain is on fire. She leaps off the sofa and switches off the TV. Her husband's race is ruined; that was that. Minttu feels like sending a text to Ferrari's management to tell them what she thinks of Sebastian Vettel's actions at the end of the start straight. She tries to calm down – impossible for a competitive person. She watches the race through Kimi-coloured glasses.

In Espoo in Finland, Paula is on edge on account of her son. She has no heart-rate monitor but she did give birth to the driver. She has a glass of water, a glass of brandy and a beer in front of her. The start is the hardest and raises the pulse sky-high. Paula has watched a few races from the paddock, but she doesn't feel that it's a place for her. It's more comfortable to watch a Grand Prix at home with a small crowd of familiar people. The Belgian Grand Prix is the only race that she attends regularly.

Kimi is driving in sixth place, his pulse slow – it's a Sunday outing. Until he's suddenly confronted with a new scenario: a collision. Max Verstappen does something silly and drives into Sebastian Vettel. The cars slide around, and in the space of three seconds everything has changed. Kimi is now third, his pulse unknown. At the same moment, Petri Vaulamo's pulse fluctuates between 105 and 115 for a few seconds. Petri bubbles with joy; he has to call his brother, who announced only half an hour ago that he will never watch another race ever again. Passion swings their moods from one extreme to another. Being a fan is a serious condition.

**The journey to the end of the year is long. A fan's heart goes into overdrive many more times before the Abu Dhabi Grand Prix, the last race, in November.**

Sami Visa is present in Shanghai. He knows that Minttu's heart is doing somersaults on Kimi's account. But what Sami doesn't know is that she switched off the TV after the first corner. He calls her to crow over Kimi's unexpected third place. Minttu, who didn't know about the turn of events, is surprised and tells him that she was unable to watch beyond the first corner. Sami sighs.

Kimi comes third in a race which, only moments before, offered him the chance of a miserable sixth place. Other drivers' bad luck and Verstappen's blunder get him a podium place. Vaulamo's pulse drops to around 70; a relieved calm descends on the man seated three metres away from the television. One Grand Prix is over, eighteen remain. The journey to the end of the year is long. A fan's heart goes into overdrive many more times before the Abu Dhabi Grand Prix, the last race, in November.

I go to Toyota Kaivoksela in Vantaa on Monday morning after the race. Sales manager Vaulamo shakes hands, his face briefly lit up by a grin. The smile hails from China, even though he has spent the whole weekend at Klaukkala. We sit down to go over the events and to look at data from the weekend's pulse measurements. A man can say what he likes, but the monitor reveals the facts.

Yesterday, the man progressed from despair to relief. During Friday's free practice, his pulse remained within moderate values, but rose at the start of Saturday's qualifying. In the final, decisive sector, Vaulamo's pulse reached 90–100 because Sebastian Vettel beat Kimi's time in the last few seconds. During the race itself, the values fluctuated between 85 and 95.

Vaulamo shows me a present he received in the morning from a business acquaintance. It's a painting depicting events at the 1982 Monaco Grand Prix. In the picture, Ayrton Senna blocks Nigel Mansell. The sales manager thinks that getting the painting right now is a mysterious coincidence, because Sebastian did just that to Kimi yesterday.

Vaulamo says he suffered greatly during the years when Kimi was a rally driver and not in Formula. The intervening years felt empty. No other driver aroused his interest. He knows that Kimi won't be driving for long but it's pointless to think about it in advance. The season is long; his pulse will rise many more times.

The season is long for Minttu Räikkönen, too, as she waits for the day when her husband no longer sets off on his travels. Minttu attended the race at Baku, observing everything from close quarters with the heart-rate monitor switched on. The readings were 74 for the first qualifying session, 128 for the second session and 156 for the third. At the start of the race, her pulse was 169.

Paula, who hasn't got a heart-rate monitor, thinks she has suffered from enough tension by now – whether caused by events on the racetrack or outside it. A normal pulse is the best pulse.

# ARE WE HERE TO DRIVE OR TO TALK?

**Baar in Switzerland. It's** the end of February and the start of the 2018 Formula season. We land at Zürich airport with Kimi's affairs manager Sami Visa and Minttu's father Kimmo Virtanen. Physiotherapist Mark Arnall joins the party on the following day, Saturday, and we fly to Barcelona where the new car is due to be tested for the first time. This is the official start of a Formula driver's working year and nomadic life.

Sami says that this is also the start of a lot of red tape. Countries outside the EU require the drivers to have work permits, and tax is deducted at source. Some countries require a work visa. Income tax is paid normally in everyone's country of domicile. The teams travel round the world like rock bands. An F1 driver's gig lasts for about five days; for the team personnel, it's a lot longer.

At Zürich airport, we're met by a slender and agile Kimi, hiding behind a cap and dark sunglasses. I last saw him in the New Year. In just under two months, his face has got thinner; his cheeks are slightly hollow.

**The team recommends that a driver wearing his race suit, shoes and helmet should weigh a maximum 73 kilos. Kimi is now well below that.**

The season is approaching and Mark Arnall's intensive training shows: Kimi has shed 3.2 kilos onto the gym floor. The team recommends that a driver wearing his race suit, shoes and helmet should weigh a maximum 73 kilos. Kimi is now well below that. One kilo has the effect of 0.1 of a second in qualifying. The insanely tiny margins force a driver to train hard and eat intelligently. This is a sport for slender men.

Kimi picks up a coffee and a croissant at the airport and skips towards his new company motor. We pack our belongings into a large Fiat Talento, the sort of practical van Kimi got used to in his karting days, though the vehicles were never new back then.

We get in. Kimi is in a good mood until Sami starts

talking about the manual gearbox. The van was ordered with an automatic gearbox but, for some reason, a manual version has been delivered. Kimi mutters that it will be exchanged straight away. We drop the subject.

Although the tests won't start until Monday, we're leaving for Barcelona in the early evening on Saturday. Kimi's work starts with the 'filming day', when material is shot for sponsors' and Ferrari's own use.

It's Saturday morning at 7.30. We woke up nice and early at six to watch a skiing competition: the men's 50-kilometre cross-country at the Winter Olympics. Finland's big hope, Iivo Niskanen, is skiing, his cheeks red with exertion. He's getting ahead of everyone else.

The doorbell rings. Who would be coming at this time of the day? Who would disrupt the tension-packed Olympic auditorium?

Minttu comes down and opens the door. An anti-doping control officer, sent by the Swiss anti-doping committee, comes in. Good timing, do step right in. We say good morning and point out that it may take a while before we can wake up the sportsman due to give the sample. The officer regrets the timing, but he does have the right to arrive early. We nod and try to watch Iivo Niskanen at the same time. Our watching helps: he wins the gold.

The officer sits awkwardly on the living-room sofa. A briefcase lies at his feet. His expression says that he's only doing his job. We learn that Mark Arnall has to send the anti-doping controllers Kimi's schedule, which will enable them to turn up when the driver is bound to be at home. If the door isn't opened, the sample – even though it hasn't been taken – is deemed to be positive.

Minttu has managed to wake Kimi up; he comes down, bad-tempered. At the same time, Iivo Niskanen is celebrating in the TV studio and exits stage left with an Olympic official. It looks like Iivo will be taking the same test as our driver here. The officer gets up from the sofa, picks up his briefcase and follows his ill-tempered, grunting subject. The deed is quickly done. The anti-doping man tells us that he has tested the Swiss skier Dario Cologna twenty times since last September. Kimi isn't interested; he goes into the kitchen, makes porridge, adds berries to it, eats and goes back to bed.

Concentration on the new season has started; Kimi needs to rest a while longer. The while proves long. It's 10.07 – no sign of the driver. Finally he comes downstairs at 13.07. The plan is to leave for Zürich airport at 15.30. Kimi went to his bedroom with Robin at eight-thirty the night before. He has been asleep for fourteen hours, minus the doping test and the quick bowl of porridge, which took about an hour. Kimi says that he had a restless night and woke up a couple of times.

At the airport we board the hired plane. I admit a slight flight phobia to the rest of the group, particularly when it's a small plane like this. Kimi says he's sorry and points out that in that particular model one of the wings doesn't always function properly. Nevertheless, he believes that I have led a good life, which I should have no problem leaving, at my age, calmly and serenely.

As soon as we land at Barcelona, Kimi cancels the 'jump out' practice session, which he deems unnecessary. The 'jump out' test of the FIA is compulsory but it would only take place the following day. In the test, a driver has to get out of a car in fifteen seconds. He or she has to pass in order to be officially allowed to carry out testing.

The huge Mobile World Congress has filled the city's hotels. Rooms have only been reserved for Kimi and Mark. Sami and I lodge on board Kimi's *Iceman* boat, which is moored at Barcelona's Port Olímpic. The actual home of the boat is in the port of Vilanova, which is located forty kilometres away. The boat is looked after by Captain Masa Kallio and Jaska Kononen, a marine engineer.

Previously I've only seen pictures and short videos of the *Iceman* yacht, manufactured by Sunseeker. Kimi bought it in 2009 and it has been looked after by Masa Kallio ever since. Jaska Kononen, in charge of the boat's technology, was employed in 2011. Jaska tells me about his first encounter with his employer:

'I had held the job for a couple of months when Kimi came to the boat to party with his friends. I watched the celebrations till five in the morning and went to bed. After half an hour, Kimi came to wake me up and said that limoncello would be served on the front deck. Well, I agreed in the end and drank limoncello with him on the afterdeck. Later, Kimi said that I would have got the sack if I hadn't started drinking with him that morning. He said that he didn't trust people who didn't drink.'

Masa has even more experience of employment relations on the *Iceman* yacht:

'I've been sacked several times. Particularly when I don't allow drunkards to ride on water scooters. I'm told that I'm cruel. Once, Kimi asked for a scooter. I said: "No, you can't get on it because you're drunk." He suggested a wrestling match. If I win, he gets to ride; if I lose, he doesn't. Of course, I didn't agree. I said blow here [in a breathalyser]. If you're in the clear, you're allowed to have a go. He blew 2.1.'

Though Masa and Jaska have seen some eye-popping events during the boat's history, they appreciate their employer's unique sense of humour. The racier times are over; the main beverage in the fridge is Vichy water. The *Iceman* yacht is in excellent condition, because its owner wants it that way. Kimi was personally involved in designing its interior. The colours, materials and small details reflect his taste.

It's early in the morning. Sami and I leave the boat for the hotel. The plan is to head for the circuit from there with Kimi and Mark, who has driven the car out of the hotel basement into the street. The only person missing is

Kimi. He's late – again. He's one of the fastest in the world on the racetrack, and one of the slowest at the hotel.

We start negotiating the morning rush hour. Mark passes a ginger and lemon drink to the driver. The drink, about a decilitre, goes down in one gulp. Kimi changes lanes without the indicator. All that's needed is a quick glance in the wing mirror to see if a gap is wide enough. Mark asks if he wants the sat nav on. No need – it's in the driver's head.

**Mark has driven the car from the hotel basement into the street. The only person missing is Kimi. He's late – again. He's one of the fastest in the world on the racetrack, and one of the slowest at the hotel.**

We arrive at the circuit for the filming day. This is when Ferrari and the sponsors can record material – action sequences, photos, interviews and other marketing stuff – for many different purposes. Kimi and Sebastian Vettel walk towards cameras on the start straight, drive the new car for around fifty kilometres, assume different expressions, and stand side by side. There are people in red everywhere, among them photographers pointing their long lenses, looking for new camera angles and changing the lighting. All this is new to an outsider; not to the drivers. The Spanish winter is the surprise element for all. It's very chilly, it's sleeting and the tests are at risk. In this weather, tyres don't heat up, the track is made wet by the conditions and the drivers feel cold in their cars. Nerves are being tested as much as the cars.

Sami takes photos of Kimi's new helmet. A driver needs between twelve and sixteen of them in a season plus replicas for the sponsors. Robin and Rianna's names have been written on the back. Kimi's nearest and dearest are included in the painting by Uffe Tägström, the helmet designer based in Tampere. Uffe has designed all of Kimi's helmets from the start. They cost around €3,000 each, with the price of the painting work on top of that.

The day turns into evening. Kimi, a son of the north, is amused by the news on all Spanish television channels, as excited reporters commentate on the grim winter that has hit the country. Italy, too, has experienced a tragedy: sleet has built up in front of the outdoor cafés. People gesticulate in a lively manner, spreading their hands. Where did this cold, filthy water come from? In Kimi's view, what they know of winter can be written on the head of a pin. All that moaning doesn't get you anywhere. Just put on your snowsuit and enjoy some ice fishing.

Everyone is hoping for better tomorrow; otherwise the tests will be aborted.

The wish is not granted. A strong wind rocks the big *Iceman* boat in the morning; sleet splashes against my face as soon as I open the door to the afterdeck. We drive to the circuit, certain that there won't be a full day's driving.

In the paddock area, we encounter a figure who is seen at virtually all of the races. He's Heikki Kulta, the sports reporter of *Turku News*. He also thought he'd be coming to a warm country from a cold one. He shivers but is enthusiastic about the new season. Bahrain will be his 350th Grand Prix, a stunning record. Kulta is a walking encyclopaedia, a combination of excited fan and analytical reporter. I ask him to identify something essential about Räikkönen.

'His ability to recover from disappointments. Kimi is quite exceptional in that,' Kulta says. He has followed Kimi from the beginning of the driver's career and has always believed in his ability even when others have doubted. Kulta was the first reporter to learn about the driver's contract with Sauber.

'I was at the Malaysian Grand Prix in 2000 and got a whiff of Kimi's contract. I immediately rang Kikka Kuosmanen, who was looking after his affairs at the time, and asked if I could interview him. Suddenly my phone rang – it was Kimi. "Räikkönen here." That's how it started: he called me. I met Joe Saward, a British reporter, in Malaysia. I gave him the news, too. Joe laughed and said it couldn't be true. He went on to say that if Kimi gets to drive in Formula 1, he'll appear at the Grand Prix dressed up as the Pope. I still haven't seen the cleric in the paddock.'

Heikki Kulta has a clear memory of the initial stages of the driver's career. Kimi was a shy, quiet boy at the centre of the most popular of all motor sports. A fish out of water.

'He would answer "I don't know" to nine out of ten questions.'

Kulta admits that he follows the races through Kimi-coloured glasses and feels the driver's wins and defeats deeply. Perhaps it's because of this sincerity that he has a good rapport with Kimi, whose relationship with the media as a whole is rather distant, verging on hostile in some cases. The driver trusts Kulta to write about the real business, not around it.

According to the reporter, Kimi is totally unique; he's natural and unaffected. He thinks before he speaks and puts what he's got to say succinctly. He's not florid, he's plain-speaking.

'These other drivers come off a different production line.' In Kulta's opinion, Kimi's special gift is his great sense of humour. 'He even gets the jokes from the Turku area' – that's the reporter's final message as he hurries forward in the paddock. He's got the chance of bump-ing into many talkative experts with weighty opinions on the season ahead, though not a single metre has yet been driven.

It's Kimi's first day of testing. Cold air and cold tyres make for a poor combination. On the first lap, Fernando Alonso's car loses a wheel and driving is interrupted for a while. During the day, Kimi drives eighty laps, a total of 372 kilometres. The race itself is sixty-six laps, so he gets some experience of the car. The following day it's Sebastian Vettel's turn, and on Wednesday it'll be Kimi again. The Finn drives the third fastest lap time, but it doesn't matter. What matters is what the car feels like. It feels good.

The tests are always the same: teams watch each other, and if their own speed is good, they may hide it from the others. And everyone thinks the same: how fast is that car *really*? Are they concealing their speed on purpose? The game is afoot.

It's the second day of testing. Today it's Sebastian's turn to drive, and Kimi comes to the boat to eat and spend time. We order Thai food, Vichy water fizzes, words fly around, freedom of speech reigns, nothing has been put on paper yet. Kimi talks, exaggerates, invents comparisons, waves his hands and spits out a traditional swearword here and there. He lets his hair down, colours his stories, breaks off, and finds a rhythm. This is how a storyteller works.

That's not the Kimi who grunts a couple of syllables to reporters and leaves in a huff. His public image is rough and fuzzy and often snapped through a bush. But it's also true. Things are what they seem. He has done some wild partying. He has thrown money around. All the same, a public image is also always blurred, overexposed and limited. And it's no wonder: Kimi has given people plenty to talk about but hasn't talked himself. That's why the difference between the public and the private is big in his case, or, to put it more precisely: it's a ravine.

The atmosphere is relaxed, and it's the right time to ask whatever springs to mind, even if there's a risk of Kimi using one of his favourite words: *kotelo* (mollusc).

It's a word he deploys to describe someone who's stupid or ignorant. I prefer to apply the latter definition to myself, and decide on asking simple questions. I haven't quite got the hang of what driving actually involves. I ask Kimi to throw a bit of light on the matter. After all, he can't even see properly out of that car.

Kimi gives me a long look but begins to explain:

'I see the top edge of the front wheels, not where the front wing is. You don't know in an ordinary car either where the front bit is going. And, yes, it's a little awkward to be almost lying down and it's hot as hell. At first, it felt strange because I was used to swaying and moving around in a microcar. In this car, you don't move at all.'

I think of another occupational extreme: crane operators sit in a small cabin high up and are connected to the builders working on the ground via a radio and a display unit.

**'Tyre pressures demand an accuracy measured in millimetres every time. An engineer once said to me that they are now "close enough". Bloody hell, in this job close enough isn't good enough.'**

Next, I want to know who Kimi chats to during a race. His face says it all: the wrong verb. You don't chat at speeds approaching 300 km/h.

'I only talk to the engineer, no one else. Not very much during the race but quite a lot otherwise. Our job is to describe how the car feels. The team observes the behaviour of the car all the time; during testing and race weekends. All of the data is online and connected to the Maranello plant, where lots of experts sit during the Grand Prix. There are guys at the scene of action and there are guys at Maranello. I call it backing up the back-up.'

'What are the important factors?'

'Gas equivalents, brakes, suspension, stability controls, etc. Tyre pressures demand an accuracy measured in millimetres every time. An engineer once said to me that they are now "close enough". Bloody hell, in this job close enough isn't good enough.'

As an outsider I'm interested in every aspect of a sport alien to me, which means I ask about wholly irrelevant things. Kimi's workplace has no toilet facilities and he has to spend a long time in it in an awkward position. What if he hasn't had a chance, for some reason, to go to the toilet before the race or the qualifying sessions?

Kimi sighs, wondering whether to answer or to let my question sink into the morass of its own tastelessness. He decides to answer. That's good, because it's always possible for the answer to be more interesting than the question.

'Nothing major has ever got inside the race suit. But I've sometimes peed in qualifying after waiting for an hour in the car. But it's virtually just water after I've been topping up all morning. And because the race suit is Ferrari red, no one really notices it. I've been lucky – I haven't had diarrhoea during a race.'

Seriously speaking, food and drink are of great importance. When Kimi gets into the car, everything has to be balanced, and that's normally the case. Mark Arnall tries to take care of every detail to make sure the driver sitting in the car is calm.

We abandon the relaxed atmosphere and move on to the next day of testing. In the garage, the mechanics bustle round the stripped-down car. Without its carbon-fibre shell and its tyres, the car resembles a complicated and messy heap of metal. It only looks like a SF71H racing car after the red shell has been lowered over it.

Eight red mechanics swarm simultaneously round the red car. Each one of them has his own task. They are paid between €3,500 and €4,000 per month, plus bonuses and daily expense allowances. The organisation includes many people whose wages don't reach that sort of level but everyone wants to work for Ferrari; everyone wants to wear the colour.

Apart from me.

Sami whispers to me that I have to leave the paddock. I follow him, bemused. He says that he has received feedback from Ferrari's management: I can't occupy this space unless I'm dressed appropriately. I'm given a red jacket. I put it on and I wear the colour for the next six hours.

The winter tests are true to their name; sleet sweeps across the landscape, and it's cold for Spain but only cool in Finnish terms. The team announces that we won't know until two o'clock if we drive today or not. We start killing time, which is made a lot easier because Ferrari's facilities are filled with people who may have something to say about Kimi. The espresso machine gurgles, strong coffee drips into small cups.

A man walks past, a man so ordinary-looking that he must be extraordinary. The most important person in an organisation is usually the one who doesn't make a lot of noise but who walks quietly in the background. He is surrounded by an aura that says he's above everything around him.

I learn that the man is Louis C. Camilleri, chairman of the board of Philip Morris International. The tobacco firm he represents is Ferrari's main funder. I ask Sami if it's possible to approach this man. Sami knows Camilleri and thinks that the matter has to be dealt with through Alberto Antonini, Ferrari's press officer. Sami approaches Antonini, who says that Camilleri may be available for an interview in about two hours. He also says at the same time that the interview with team boss Maurizio Arrivabene, agreed the day before, could take place now.

Arrivabene sits opposite me with the press officer next to him. I switch on the Dictaphone and so does Antonini. Ferrari documents everything.

The team boss says that he met Kimi for the first time in the driver's championship year in 2007. He says that he noticed something that has become the foundation of Kimi's professional identity. 'Kimi is different from the others in that he finds out first and speaks only then.' It's generally known that Arrivabene and Kimi get on well. It's not surprising because this man, too, speaks with deliberation and likes to use precise expressions. He thinks that Kimi doesn't try to be a star and that's why he is like he is.

I recall a paradox that I noted at the Malaysian Grand

Prix: Kimi gives very little to his fans, and yet the fans feel they get a great deal. Arrivabene suppresses a laugh when he remembers a Chinese trip.

'Kimi came out of the airport gate with hundreds of people waiting for him. He wore dark glasses and a black rucksack and everyone hoped he would say something. He said: "Hello."'

Arrivabene mentions one more thing that has become a solid ingredient in the driver's relationship with the team: Kimi is loyal. After saying it, the team boss is silent for a moment, as if wanting to pay homage to the word. Kimi has been loyal to all his teams in good times and bad, in the pit lane and at every corner.

Louis C. Camilleri walks past and gives me a look that tells me we could have the chat now; I don't need to wait for two hours. I thank Arrivabene for the interview. His handshake is firm.

When Camilleri takes his turn, he says that he met Kimi for the first time in 2006, in Paris, when the driver's managers Dave and Steve Robertson were negotiating the Ferrari contract at Jean Todt's home. Todt was Ferrari's team boss at the time.

'Kimi seemed like a smart chap. I like people who listen. We're born with two ears, two eyes but just one mouth. This fellow uses them in the right ratio.'

I remember Jean Todt talking to me about the same thing using different words. Kimi is reserved and shy but direct. Camilleri says that he has become friends with the driver over the years. They've been to an ice hockey match in his home city, New York, and Kimi has also visited his vineyard.

'He doesn't differentiate between people. He treats everyone the same, whether it's a director or a cleaner. He's emotionally intelligent. There's a lot of superciliousness in Formula 1; he has none.'

Finally, Camilleri describes an interesting detail about Kimi's wedding: 'All of a sudden, Kimi stood up and gave a speech which he hadn't written down. It really sticks in my memory – it touched me. It's one of the most beautiful speeches I've ever heard. He spoke for something like ten minutes.'

Camilleri has to go to another meeting. I thank him for the chat. Kimi, hidden behind dark glasses, walks past. He disappears into his small room to take a nap. Maybe there will be no testing today, no driving. Are we here to drive or to talk? This time, it was to talk.

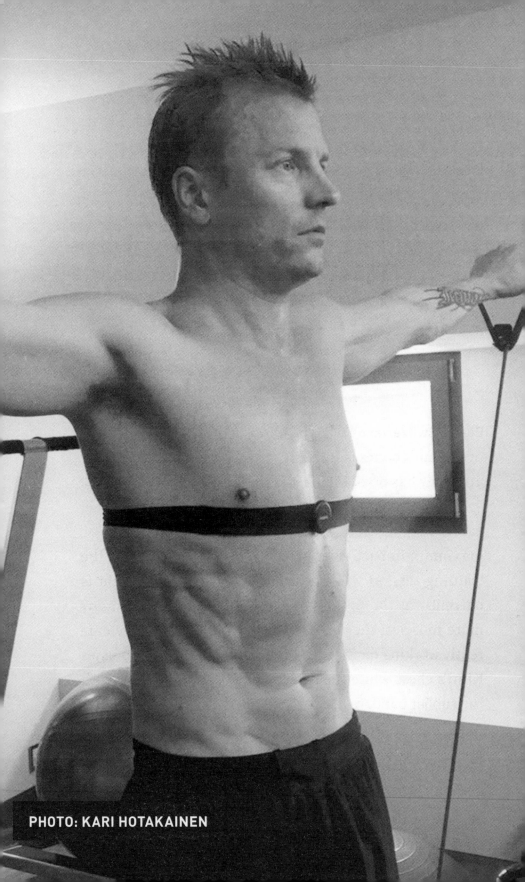

PHOTO: KARI HOTAKAINEN

# AN END IS A BEGINNING

**Baar in Switzerland at** the end of April 2018. The layer of flesh over Kimi's bones is thin and glistens with drops of sweat. The body has no opinions, or at least no one asks if it does.

Physiotherapist Mark Arnall sifts through the elastic bands hanging on his arm. He's looking for one that has a maximum impact when stretched. It's eleven o'clock; the training session will last another hour. Kimi's weight is currently at the optimum level and he doesn't want any more muscles; they are too heavy. The two men are currently working on the upper body and hands. Mark presses Kimi's chest while the driver executes a movement with the rubber band, repeating it fifteen times. Another movement follows and is repeated twelve times. Next, Kimi holds a 5-kilo weight in each hand. He moves his hands sideways to the front and performs eight repetitions. After a break, he lies on his back on the floor and stretches the band, raising his hips at the same time. The exercise is repeated twelve times.

Kimi is on his way to Azerbaijan and doesn't spare the flesh. The Baku race is due in a week's time. How long will this torture carry on? No one knows but, at this point in time, mortifying the flesh and making car tyres squeal still seem good to Kimi.

**'It won't be hard for me to give up this job. I'll be relieved when the travelling and shit-mongering that go with the sport come to an end. Driving is great – unlike all the rest that goes with it.'**

Ending a sports career isn't easy. The quitter is often at the halfway stage of his or her life, or even younger. A lot has happened; at least half as much is yet to come. The end is the beginning of something new. It's the start of a new life.

Some have processed their experiences into words and

sentences, which are used at life management seminars. We won't see Kimi Räikkönen at management training events talking about resources and body language. It's quite certain we won't see him commentating on F1 races at the circuits. He has led a tightly scheduled life, rushing from one place to the next. When he quits F1, he'll stay put for a bit.

He was born with grease on his hands. He has the soul of a mechanic and the physique of a motorist, so alternative motor sports would be the most natural progression. But nothing is set in stone – except he won't miss anything about the job.

'It won't be hard for me to quit this job. I'll be relieved when the travelling and shit-mongering come to an end. Driving is great – unlike all the rest that goes with it.'

Kimi's voice is determined and defiant but he doesn't raise it.

Right now everyday life is much more eventful than a racetrack. Robin, aged three, and Rianna, aged one, develop at a faster pace than F1. Robin says a new word for the first time only once and it would be great to be there to catch it. When Rianna takes her first steps, her dad may well be at the interview that follows Friday's free practice, scratching his neck and hiding his irritation.

Kimi hasn't yet decided what he'll do after the end of his career. He only knows what he definitely *won't* do.

It's Hyvinkää, 5 October 2010. The phone of Antti

Pyrhönen, a professional motocross rider, rings at 3am. It's Kimi Räikkönen on the other end. The motocross rider has followed Kimi's career from the beginning, and has often felt that their paths would yet cross. All the same, Pyrhönen finds it hard to believe his ears. It really is Räikkönen himself on the phone, saying that he would like to meet up. He's planning to set up his own moto-cross team. Pyrhönen answers that a meeting would be OK, but when? Straight away, says Kimi. The motocross rider thinks that Kimi is calling from Espoo but Kimi says that he's in Switzerland. Pyrhönen thinks he might be able to come in a month's time. Kimi thinks that he should make it immediately, on the same day. Or actually tomorrow. It's night time at the moment – what is the time? It's tomorrow already, and Pyrhönen says that he'll come right away.

'It was just like a dream. I was being rehabilitated fol-lowing a serious injury. I left home in central Hyvinkää and wondered whether to take with me the only CD in my possession. It was Vesa-Matti Loiri's *Good Wood*, which I listened to lots of times during my rehabilitation. I played ping-pong and listened to that CD. It was already in my hand when I was leaving but I decided not to take it after all. I was really nervous. Kimi was there to meet me in Switzerland with a relaxed greeting: "Hi there, Ana." We sat down on a large settee. Kimi fiddled around with YouTube and put on Loiri's *Good Wood*. I thought that this can't be real. We drank coffee and chatted. Then Kimi suggested that we go downstairs and have a game of ping-pong. Then I thought that there's something fateful about all this. I felt as if we had always known each other.'

The encounter led to Kimi calling Pyrhönen later on to ask him to head the Ice One Racing team based in Belgium. Pyrhönen has been employed as team boss since autumn 2012. He is also godfather to Kimi's daughter Rianna.

Kimi was three when he first mounted a children's Italjet motocross bike. Now, thirty-six years later, he owns a motocross team. The circle has closed, the sound of a bike revving carries on.

Kimi, together with Pyrhönen, was able to plan everything for Ice One Racing from the start. The 'workshop' – the name they gave to the team's head-quarters – is located at Lommel in Belgium. It forms a carefully thought-out unit; the 2,500-square-metre space is a modern, almost clinical entity. According to the insurance inspector's report, it is like a hospital, so clean that you could eat off the floor. The building embodies Kimi's perfectionism. The reverse side of the tearaway is his precision and longing for harmony.

Ice One Racing is Husqvarna's factory team, which competes in the elite class of motocross, MXGP. The team has been second in the Manufacturers' World Championship once and third twice. It employs fifteen people, including the drivers.

According to Pyrhönen, Kimi keeps tabs on everything, makes decisions quickly and knows an awful lot about the sport. The two men think alike, which facilitates decision-making. Pyrhönen doesn't think that running the motocross team will be enough for Kimi.

Will it be enough? Kimi doesn't know the answer. That means it won't. Once the current career is over, everything will be wide open.

One thing is clear: the something new must be his own thing and he must be passionate about it. Kimi doesn't want to do anything half-heartedly. He respected Nico Rosberg, who said he was giving up driving to spend time with his family.

'It was cool, I thought. And now he stands there in the paddock commentating on races. I don't get it; not long ago he said that he wanted to move away from those circles.'

Kimi is interested in at least two things: planning and marketing. He has observed the latter from close quarters during the whole of his career.

'I'm interested in doing something in which I can be involved body and soul and which I can influence. I don't want to stand somewhere holding a bottle of oil, praising its suitability for winter conditions. And I don't want to stand in a race suit in the corner of a shopping centre and say into a mike that this is a really good shampoo.'

He met Hartwall's representatives and the beverage company's Chinese and Japanese partners at the Chinese

Grand Prix. The topic under discussion was a long drink, which was marketed in Asia with Kimi's support. Those present were taken by surprise at the driver's unique way of explaining how the drink should be sold to new countries. His delivery at the event was straightforward, eschewing jargon. It made an impact on the audience. They got the impression that Kimi was really behind the drink and didn't just stand in a rigid cardboard picture with a can in hand.

> **'I could be involved in developing a passenger car. I could do it behind the scenes, not in public. I could test those vehicles – I do have a bit of experience of cars.'**

I recall our visit to Ferrari's car factory. Kimi was interested in the operation of the assembly lines and the manual work carried out by the workers. He was thinking of creating a video which would help him assemble a car, purchased by him, together with the rest of the workforce.

'I could be involved in developing a passenger car. I could do it behind the scenes, not in public. I could test those vehicles – I do have a bit of experience of cars.'

Kimi isn't worried about the ending of his career. He doesn't understand why some people get stuck in a groove. Lots of people have come to tell him to enjoy himself while he can; he doesn't know how dull life will be when he's no longer on the racetrack.

'I don't get it. I'm perfectly capable of staying indoors at home for a week without going anywhere. I enjoy just existing. I don't think of Formula 1 for twenty-four hours a day. During the Mexican Grand Prix, I bumped into Jeff Gordon, who won the NASCAR championship four times. He had just ended his career and looked miserable. It was obviously still bothering him.'

We're in Baar, outside Kimi's home, near the swimming pool. Kimi breaks into a run, leaps over a big water toy and splashes into the water. Minttu takes a picture of the jump. In half an hour's time, it'll appear on Instagram. The account currently has around 700,000 followers. For this contact, Kimi didn't have to go anywhere, and he didn't have to say a word. His future is open. Follow it.

# DAD, WHO ARE YOU?

**The new car will** be launched on 30 January. The arrival of a new human being is expected to take place around the same time. This arrival is induced to ensure Dad can be present before he has to take off in order to stand next to the new car. Speedy action is required.

The induction process starts; the new person is reluctant to come out. A vacuum extractor is deployed and makes a horrible noise. The sound is followed by a human being, who makes a good sound. There's joy, relief, happiness. Now the new arrival is in Switzerland and out in the world.

The human being turns out to have a yellowy hue. The unusual colour is caused by an accumulation of a substance called bilirubin in his bloodstream. It's not a problem: he's placed in a box with a blue light. The yellow colour is brought about by the dispersal of a bruise, caused by the suction cup. Dad stretches his hand into the box through a narrow slit and holds the baby's hand, trying to soothe. He didn't realise what fatherhood prepares him for: constant worry.

Finally, the yellow hue disappears and the baby assumes his natural colour. Dad leaves to take a look at the new car; it's red.

Mum and Dad are novices; everything is new and frightening. The baby doesn't have to do anything to get all that an adult strives for: food, love, warmth. He fills the whole home, though he doesn't yet move.

Then Dad has to go off to test the red car. When he returns, he doesn't want to leave ever again. The cars remain more or less the same, while the baby changes every day. He tests his parents round the clock; every noise he makes sounds ten times louder in their ears. A car squeals and creates a racket, but it can be adjusted. The baby can be pacified with food and sleep but, after that, everything else is guesswork. He doesn't yet have any understanding of Dad's comings and goings, but can sense them already and will react to them in a year's time.

The baby is a boy and he's called Robin Ace Matias Räikkönen. Now Robin is three and cross with his dad. He's especially angry during the first couple of days after Dad has come home following a long stint of racing. The healthy son has a clear sense of priorities: Dad needs to be at home, not driving round a distorted circle on the other side of the world.

**He didn't have to worry during races, because he knew that Minttu was at home. But the back of his mind was throbbing with the thought that he should be there too.**

The man sitting in this room isn't, at the moment, an F1 driver. Kimi isn't looking at the track but through the window. He looks out at the greenery and recalls the early days of Robin's life.

'Straight away I was thinking, *Will everything work out? Can I do anything right? Dare I touch him? I daren't dress him, he'll fall apart.* He didn't. First I wished he'd go to sleep and then I had to listen to make sure he was still breathing. And what if he turns over onto his tummy and doesn't get any oxygen? When Robin got a bit older, these anxieties started fading.'

He didn't have to worry during races, because he knew that Minttu was at home. But the back of his mind was throbbing with the thought that he should be there too.

'I would just like to be there, to be at home. That's the most important thing, not what I do with the children.

We were always together in my family, because we were all into motor sports. That's bound to be one of the reasons I feel like this.'

Kimi was thirty-six when Robin was born. It was just the right age for him. In his previous marriage, the thought of having a child was virtually impossible, though Kimi and Jenni Dahlman were officially married for ten years.

'The whole marriage was more or less a rollercoaster ride from my part. I never thought that it could include children – you can't fix a relationship that way. There was no firm basis for children.'

Kimi doesn't want to say anything more about his first marriage and neither does Jenni. When they met, Jenni was nineteen and Kimi twenty-one. The marriage took place in 2004 and the divorce went through in 2014. The relationship was effectively over much earlier.

Kimi is now the father of two children and he knows a fair amount about parenthood. Once you have children, you can't send them back; they are nothing like a successful Grand Prix or a World Championship; such achievements fade over the years. Children are a permanent twinkle in your eye; they shine throughout your life and allow emotions to show through the stale crust of everyday life.

'It feels horrible to leave with Robin hanging onto my leg. It's just so painful. What's good, though, is that when

I've been away for a week or two, I see how they've grown and learnt new things.'

Life moulds a person as it wishes. It doesn't ask any questions. Success and fame are fine things that can become insignificant in the blink of an eye. Kimi has achieved a great deal, including celebrity and wealth. He also lost three significant people in the space of a few years: his father, Matti Räikkönen, in December 2010; his manager, David Robertson, in February 2014, and his doctor, Aki Hintsa, in November 2016.

Successes provide the icing on the cake; they also peel away layers and reveal what's essential. Now Kimi has got a family. The children are old enough to ask where Dad is, but they don't yet ask *who* he is.

A human being is realised in his actions, words, gestures and relationships with other people. He can tell us what he's like himself but then, in that case, we invariably hear from an unreliable narrator. The true picture of a person is created by others: from the way they talk about him, see him or hear him. All the same, it's worth asking the man: what are you like?

The question makes Kimi sink deeper into the sofa. He can't say. A fair number of people can, or at least like to think they can, answer the question even if they can't. Someone who claims to know himself thoroughly is lying, or painting a favourable picture of himself, or putting on an act. You may know yourself to some degree, but not exhaustively.

Kimi Räikkönen, what kind of a person are you?

'You should ask someone else, I think. Hard to say. I'm not interested in what I'm like. Everyone's a prick at times. Something's wrong if you're never a prick. And people like to call you a prick pretty quickly if you disagree with them. You're a doormat if you've got no opinions of your own.'

Robin comes to the door, peeks in and giggles. Dad's talking to the man, into a small box between them. Robin isn't interested in talking or boxes. Playing would be interesting. The boy calls out a sentence in a mixture of Finnish and English from the door. The meaning of the sentence is clear: stop nattering.

Robin makes Kimi think of fatherhood.

'My brother Rami is a perfect dad. I've been thinking that I'd be happy if I could be half as good. I've been looking at the way he is with his kids. He's with them all the time doing all sorts of things. It'll be good if I manage 50 per cent of it.'

As Kimi can't think of anything to say about himself, I recall some of the stories told by his friends. Gino Rosato is the mysterious general manager at Ferrari, the Director of F1 Operations. But in the present context he's Robin's godfather, who has known Kimi for twelve years. Gino is Canadian-Italian – he comes originally from Canada but currently lives in Italy, near Maranello. Gino says that, during the Montreal Grand Prix, Kimi would always visit

Gino's mother, who lives in the town of Laval, twenty-five kilometres from Montreal. Kimi knew that it meant a lot to the mother. According to Gino, many people in the Formula 1 business change and begin to associate only with important people. Kimi, however, never socialises with anyone to gain an advantage.

He says nothing about the driver being a prick but Kimi's own characterisation carries some weight. Here I have to cite a story told about Henry Kissinger, former US Secretary of State. Kissinger wanted to know the background of some issue and asked his aides to gather the information. The aides did the research and brought the paperwork to the Secretary of State. He looked at the documents and said: 'Don't give me facts. Tell me what they mean.'

In Kimi's case, it's a fact that he has travelled for around 140 days a year for eighteen years. Those days amount to approximately seven years. What does this fact mean? It means that he hasn't been continuously at home; he's been coming and going. It affects his psyche; his nervous system is never completely at rest. The suitcase is emptied into the washing machine, and shortly after the clothes have dried they're folded back into the case. On this sort of merry-go-round a person becomes impatient and may behave brusquely. He may become a prick, at least temporarily, at least towards the outside world, and sometimes towards his nearest and dearest.

No wonder Kimi longs for a time when he doesn't have to go anywhere.

At this stage we know this: Kimi is both kind-hearted and a prick. He loves children and has a sense of humour – provided his audience happens to share his kind of humour. We should never think that our own sense of humour is a global truth.

What else is he?

'Reserved, shy and direct,' says Jean Todt, the former team boss of Ferrari and the current chairman of the FIA.

'Funny and a darling,' says Minttu.

'He doesn't make a song and dance about what happens in a race,' says Sebastian Vettel.

'Big and familiar and picks me up,' thinks Rianna.

'He's got nerves of steel, otherwise he would never have won the championship,' says Jean Todt.

'I never thought that I was a star of any kind,' he says himself.

I ask him what he dislikes.

'Let's say the phone. In 90 per cent of all calls, no one has got anything important to say. In the '90s, with landlines, you were bound to have something to say. For example, people might suggest going out; they didn't ring just for the fun of it. That's why my phone has been on silent for years. I can't be bothered to answer when the voice at the other end says that it's nothing really, I just called to ask how you were.'

That's clear now. Let's not phone each other.

Where does Kimi come from?

An individual can't choose his family when he's born and he can't swap it as a child. Some are born with a silver spoon in their mouths, others with a spanner in their hands. A person's start in life gets forgotten and vanishes beyond the horizon but, sometimes, it can be glimpsed clearly. A spanner sticks out of Kimi's back pocket and this is not a cheap metaphor. You can tell from the way he acts, talks and moves where he comes from.

Ron Dennis, McLaren's team boss, tried at one time to infiltrate Kimi into high society but the attempt failed. A square peg didn't fit into a round hole. There's a saying: Don't blame the mirror if your face is crooked. In the case of Formula 1, you could call the mirror crooked, or something worse. In that world, big money and bad taste have often formed a charming alliance. It's no wonder a grease monkey from Karhusuo, Espoo, has felt like a fish out of water in the glamorous world of F1 outside the racetrack.

Kimi could compare himself – if he so wished – to Charlie Watts, the drummer of the Rolling Stones. Watts has played the drums for fifty-three years in a group from whose fame and glamour he has distanced himself. From time to time, the drummer still wonders what he is doing in a band that began by playing blues and should have been disbanded by its own impossibility within two or three years. Watts sits on his drum stool in his tailor-made suit, producing a lazy but precise rhythm with a touch of jazz.

Kimi must have rubbed his eyes a few times when looking at the world he has drifted into as a result of steering a car with precision and assessing its behaviour accurately. He ended up in this world even though he only wanted to drive.

'I hadn't even seen a live Formula Grand Prix before I went and drove in one myself.'

Since you don't really know what you're like, I say to him, at least tell me what you like doing. A man is also revealed in his actions, after all.

'I like using my hands. I like to fix and mend, to build and to plan. I come up with a solution pretty quickly if something's broken.'

I remember a story told by Sami Visa about the 2017 tests at Barcelona. Kimi noticed that the toilet of the Ferrari bus didn't work properly. He went to ask the staff for tools. The incredulous workers handed an implement to the star driver. During his investigation, Kimi remarked that his boat had a similar system. He crawled under the bus and repaired the toilet in no time at all. The staff were left with their mouths open.

Kimi is good with his hands, and talkative. But now he's beginning to run out of words. Robin opens the door again and looks at his dad. He's too shy to say anything but Dad understands his expression. Let's go and have a nap.

The following morning Kimi sleeps late. Robin is already awake and sits quietly on Minttu's lap. Then he says something in a mixture of Finnish and English, jumps down and starts driving a small car along the hallway. Robin gives a running commentary on his actions. Words and deeds are in balance.

# STATISTICS 2001–2018

Number in brackets after qualifying refers to a changed place on the grid.

## 2001

| DRIVER | TEAM | TIME |
|---|---|---|
| **AUSTRALIAN GP** | | |
| 1. Michael Schumacher | Ferrari | 1.38.26,533 |
| 2. David Coulthard | McLaren-Mercedes | +1,717 |
| 3. Rubens Barrichello | Ferrari | +33,491 |
| **6. Kimi Räikkönen** | **Sauber-Petronas** | **+1.24,143** |

Australian GP, qualifying
13. Kimi Räikkönen    Sauber-Petronas    1.28,993

| **MALAYSIAN GP** | | |
|---|---|---|
| 1. Michael Schumacher | Ferrari | 1.47.34,801 |
| 2. Rubens Barrichello | Ferrari | +23,660 |
| 3. David Coulthard | McLaren-Mercedes | +28,555 |

**Kimi Räikkönon (Sauber-Petronas) retired on lap 1.**

Malaysian GP, qualifying
14. Kimi Räikkönen    Sauber-Petronas    1.37,728

| **BRAZILIAN GP** | | |
|---|---|---|
| 1. David Coulthard | McLaren-Mercedes | 1.39.00,834 |
| 2. Michael Schumacher | Ferrari | +16,164 |
| 3. Nick Heidfeld | Sauber-Petronas | +1 lap |

**Kimi Räikkönen (Sauber-Petronas) retired on lap 55.**

Brazilian GP, qualifying
10. Kimi Räikkönen    Sauber-Petronas    1.14,924

| **SAN MARINO GP** | | |
|---|---|---|
| 1. Ralf Schumacher | Williams-BMW | 1.30.44,817 |
| 2. David Coulthard | McLaren-Mercedes | +4,352 |
| 3. Rubens Barrichello | Ferrari | +34,766 |

**Kimi Räikkönen (Sauber-Petronas) retired on lap 17.**

San Marino GP, qualifying
10. Kimi Räikkönen    Sauber-Petronas    1.24,71

| **SPANISH GP** | | |
|---|---|---|
| 1. Michael Schumacher | Ferrari | 1.31.03,305 |
| 2. Juan Pablo Montoya | Williams-BMW | +40,738 |
| 3. Jacques Villeneuve | BAR-Honda | +49,626 |
| **8. Kimi Räikkönen** | **Sauber-Petronas** | **+1.19,808** |

Spanish GP, qualifying
9. Kimi Räikkönen    Sauber-Petronas    1.19,229

| **AUSTRIAN GP** | | |
|---|---|---|
| 1. David Coulthard | McLaren-Mercedes | 1.27.45,927 |
| 2. Michael Schumacher | Ferrari | +2,190 |
| 3. Rubens Barrichello | Ferrari | +2,527 |
| **4. Kimi Räikkönen** | **Sauber-Petronas** | **+41,593** |

Austrian GP, qualifying
9. Kimi Räikkönen    Sauber-Petronas    1.10,396

| **MONACO GP** | | |
|---|---|---|
| 1. Michael Schumacher | Ferrari | 1.47.22,561 |
| 2. Rubens Barrichello | Ferrari | +0,431 |
| 3. Eddie Irvine | Jaguar-Cosworth | +30,698 |
| **10. Kimi Räikkönen** | **Sauber-Petronas** | **+5 laps** |

Monaco GP, qualifying
15. Kimi Räikkönen    Sauber-Petronas    1.20,081

| **CANADIAN GP** | | |
|---|---|---|
| 1. Ralf Schumacher | Williams-BMW | 1.34.31,522 |
| 2. Michael Schumacher | Ferrari | +20,235 |
| 3. Mika Häkkinen | McLaren-Mercedes | +40,672 |
| **4. Kimi Räikkönen** | **Sauber-Petronas** | **+1.08,116** |

Canadian GP, qualifying
7. Kimi Räikkönen    Sauber-Petronas    1.16,875

| **EUROPEAN GP** | | |
|---|---|---|
| 1. Michael Schumacher | Ferrari | 1.29.42,724 |
| 2. Juan Pablo Montoya | Williams-BMW | +4,127 |
| 3. David Coulthard | McLaren-Mercedes | +24,993 |
| **10. Kimi Räikkönen** | **Sauber-Petronas** | **+1 lap** |

European GP, qualifying
9. Kimi Räikkönen    Sauber-Petronas    1.16,402

| **FRENCH GP** | | |
|---|---|---|
| 1. Michael Schumacher | Ferrari | 1.33.35,636 |
| 2. Ralf Schumacher | Williams-BMW | +10,399 |
| 3. Rubens Barrichello | Ferrari | +16,381 |
| **7. Kimi Räikkönen** | **Sauber-Petronas** | **+1 lap** |

French GP, qualifying
13. Kimi Räikkönen    Sauber-Petronas    1.14,536

## BRITISH GP

| | | | |
|---|---|---|---|
| 1. | Mika Häkkinen | McLaren-Mercedes | 1.25.33,770 |
| 2. | Michael Schumacher | Ferrari | +33,646 |
| 3. | Rubens Barrichello | Ferrari | +59,281 |
| **5.** | **Kimi Räikkönen** | **Sauber-Petronas** | **+1 lap** |

British GP, qualifying

| | | | |
|---|---|---|---|
| 7. | Kimi Räikkönen | Sauber-Petronas | 1.22,023 |

## GERMAN GP

| | | | |
|---|---|---|---|
| 1. | Ralf Schumacher | Williams-BMW | 1.18.17,873 |
| 2. | Rubens Barrichello | Ferrari | +46,117 |
| 3. | Jacques Villeneuve | BAR-Honda | +1.02,806 |

**Kimi Räikkönen (McLaren-Mercedes) retired on lap 16.**

German GP, qualifying

| | | | |
|---|---|---|---|
| 8. | Kimi Räikkönen | Sauber-Petronas | 1.40,072 |

## HUNGARIAN GP

| | | | |
|---|---|---|---|
| 1. | Michael Schumacher | Ferrari | 1.41.49,675 |
| 2. | Rubens Barrichello | Ferrari | +3,363 |
| 3. | David Coulthard | McLaren-Mercedes | +3,940 |
| **7.** | **Kimi Räikkönen** | **Sauber-Petronas** | **+1 lap** |

Hungarian GP, qualifying

| | | | |
|---|---|---|---|
| 9. | Kimi Räikkönen | Sauber-Petronas | 1.15,906 |

## BELGIAN GP

| | | | |
|---|---|---|---|
| 1. | Michael Schumacher | Ferrari | 1.08.05,002 |
| 2. | David Coulthard | McLaren-Mercedes | +10,098 |
| 3. | Giancarlo Fisichella | Benetton-Renault | +27,742 |

**Kimi Räikkönen (Sauber-Petronas) retired on lap 1.**

Belgian GP, qualifying

| | | | |
|---|---|---|---|
| 12. | Kimi Räikkönen | Sauber-Petronas | 1.59,050 |

## ITALIAN GP

| | | | |
|---|---|---|---|
| 1. | Juan Pablo Montoya | Williams-BMW | 1.16.58,493 |
| 2. | Rubens Barrichello | Ferrari | +5,175 |
| 3. | Ralf Schumacher | Williams-BMW | +17,335 |
| **3.** | **Kimi Räikkönen** | **McLaren-Mercedes** | **+1.23,107** |

Italian GP, qualifying

| | | | |
|---|---|---|---|
| 9. | Kimi Räikkönen | Sauber-Petronas | 1.23,595 |

## UNITED STATES GP

| | | | |
|---|---|---|---|
| 1. | Mika Häkkinen | McLaren-Mercedes | 1.32.42,840 |
| 2. | Michael Schumacher | Ferrari | +11,046 |
| 3. | David Coulthard | McLaren-Mercedes | +12,043 |

**Kimi Räikkönen (Sauber-Petronas) retired on lap 2.**

United States GP, qualifying

| | | | |
|---|---|---|---|
| 11. | Kimi Räikkönen | Sauber-Petronas | 1.12,881 |

## JAPANESE GP

| | | | |
|---|---|---|---|
| 1. | Michael Schumacher | Ferrari | 1.27.33,298 |
| 2. | Juan Pablo Montoya | Williams-BMW | +3,154 |
| 3. | David Coulthard | McLaren-Mercedes | +23,262 |

**Kimi Räikkönen (McLaren-Mercedes) retired on lap 5.**

Japanese GP, qualifying

| | | | |
|---|---|---|---|
| 12. | Kimi Räikkönen | Sauber-Petronas | 1.34,581 |

# 2002

## AUSTRALIAN GP

| | | | |
|---|---|---|---|
| 1. | Michael Schumacher | Ferrari | 1.35.36,792 |
| 2. | Juan Pablo Montoya | Williams-BMW | +18,628 |
| **3.** | **Kimi Räikkönen** | **McLaren-Mercedes** | **+25,067** |

Australian GP, qualifying

| | | | |
|---|---|---|---|
| 5. | Kimi Räikkönen | McLaren-Mercedes | 1.27,161 |

## MALAYSIAN GP

| | | | |
|---|---|---|---|
| 1. | Ralf Schumacher | Williams-BMW | 1.34.12,912 |
| 2. | Juan Pablo Montoya | Williams-BMW | +39,700 |
| 3. | Michael Schumacher | Ferrari | +1.01,795 |

**Kimi Räikkönen (McLaren-Mercedes) retired on lap 24.**

Malaysian GP, qualifying

| | | | |
|---|---|---|---|
| 5. | Kimi Räikkönen | McLaren-Mercedes | 1.36,468 |

## BRAZILIAN GP

| | | | |
|---|---|---|---|
| 1. | Michael Schumacher | Ferrari | 1.31.43,662 |
| 2. | Ralf Schumacher | Williams-BMW | +0,588 |
| 3. | David Coulthard | McLaren-Mercedes | +59,109 |

**Kimi Räikkönen (McLaren-Mercedes) retired on lap 67 but came 12th.**

Brazilian GP, qualifying

| | | | |
|---|---|---|---|
| 5. | Kimi Räikkönen | McLaren-Mercedes | 1.13,595 |

## SAN MARINO GP

| | | | |
|---|---|---|---|
| 1. | Michael Schumacher | Ferrari | 1.29.10,789 |
| 2. | Rubens Barrichello | Ferrari | +17,907 |
| 3. | Ralf Schumacher | Williams-BMW | +19,755 |

**Kimi Räikkönen (McLaren-Mercedes) retired on lap 44.**

San Marino GP, qualifying

| | | | |
|---|---|---|---|
| 5. | Kimi Räikkönen | McLaren-Mercedes | 1.22,1041 |

## SPANISH GP

| | | | |
|---|---|---|---|
| 1. | Michael Schumacher | Ferrari | 1.30.29,981 |
| 2. | Juan Pablo Montoya | Williams-BMW | +35,630 |
| 3. | David Coulthard | McLaren-Mercedes | +42,623 |

**Kimi Räikkönen (McLaren-Mercedes) retired on lap 4.**

Spanish GP, qualifying

| | | | |
|---|---|---|---|
| 5. | Kimi Räikkönen | McLaren-Mercedes | 1.17,519 |

## AUSTRIAN GP

1. Michael Schumacher    Ferrari    1.33.51,562
2. Rubens Barrichello    Ferrari    +0,182
3. Juan Pablo Montoya    Williams-BMW    +17,730

**Kimi Räikkönen (McLaren-Mercedes) retired on lap 5.**

Austrian GP, qualifying
6. Kimi Räikkönen    McLaren-Mercedes    1.09,154

## MONACO GP

1. David Coulthard    McLaren-Mercedes    1.45.39,055
2. Michael Schumacher    Ferrari    +1,050
3. Ralf Schumacher    Williams-BMW    +1.07,450

**Kimi Räikkönen (McLaren-Mercedes) retired on lap 41.**

Monaco GP, qualifying
7. (6) Kimi Räikkönen    McLaren-Mercedes    1.17,660

## CANADIAN GP

1. Michael Schumacher    Ferrari    1.33.36,111
2. David Coulthard    McLaren-Mercedes    +1,132
3. Rubens Barrichello    Ferrari    +7,082
4. **Kimi Räikkönen**    **McLaren-Mercedes**    **+37,563**

Canadian GP, qualifying
5. Kimi Räikkönen    McLaren-Mercedes    1.13,898

## EUROPEAN GP

1. Rubens Barrichello    Ferrari    1.35.07,426
2. Michael Schumacher    Ferrari    +0,294
3. **Kimi Räikkönen**    **McLaren-Mercedes**    **+46,435**

European GP, qualifying
6. Kimi Räikkönen    McLaren-Mercedes    1.30,591

## BRITISH GP

1. Michael Schumacher    Ferrari    1.31.45,015
2. Rubens Barrichello    Ferrari    +14,578
3. Juan Pablo Montoya    Williams-BMW    +31,661

**Kimi Räikkönen (McLaren-Mercedes) retired on lap 44.**

British GP, qualifying
5. Kimi Räikkönen    McLaren-Mercedes    1.20,133

## FRENCH GP

1. Michael Schumacher    Ferrari    1.32.09,837
2. **Kimi Räikkönen**    **McLaren-Mercedes**    **+1,104**
3. David Coulthard    McLaren-Mercedes    +31,975

French GP, qualifying
4. Kimi Räikkönen    McLaren-Mercedes    1.12,244

## GERMAN GP

1. Michael Schumacher    Ferrari    1.27.52,078
2. Juan Pablo Montoya    Williams-BMW    +10,503
3. Ralf Schumacher    Williams-BMW    +14,466

**Kimi Räikkönen (McLaren-Mercedes) retired on lap 59.**

German GP, qualifying
5. Kimi Räikkönen    McLaren-Mercedes    1.15,639

## HUNGARIAN GP

1. Rubens Barrichello    Ferrari    1.41.49,001
2. Michael Schumacher    Ferrari    +0,434
3. Ralf Schumacher    Williams-BMW    +13,355
4. **Kimi Räikkönen**    **McLaren-Mercedes**    **+29,479**

Hungarian GP, qualifying
11. Kimi Räikkönen    McLaren-Mercedes    1.15,243

## BELGIAN GP

1. Michael Schumacher    Ferrari    1.21.20,634
2. Rubens Barrichello    Ferrari    +1,977
3. Juan Pablo Montoya    Williams-BMW    +18,445

**Kimi Räikkönen (McLaren-Mercedes) retired on lap 35.**

Belgian GP, qualifying
2. Kimi Räikkönen    McLaren-Mercedes    1.44,150

## ITALIAN GP

1. Rubens Barrichello    Ferrari    1.16.19,982
2. Michael Schumacher    Ferrari    +0,255
3. Eddie Irvine    Jaguar-Cosworth    +52,579

**Kimi Räikkönen (McLaren-Mercedes) retired on lap 29.**

Italian GP, qualifying
6. Kimi Räikkönen    McLaren-Mercedes    1.21,712

## UNITED STATES GP

1. Rubens Barrichello    Ferrari    1.31.08,0
2. Michael Schumacher    Ferrari    +0,011
3. David Coulthard    McLaren-Mercedes    +7,799

**Kimi Räikkönen (McLaren-Mercedes) retired on lap 50.**

United States GP, qualifying
6. Kimi Räikkönen    McLaren-Mercedes    1.11,633

## JAPANESE GP

1. Michael Schumacher    Ferrari    1.26.59,698
2. Rubens Barrichello    Ferrari    +0,506
3. **Kimi Räikkönen**    **McLaren-Mercedes**    **+23,292**

Japanese GP, qualifying
4. Kimi Räikkönen    McLaren-Mercedes    1.32,197

**279**

# 2003

## AUSTRALIAN GP
1. David Coulthard    McLaren-Mercedes    1.34.42,124
2. Juan Pablo Montoya    Williams-BMW    +8,675
3. **Kimi Räikkönen**    **McLaren-Mercedes**    **+9,192**

Australian GP, qualifying
15. Kimi Räikkönen    McLaren-Mercedes    1.29,470

## MALAYSIAN GP
1. **Kimi Räikkönen**    **McLaren-Mercedes**    **1.32.22,195**
2. Rubens Barrichello    Ferrari    +39,286
3. Fernando Alonso    Renault    +1.04,007

Malaysian GP, qualifying
7. Kimi Räikkönen    McLaren-Mercedes    1.37,858

## BRAZILIAN GP
1. Giancarlo Fisichella    Jordan-Ford    1.31.17,748
2. **Kimi Räikkönen**    **McLaren-Mercedes**    **+0,945**
3. Fernando Alonso    Renault    +6,348

Brazilian GP, qualifying
4. Kimi Räikkönen    McLaren-Mercedes    1.13,866

## SAN MARINO GP
1. Michael Schumacher    Ferrari    1.28.12,058
2. **Kimi Räikkönen**    **McLaren-Mercedes**    **+1,882**
3. Rubens Barrichello    Ferrari    +2,291

San Marino GP, qualifying
6. Kimi Räikkönen    McLaren-Mercedes    1.23,148

## SPANISH GP
1. Michael Schumacher    Ferrari    1.33.46,933
2. Fernando Alonso    Renault    +5,716
3. Rubens Barrichello    Ferrari    +18,001
**Kimi Räikkönen (McLaren-Mercedes) retired on lap 1.**

Spanish GP, qualifying
20. Kimi Räikkönen    McLaren-Mercedes    1.31,900

## AUSTRIAN GP
1. Michael Schumacher    Ferrari    1.24.04,888
2. **Kimi Räikkönen**    **McLaren-Mercedes**    **+3,362**
3. Rubens Barrichello    Ferrari    +3,951

Austrian GP, qualifying
2. Kimi Räikkönen    McLaren-Mercedes    1.09,189

## MONACO GP
1. Juan Pablo Montoya    Williams-BMW    1.42.19,010
2. **Kimi Räikkönen**    **McLaren-Mercedes**    **+0,602**
3. Michael Schumacher    Ferrari    +1,720

Monaco GP, qualifying
2. Kimi Räikkönen    McLaren-Mercedes    1.15,295

## CANADIAN GP
1. Michael Schumacher    Ferrari    1.31.13,591
2. Ralf Schumacher    Williams-BMW    +0,784
3. Juan Pablo Montoya    Williams-BMW    +1,355
6. **Kimi Räikkönen**    **McLaren-Mercedes**    **+1.10,502**

Canadian GP, qualifying
20. Kimi Räikkönen    McLaren-Mercedes    no time

## EUROPEAN GP
1. Ralf Schumacher    Williams-BMW    1.34.43,622
2. Juan Pablo Montoya    Williams-BMW    +16,821
3. Rubens Barrichello    Ferrari    +39,673
**Kimi Räikkönen (McLaren-Mercedes) retired on lap 25.**

European GP, qualifying
1. Kimi Räikkönen    McLaren-Mercedes    1.31,523

## FRENCH GP
1. Ralf Schumacherr    Williams-BMW    1.30.49,213
2. Juan Pablo Montoya    Williams-BMW    +13,813
3. Michael Schumacher    Ferrari    +19,568
4. **Kimi Räikkönen**    **McLaren-Mercedes**    **+38,047**

French GP, qualifying
4. Kimi Räikkönen    McLaren-Mercedes    1.15,533

## BRITISH GP
1. Rubens Barrichello    Ferrari    1.28.37,554
2. Juan Pablo Montoya    Williams-BMW    +5,462
3. **Kimi Räikkönen**    **McLaren-Mercedes**    **+10,656**

British GP, qualifying
3. Kimi Räikkönen    McLaren-Mercedes    1.21,695

## GERMAN GP
1. Juan Pablo Montoya    Williams-BMW    1.28.48,769
2. David Coulthard    McLaren-Mercedes    +1.05,459
3. Jarno Trulli    Renault    +1.09,060
**Kimi Räikkönen retired on lap 1.**

German GP, qualifying
5. Kimi Räikkönen    McLaren-Mercedes    1.15,874

## HUNGARIAN GP

1. Fernando Alonso — Renault — 1.39.01,460
2. **Kimi Räikkönen** — **McLaren-Mercedes** — **+16,768**
3. Juan Pablo Montoya — Williams-BMW — +34,537

Hungarian GP, qualifying
6. Kimi Räikkönen — McLaren-Mercedes — 1.22,742

## ITALIAN GP

1. Michael Schumacher — Ferrari — 1.14.19,838
2. Juan Pablo Montoya — Williams-BMW — +5,294
3. Rubens Barrichello — Ferrari — +11,835
4. **Kimi Räikkönen** — **McLaren-Mercedes** — **+12,834**

Italian GP, qualifying
4. Kimi Räikkönen — McLaren-Mercedes — 1.21,466

## UNITED STATES GP

1. Michael Schumacher — Ferrari — 1.33.35,997
2. **Kimi Räikkönen** — **McLaren-Mercedes** — **+18,258**
3. Heinz-Harald Frentzen — Sauber-Petronas — +37,964

United States GP, qualifying
1. Kimi Räikkönen — McLaren-Mercedes — 1.11,670

## JAPANESE GP

1. Rubens Barrichello — Ferrari — 1.25.11,743
2. **Kimi Räikkönen** — **McLaren-Mercedes** — **+11,085**
3. David Coulthard — McLaren-Mercedes — +11,614

Japanese GP, qualifying
8. Kimi Räikkönen — McLaren-Mercedes — 1.33,272

## 2004

## AUSTRALIAN GP

1. Michael Schumacher — Ferrari — 1.24.15,757
2. Rubens Barrichello — Ferrari — +13,605
3. Fernando Alonso — Renault — +34,673
**Kimi Räikkönen (McLaren-Mercedes) retired on lap 9.**

Australian GP, qualifying
10. Kimi Räikkönen — McLaren-Mercedes — 1.26,297

## MALAYSIAN GP

1. Michael Schumacher — Ferrari — 1.31.07,490
2. Juan Pablo Montoya — Williams-BMW — +5,022
3. Jenson Button — BAR-Honda — +11,568
**Kimi Räikkönen (McLaren-Mercedes) retired on lap 42.**

Malaysian GP, qualifying
5. Kimi Räikkönen — McLaren-Mercedes — 1.34,164

## BAHRAIN GP

1. Michael Schumacher — Ferrari — 1.28.34,875
2. Rubens Barrichello — Ferrari — +1,367
3. Jenson Button — BAR-Honda — +26,687
**Kimi Räikkönen (McLaren-Mercedes) retired on lap 7.**

Bahrain GP, qualifying
20. Kimi Räikkönen — McLaren-Mercedes — no time

## SAN MARINO GP

1. Michael Schumacher — Ferrari — 1.26.19,670
2. Jenson Button — BAR-Honda — +9,702
3. Juan Pablo Montoya — Williams-BMW — +21,617
8. **Kimi Räikkönen** — **McLaren-Mercedes** — **+1 lap**

San Marino GP, qualifying
20. Kimi Räikkönen — McLaren-Mercedes — no time

## SPANISH GP

1. Michael Schumacher — Ferrari — 1.27.32,841
2. Rubens Barrichello — Ferrari — +13,290
3. Jarno Trulli — Renault — +32,294
11. **Kimi Räikkönen** — **McLaren-Mercedes** — **+1 lap**

Spanish GP, qualifying
13. Kimi Räikkönen — McLaren-Mercedes — 1.17,445

## MONACO GP

1. Jarno Trulli — Renault — 1.45.46,601
2. Jenson Button — BAR-Honda — +0,497
3. Rubens Barrichello — Ferrari — +1.15,766
**Kimi Räikkönen (McLaren-Mercedes) retired on lap 27.**

Monaco GP, qualifying
6. (5) Kimi Räikkönen — McLaren-Mercedes — 1.14,592

## EUROPEAN GP

1. Michael Schumacher — Ferrari — 1.32.35,101
2. Rubens Barrichello — Ferrari — +17,989
3. Jenson Button — BAR-Honda — +22,533
**Kimi Räikkönen (McLaren-Mercedes) retired on lap 9.**

European GP, qualifying
4. Kimi Räikkönen — McLaren-Mercedes — 1.29,137

## CANADIAN GP

1. Michael Schumacher — Ferrari — 1.28.24,803
2. Rubens Barrichello — Ferrari — +5,108
3. Jenson Button — BAR-Honda — +20,409
5. **Kimi Räikkönen** — **McLaren-Mercedes** — **+1 lap**

Canadian GP, qualifying
8. Kimi Räikkönen — McLaren-Mercedes — 1.13,595

## UNITED STATES GP

1. Michael Schumacher    Ferrari    1.40.29,914
2. Rubens Barrichello    Ferrari    +2,950
3. Takuma Sato    BAR-Honda    +22,036
6. **Kimi Räikkönen**    **McLaren-Mercedes**    **+1 lap**

United States GP, qualifying
7. Kimi Räikkönen    McLaren-Mercedes    1.11,137

## FRENCH GP

1. Michael Schumacher    Ferrari    1.30.18,133
2. Fernando Alonso    Renault    +8,329
3. Rubens Barrichello    Ferrari    +31,622
7. **Kimi Räikkönen**    **McLaren-Mercedes**    **+36,230**

French GP, qualifying
9. Kimi Räikkönen    McLaren-Mercedes    1.14,346

## BRITISH GP

1. Michael Schumacher    Ferrari    1.24.42,700
2. **Kimi Räikkönen**    **McLaren-Mercedes**    **+2,130**
3. Rubens Barrichello    Ferrari    +3,114

British GP, qualifying
1. Kimi Räikkönen    McLaren-Mercedes    1.18,233

## GERMAN GP

1. Michael Schumacher    Ferrari    1.23.54,848
2. Jenson Button    BAR-Honda    +8,388
3. Fernando Alonso    Renault    +16,351

**Kimi Räikkönen (McLaren-Mercedes) retired on lap 13.**

German GP, qualifying
4. (3) Kimi Räikkönen    McLaren-Mercedes    1.13,690

## HUNGARIAN GP

1. Michael Schumacher    Ferrari    1.35.26,131
2. Rubens Barrichello    Ferrari    +4,696
3. Fernando Alonso    Renault    +44,599

**Kimi Räikkönen (McLaren-Mercedes) retired on lap 13.**

Hungarian GP, qualifying
10. Kimi Räikkönen    McLaren-Mercedes    1.20,570

## BELGIAN GP

1. **Kimi Räikkönen**    **McLaren-Mercedes**    **1.32.35,274**
2. Michael Schumacher    Ferrari    +3,132
3. Rubens Barrichello    Ferrari    +4,371

Belgian GP, qualifying
10. Kimi Räikkönen    McLaren-Mercedes    1.59,635

## ITALIAN GP

1. Rubens Barrichello    Ferrari    1.15.18,448
2. Michael Schumacher    Ferrari    +1,347
3. Jenson Button    BAR-Honda    +10,197

**Kimi Räikkönen (McLaren-Mercedes) retired on lap 13.**

Italian GP, qualifying
7. Kimi Räikkönen    McLaren-Mercedes    1.20,877

## CHINESE GP

1. Rubens Barrichello    Ferrari    1.29.12,420
2. Jenson Button    BAR-Honda    +1,035
3. **Kimi Räikkönen**    **McLaren-Mercedes**    **+1,469**

Chinese GP, qualifying
2. Kimi Räikkönen    McLaren-Mercedes    1.34,178

## JAPANESE GP

1. Michael Schumacher    Ferrari    1.24.26,985
2. Ralf Schumacher    Williams-BMW    +14,098
3. Jenson Button    BAR-Honda    +19,662
6. **Kimi Räikkönen**    **McLaren-Mercedes**    **+39,362**

Japanese GP, qualifying
12. Kimi Räikkönen    McLaren-Mercedes    1.36,820

## BRAZILIAN GP

1. Juan Pablo Montoya    Williams-BMW    1.28.01,451
2. **Kimi Räikkönen**    **McLaren-Mercedes**    **+1,022**
3. Rubens Barrichello    Ferrari    +24,099

Brazilian GP, qualifying
3. Kimi Räikkönen    McLaren-Mercedes    1.10,892

# 2005

## AUSTRALIAN GP

1. Giancarlo Fisichella    Renault    1.24.17,336
2. Rubens Barrichello    Ferrari    +5,553
3. Fernando Alonso    Renault    +6,712
8. **Kimi Räikkönen**    **McLaren-Mercedes**    **+39,633**

Australian GP, qualifying
10. Kimi Räikkönen    McLaren-Mercedes    3.15,558

## MALAYSIAN GP

1. Fernando Alonso    Renault    1.31.33,736
2. Jarno Trulli    Toyota    +24,327
3. Nick Heidfeld    Williams-BMW    +32,188
9. **Kimi Räikkönen**    **McLaren-Mercedes**    **+1.21,580**

Malaysian GP, qualifying
6. Kimi Räikkönen    McLaren-Mercedes    1.36,644

## BAHRAIN GP

1. Fernando Alonso    Renault    1.29.18,531
2. Jarno Trulli    Toyota    +13,409
3. **Kimi Räikkönen**    **McLaren-Mercedes**    **+32,063**

Bahrain GP, qualifying
9. Kimi Räikkönen    McLaren-Mercedes    3.03,524

## SAN MARINO GP

1. Fernando Alonso    Renault    1.27.41,921
2. Michael Schumacher    Ferrari    +0,215
3. Alexander Wurz    McLaren-Mercedes    +27,554
**Kimi Räikkönen retired on lap 9.**

San Marino GP, qualifying
1. Kimi Räikkönen    McLaren-Mercedes    2.42,880

## SPANISH GP

1. **Kimi Räikkönen**    **McLaren-Mercedes**    **1.27.16,830**
2. Fernando Alonso    Renault    +27,652
3. Jarno Trulli    Toyota    +45,947

Spanish GP, qualifying
1. Kimi Räikkönen    McLaren-Mercedes    2.31,421

## MONACO GP

1. **Kimi Räikkönen**    **McLaren-Mercedes**    **1.45.15,556**
2. Nick Heidfeld    Williams-BMW    +13,877
3. Mark Webber    Williams-BMW    +18,484

Monaco GP, qualifying
1. Kimi Räikkönen    McLaren-Mercedes    2.30,325

## EUROPEAN GP

1. Fernando Alonso    Renault    1.31.46,648
2. Nick Heidfeld    Williams-BMW    +16,567
3. Rubens Barrichello    Ferrari    +18,549
11. **Kimi Räikkönen**    **McLaren-Mercedes**    **+1 lap**

European GP, qualifying
2. Kimi Räikkönen    McLaren-Mercedes    1.30,197

## CANADIAN GP

1. **Kimi Räikkönen**    **McLaren-Mercedes**    **1.32.09,290**
2. Michael Schumacher    Ferrari    +1,137
3. Rubens Barrichello    Ferrari    +40,483

Canadian GP, qualifying
7. Kimi Räikkönen    McLaren-Mercedes    1.15,923

## UNITED STATES GP

1. Michael Schumacher    Ferrari    1.29.43,181
2. Rubens Barrichello    Ferrari    +1,522
3. Tiago Monteiro    Jordan-Toyota    +1 lap
**Kimi Räikkönen (McLaren-Mercedes) did not drive the GP.**

United States GP, qualifying
2. Kimi Räikkönen    McLaren-Mercedes    1.10,694

## FRENCH GP

1. Fernando Alonso    Renault    1.31.22,232
2. **Kimi Räikkönen**    **McLaren-Mercedes**    **+11,805**
3. Michael Schumacher    Ferrari    +1.21,914

French GP, qualifying
3. (13) Kimi Räikkönen    McLaren-Mercedes    3.15,558

## BRITISH GP

1. Juan Pablo Montoya    McLaren-Mercedes    1.24.29,588
2. Fernando Alonso    Renault    +2,739
3. **Kimi Räikkönen**    **McLaren-Mercedes**    **+14,436**

British GP, qualifying
2. (12) Kimi Räikkönen    McLaren-Mercedes    1.19,932

## GERMAN GP

1. Fernando Alonso    Renault    1.26.28,599
2. Juan Pablo Montoya    McLaren-Mercedes    +22,569
3. Jenson Button    BAR-Honda    +24,422
**Kimi Räikkönen (McLaren-Mercedes) retired on lap 32.**

German GP, qualifying
1. Kimi Räikkönen    McLaren-Mercedes    1.14,320

## HUNGARIAN GP

1. **Kimi Räikkönen**    **McLaren-Mercedes**    **1.37.25,552**
2. Rubens Barrichello    Ferrari    +35,581
3. Ralf Schumacher    Toyota    +36,129

Hungarian GP, qualifying
4. Kimi Räikkönen    McLaren-Mercedes    1.20,891

## TURKISH GP

1. **Kimi Räikkönen**    **McLaren-Mercedes**    **1.24.34,454**
2. Fernando Alonso    Renault    +18,609
3. Juan Pablo Montoya    McLaren-Mercedes    +19,635

Turkish GP, qualifying
1. Kimi Räikkönen    McLaren-Mercedes    1.26,797

## ITALIAN GP

1. Juan Pablo Montoya — McLaren-Mercedes — 1.14.28,659
2. Fernando Alonso — Renault — +2,479
3. Giancarlo Fisichella — Renault — +17,975
4. **Kimi Räikkönen** — **McLaren-Mercedes** — **+22,775**

Italian GP, qualifying
1. (11) Kimi Räikkönen — McLaren-Mercedes — 1.20,878

## BELGIAN GP

1. **Kimi Räikkönen** — **McLaren-Mercedes** — **1.30.01,295**
2. Fernando Alonso — Renault — +28,394
3. Jenson Button — BAR-Honda — +32,077

Belgian GP, qualifying
2. Kimi Räikkönen — McLaren-Mercedes — 1.46,440

## BRAZILIAN GP

1. Juan Pablo Montoya — McLaren-Mercedes — 1.29.20,574
2. **Kimi Räikkönenr** — **McLaren-Mercedes** — **+2,527**
3. Fernando Alonso — Renault — +24,840

Brazilian GP, qualifying
5. Kimi Räikkönen — McLaren-Mercedes — 1.12,781

## JAPANESE GP

1. **Kimi Räikkönen** — **McLaren-Mercedes** — **1.29.02,212**
2. Giancarlo Fisichella — Renault — +1,633
3. Fernando Alonso — Renault — +17,456

Japanese GP, qualifying
17. Kimi Räikkönen — McLaren-Mercedes — 2.02,309

## CHINESE GP

1. Fernando Alonso — Renault — 1.39.53,618
2. **Kimi Räikkönen** — **McLaren-Mercedes** — **+4,015**
3. Ralf Schumacher — Toyota — +25,376

Chinese GP, qualifying
3. Kimi Räikkönen — McLaren-Mercedes — 1.34,488

# 2006

## BAHRAIN GP

1. Fernando Alonso — Renault — 1.29.46,205
2. Michael Schumacher — Ferrari — +1,246
3. **Kimi Räikkönen** — **McLaren-Mercedes** — **+19,360**

Bahrain GP, qualifying
22. Kimi Räikkönen — McLaren-Mercedes — no time

## MALAYSIAN GP

1. Giancarlo Fisichella — Renault — 1.30.40,529
2. Fernando Alonso — Renault — +4,585
3. Jenson Button — Honda — +9,631
**Kimi Räikkönen (McLaren-Mercedes) retired on lap 1.**

Malaysian GP, qualifying
7. (6) Kimi Räikkönen — McLaren-Mercedes — 1.34,983

## AUSTRALIAN GP

1. Fernando Alonso — Renault — 1.34.27,870
2. **Kimi Räikkönen** — **McLaren-Mercedes** — **+1,829**
3. Ralf Schumacher — Toyota — +24,824

Australian GP, qualifying
4. Kimi Räikkönen — McLaren-Mercedes — 1.25,822

## SAN MARINO GP

1. Michael Schumacher — Ferrari — 1.31.06,486
2. Fernando Alonso — Renault — +2,096
3. Juan Pablo Montoya — McLaren-Mercedes — +15,868
5. **Kimi Räikkönen** — **McLaren-Mercedes** — **+17,524**

San Marino GP, qualifying
8. Kimi Räikkönen — McLaren-Mercedes — 1.24,158

## EUROPEAN GP

1. Michael Schumacher — Ferrari — 1.35.58,765
2. Fernando Alonso — Renault — +3,751
3. Felipe Massa — Ferrari — +4,447
4. **Kimi Räikkönen** — **McLaren-Mercedes** — **+4,879**

European GP, qualifying
5. Kimi Räikkönen — McLaren-Mercedes — 1.31,263

## SPANISH GP

1. Fernando Alonso — Renault — 1.26.21,759
2. Michael Schumacher — Ferrari — +18,502
3. Giancarlo Fisichella — Renault — +23,951
5. **Kimi Räikkönen** — **McLaren-Mercedes** — **+56,875**

Spanish GP, qualifying
9. Kimi Räikkönen — McLaren-Mercedes — 1.16,613

## MONACO GP

1. Fernando Alonso — Renault — 1.43.43,116
2. Juan Pablo Montoya — McLaren-Mercedes — +14,567
3. David Coulthard — Red Bull-Ferrari — +52,298
**Kimi Räikkönen (McLaren-Mercedes) retired on lap 50.**

Monaco GP, qualifying
3. Kimi Räikkönen — McLaren-Mercedes — 1.13,887

## BRITISH GP

| 1. Fernando Alonso | Renault | 1.25.51,927 |
|---|---|---|
| 2. Michael Schumacher | Ferrari | +13,951 |
| **3. Kimi Räikkönen** | **McLaren-Mercedes** | **+18,672** |

British GP, qualifying

| 2. Kimi Räikkönen | McLaren-Mercedes | 1.20,397 |
|---|---|---|

## CANADIAN GP

| 1. Fernando Alonso | Renault | 1.34.37,308 |
|---|---|---|
| 2. Michael Schumacher | Ferrari | +2,111 |
| **3. Kimi Räikkönen** | **McLaren-Mercedes** | **+8,813** |

Canadian GP, qualifying

| 3. Kimi Räikkönen | McLaren-Mercedes | 1.15,376 |
|---|---|---|

## UNITED STATES GP

| 1. Michael Schumacher | Ferrari | 1.34.35,199 |
|---|---|---|
| 2. Felipe Massa | Ferrari | +7,984 |
| 3. Giancarlo Fisichella | Renault | +16,595 |

**Kimi Räikkönen (McLaren-Mercedes) retired on lap 1.**

United States GP, qualifying

| 9. Kimi Räikkönen | McLaren-Mercedes | 1.13,174 |
|---|---|---|

## FRENCH GP

| 1. Michael Schumacher | Ferrari | 1.32.07,803 |
|---|---|---|
| 2. Fernando Alonso | Renault | +10,131 |
| 3. Felipe Massa | Ferrari | +22,546 |
| **5. Kimi Räikkönen** | **McLaren-Mercedes** | **+33,006** |

French GP, qualifying

| 6. Kimi Räikkönen | McLaren-Mercedes | 1.16,281 |
|---|---|---|

## GERMAN GP

| 1. Michael Schumacher | Ferrari | 1.27.51,693 |
|---|---|---|
| 2. Felipe Massa | Ferrari | +0,720 |
| **3. Kimi Räikkönen** | **McLaren-Mercedes** | **+13,206** |

German GP, qualifying

| 1. Kimi Räikkönen | McLaren-Mercedes | 1.14,070 |
|---|---|---|

## HUNGARIAN GP

| 1. Jenson Button | Honda | 1.52.20,941 |
|---|---|---|
| 2. Pedro de la Rosa | McLaren-Mercedes | +30,837 |
| 3. Nick Heidfeld | BMW Sauber | +43,822 |

**Kimi Räikkönen (McLaren-Mercedes) retired on lap 25.**

Hungarian GP, qualifying

| 1. Kimi Räikkönen | McLaren-Mercedes | 1.19,599 |
|---|---|---|

## TURKISH GP

| 1. Felipe Massa | Ferrari | 1.28.51,082 |
|---|---|---|
| 2. Fernando Alonso | Renault | +5,575 |
| 3. Michael Schumacher | Ferrari | +5,656 |

**Kimi Räikkönen (McLaren-Mercedes) retired on lap 2.**

Turkish GP, qualifying

| 8. (7) Kimi Räikkönen | McLaren-Mercedes | 1.27,866 |
|---|---|---|

## ITALIAN GP

| 1. Michael Schumacher | Ferrari | 1.14.51,975 |
|---|---|---|
| **2. Kimi Räikkönen** | **McLaren-Mercedes** | **+8,046** |
| 3. Robert Kubica | BMW Sauber | +26,414 |

Italian GP, qualifying

| 1. Kimi Räikkönen | McLaren-Mercedes | 1.21,484 |
|---|---|---|

## CHINESE GP

| 1. Michael Schumacher | Ferrari | 1.37.32,747 |
|---|---|---|
| 2. Fernando Alonso | Renault | +3,121 |
| 3. Giancarlo Fisichella | Renault | +44,197 |

**Kimi Räikkönen (McLaren-Mercedes) retired on lap 18.**

Chinese GP, qualifying

| 5. Kimi Räikkönen | McLaren-Mercedes | 1.45,754 |
|---|---|---|

## JAPANESE GP

| 1. Fernando Alonso | Renault | 1.23.52,413 |
|---|---|---|
| 2. Felipe Massa | Ferrari | +16,151 |
| 3. Giancarlo Fisichella | Renault | +23,953 |
| **5. Kimi Räikkönen** | **McLaren-Mercedes** | **+43,596** |

Japanese GP, qualifying

| 11. Kimi Räikkönen | McLaren-Mercedes | 1.30,827 |
|---|---|---|

## BRAZILIAN GP

| 1. Felipe Massa | Ferrari | 1.31.53,751 |
|---|---|---|
| 2. Fernando Alonso | Renault | +18,658 |
| 3. Jenson Button | Honda | +19,394 |
| **5. Kimi Räikkönen** | **McLaren-Mercedes** | **+28,503** |

Brazilian GP, qualifying

| 2. Kimi Räikkönen | McLaren-Mercedes | 1.11,299 |
|---|---|---|

## 2007

## AUSTRALIAN GP

| **1. Kimi Räikkönen** | **Ferrari** | **1.25.28,770** |
|---|---|---|
| 2. Fernando Alonso | McLaren-Mercedes | +7,242 |
| 3. Lewis Hamilton | McLaren-Mercedes | +18,595 |

Australian GP, qualifying

| 1. Kimi Räikkönen | Ferrari | 1.26,072 |
|---|---|---|

## MALAYSIAN GP
| 1. | Fernando Alonso | McLaren-Mercedes | 1.32.14,930 |
| 2. | Lewis Hamilton | McLaren-Mercedes | +17,557 |
| **3.** | **Kimi Räikkönen** | **Ferrari** | **+18,339** |

Malaysian GP, qualifying
| 3. | Kimi Räikkönen | Ferrari | 1.35,479 |

## BAHRAIN GP
| 1. | Felipe Massa | Ferrari | 1.33.27,515 |
| 2. | Lewis Hamilton | McLaren-Mercedes | +2,360 |
| **3.** | **Kimi Räikkönen** | **Ferrari** | **+10,839** |

Bahrain GP, qualifying
| 3. | Kimi Räikkönen | Ferrari | 1.33,131 |

## SPANISH GP
| 1. | Felipe Massa | Ferrari | 1.31.36,230 |
| 2. | Lewis Hamilton | McLaren-Mercedes | +6,790 |
| 3. | Fernando Alonso | McLaren-Mercedes | +17,456 |

**Kimi Räikkönen (Ferrari) retired on lap 9.**

Spanish GP, qualifying
| 3. | Kimi Räikkönen | Ferrari | 1.21,723 |

## MONACO GP
| 1. | Fernando Alonso | McLaren-Mercedes | 1.40.29,329 |
| 2. | Lewis Hamilton | McLaren-Mercedes | + 4,095 |
| 3. | Felipe Massa | Ferrari | +1.09,114 |
| **8.** | **Kimi Räikkönen** | **Ferrari** | **+1 lap** |

Monaco GP, qualifying
| 16. | Kimi Räikkönen | Ferrari | no time |

## CANADIAN GP
| 1. | Lewis Hamilton | McLaren-Mercedes | 1.44.11,292 |
| 2. | Nick Heidfeld | BMW Sauber | +4,343 |
| 3. | Alexander Wurz | Williams-Toyota | +5,325 |
| **5.** | **Kimi Räikkönen** | **Ferrari** | **+13,007** |

Canadian GP, qualifying
| 4. | Kimi Räikkönen | Ferrari | 1.16,411 |

## UNITED STATES GP
| 1. | Lewis Hamilton | McLaren-Mercedes | 1.31.09,965 |
| 2. | Fernando Alonso | McLaren-Mercedes | +1,518 |
| 3. | Felipe Massa | Ferrari | +12,842 |
| **4.** | **Kimi Räikkönen** | **Ferrari** | **+15,422** |

United States GP, qualifying
| 4. | Kimi Räikkönen | Ferrari | 1.12,839 |

## FRENCH GP
| **1.** | **Kimi Räikkönen** | **Ferrari** | **1.30.54,200** |
| 2. | Felipe Massa | Ferrari | +2,414 |
| 3. | Lewis Hamilton | McLaren-Mercedes | +32,153 |

French GP, qualifying
| 3. | Kimi Räikkönen | Ferrari | 1.15,257 |

## BRITISH GP
| **1.** | **Kimi Räikkönen** | **Ferrari** | **1.21.43,074** |
| 2. | Fernando Alonso | McLaren-Mercedes | +2,459 |
| 3. | Lewis Hamilton | McLaren-Mercedes | +39,373 |

British GP, qualifying
| 2. | Kimi Räikkönen | Ferrari | 1.20,099 |

## EUROPEAN GP
| 1. | Fernando Alonso | McLaren-Mercedes | 2.06.26,358 |
| 2. | Felipe Massa | Ferrari | +8,155 |
| 3. | Mark Webber | Red Bull-Renault | +1.05,674 |

**Kimi Räikkönen (Ferrari) retired on lap 34.**

European GP, qualifying
| 1. | Kimi Räikkönen | Ferrari | 1.31,450 |

## HUNGARIAN GP
| 1. | Lewis Hamilton | McLaren-Mercedes | 1.35.52,991 |
| **2.** | **Kimi Räikkönen** | **Ferrari** | **+0,715** |
| 3. | Nick Heidfeld | BMW Sauber | +43,129 |

Hungarian GP, qualifying
| 4. | (3) Kimi Räikkönen | Ferrari | 1.20,410 |

## TURKISH GP
| 1. | Felipe Massa | Ferrari | 1.26.42,161 |
| **2.** | **Kimi Räikkönen** | **Ferrari** | **+2,275** |
| 3. | Fernando Alonso | McLaren-Mercedes | +26,181 |

Turkish GP, qualifying
| 3. | Kimi Räikkönen | Ferrari | 1.27,546 |

## ITALIAN GP
| 1. | Fernando Alonso | McLaren-Mercedes | 1.18.37,806 |
| 2. | Lewis Hamilton | McLaren-Mercedes | +6,062 |
| **3.** | **Kimi Räikkönen** | **Ferrari** | **+27,325** |

Italian GP, qualifying
| 5. | Kimi Räikkönen | Ferrari | 1.23,183 |

## BELGIAN GP

| | | |
|---|---|---|
| 1. **Kimi Räikkönen** | **Ferrari** | **1.20.39,066** |
| 2. Felipe Massa | Ferrari | +4,695 |
| 3. Fernando Alonso | McLaren-Mercedes | +14,343 |

Belgian GP, qualifying

| | | |
|---|---|---|
| 1. Kimi Räikkönen | Ferrari | 1.45,994 |

## JAPANESE GP

| | | |
|---|---|---|
| 1. Lewis Hamilton | McLaren-Mercedes | 2.00.34,579 |
| 2. Heikki Kovalainen | Renault | +8,377 |
| 3. **Kimi Räikkönen** | **Ferrari** | **+9,478** |

Japanese GP, qualifying

| | | |
|---|---|---|
| 3. Kimi Räikkönen | Ferrari | 1.25,516 |

## CHINESE GP

| | | |
|---|---|---|
| 1. **Kimi Räikkönen** | **Ferrari** | **1.37.58,395** |
| 2. Fernando Alonso | McLaren-Mercedes | +9,806 |
| 3. Felipe Massa | Ferrari | +12,891 |

Chinese GP, qualifying

| | | |
|---|---|---|
| 2. Kimi Räikkönen | Ferrari | 1.36,044 |

## BRAZILIAN GP

| | | |
|---|---|---|
| 1. **Kimi Räikkönen** | **Ferrari** | **1.28.15,270** |
| 2. Felipe Massa | Ferrari | +1,493 |
| 3. Fernando Alonso | McLaren-Mercedes | +57,019 |

Brazilian GP, qualifying

| | | |
|---|---|---|
| 3. Kimi Räikkönen | Ferrari | 1.12,322 |

## 2008

## AUSTRALIAN GP

| | | |
|---|---|---|
| 1. Lewis Hamilton | McLaren-Mercedes | 1.34.50,616 |
| 2. Nick Heidfeld | BMW Sauber | +5,478 |
| 3. Nico Rosberg | Williams-Toyota | +8,163 |

**Kimi Räikkönen (Ferrari) retired on lap 53 but was 8th qualifying.**

Australian GP, qualifying

| | | |
|---|---|---|
| 16. (15) Kimi Räikkönen | Ferrari | no time |

## MALAYSIAN GP

| | | |
|---|---|---|
| 1. **Kimi Räikkönen** | **Ferrari** | **1.31.18,555** |
| 2. Robert Kubica | BMW Sauber | +19,750 |
| 3. Heikki Kovalainen | McLaren-Mercedes | +38,450 |

Malaysian GP, qualifying

| | | |
|---|---|---|
| 2. Kimi Räikkönen | Ferrari | 1.36,230 |

## BAHRAIN GP

| | | |
|---|---|---|
| 1. Felipe Massa | Ferrari | 1.31.06,970 |
| 2. **Kimi Räikkönen** | **Ferrari** | **+3,339** |
| 3. Robert Kupica | BMW Sauber | +4,998 |

Bahrain GP, qualifying

| | | |
|---|---|---|
| 4. Kimi Räikkönen | Ferrari | 1.33,418 |

## SPANISH GP

| | | |
|---|---|---|
| 1. **Kimi Räikkönen** | **Ferrari** | **1.38.19,051** |
| 2. Felipe Massa | Ferrari | +6,790 |
| 3. Lewis Hamilton | McLaren-Mercedes | +4,187 |

Spanish GP, qualifying

| | | |
|---|---|---|
| 1. Kimi Räikkönen | Ferrari | 1.21,813 |

## TURKISH GP

| | | |
|---|---|---|
| 1. Felipe Massa | Ferrari | 1.26.49,451 |
| 2. Lewis Hamilton | McLaren-Mercedes | +3,779 |
| 3. **Lewis Hamilton** | **Ferrari** | **+4,271** |

Turkish GP, qualifying

| | | |
|---|---|---|
| 3. Kimi Räikkönen | Ferrari | 1.27,936 |

## MONACO GP

| | | |
|---|---|---|
| 1. Lewis Hamilton | McLaren-Mercedes | 2.00.42,742 |
| 2. Robert Kupica | BMW Sauber | +3,064 |
| 3. Felipe Massa | Ferrari | +4,811 |
| 9. **Kimi Räikkönen** | **Ferrari** | **+33,792** |

Monaco GP, qualifying

| | | |
|---|---|---|
| 2. Kimi Räikkönen | Ferrari | 1.15,815 |

## CANADIAN GP

| | | |
|---|---|---|
| 1. Robert Kupica | BMW Sauber | 1.36.24,227 |
| 2. Nick Heidfeld | BMW Sauber | +16,495 |
| 3. David Coulthard | Red Bull-Renault | +23,352 |

**Kimi Räikkönen (Ferrari) retired on lap 19.**

Canadian GP, qualifying

| | | |
|---|---|---|
| 3. Kimi Räikkönen | Ferrari | 1.18,735 |

## FRENCH GP

| | | |
|---|---|---|
| 1. Felipe Massa | Ferrari | 1.31.50,245 |
| 2. **Kimi Räikkönen** | **Ferrari** | **+17,984** |
| 3. Jarno Trulli | Toyota | +28,250 |

French GP, qualifying

| | | |
|---|---|---|
| 1. Kimi Räikkönen | Ferrari | 1.16,449 |

## BRITISH GP

1. Lewis Hamilton — McLaren-Mercedes — 1.39.09,440
2. Nick Heidfeld — BMW Sauber — +1.08,577
3. Rubens Barrichello — Honda — +1.22,273
9. **Kimi Räikkönen** — **Ferrari** — **+1 lap**

British GP, qualifying
3. Kimi Räikkönen — Ferrari — 1.16,449

## GERMAN GP

1. Lewis Hamilton — McLaren-Mercedes — 1.37.27,067
2. Nelson Piquet Jr. — Renault — +5,586
3. Felipe Massa — Ferrari — +9,339
6. **Kimi Räikkönen** — **Ferrari** — **+14,403**

German GP, qualifying
6. Kimi Räikkönen — Ferrari — 1.16,389

## HUNGARIAN GP

1. Heikki Kovalainen — McLaren-Mercedes — 2.00.42,742
2. Timo Glock — Toyota — +11,061
3. **Kimi Räikkönen** — **Ferrari** — **+16,856**

Hungarian GP, qualifying
6. Kimi Räikkönen — Ferrari — 1.21,516

## EUROPEAN GP

1. Felipe Massa — Ferrari — 1.35.32,339
2. Lewis Hamilton — McLaren-Mercedes — +5,611
3. Robert Kubica — BMW Sauber — +37,353
**Kimi Räikkönen interrupted on lap 34.**

European GP, qualifying
1. Kimi Räikkönen — Ferrari — 1.31,450

## BELGIAN GP

1. Felipe Massa — Ferrari — 1.22.59,394
2. Nick Heidfeld — BMW Sauber — +9,383
3. Lewis Hamilton — McLaren-Mercedes — +10,539
**Kimi Räikkönen retired on lap 42 but was 18th.**

Belgian GP, qualifying
4. Kimi Räikkönen — Ferrari — 1.47,992

## ITALIAN GP

1. Sebastian Vettel — Toro Rosso-Ferrari — 1.26.47,494
2. Heikki Kovalainen — McLaren-Mercedes — +12,512
3. Robert Kubica — BMW Sauber — +20,471
9. **Kimi Räikkönen** — **Ferrari** — **+39,468**

Italian GP, qualifying
14. Kimi Räikkönen — Ferrari — 1.37,522

## SINGAPORE GP

1. Fernando Alonso — Renault — 1.57.16,304
2. Nico Rosberg — Williams-Toyota — +2,957
3. Lewis Hamilton — McLaren-Mercedes — +5,917
**Kimi Räikkönen retired on lap 57 but was 15th.**

Singapore GP, qualifying
3. Kimi Räikkönen — Ferrari — 1.45,617

## JAPANESE GP

1. Fernando Alonso — Renault — 1.30.21,892
2. Robert Kubica — BMW Sauber — +5,283
3. **Kimi Räikkönen** — **Ferrari** — **+6,400**

Japanese GP, qualifying
6. Kimi Räikkönen — Ferrari — 1.18,644

## CHINESE GP

1. Lewis Hamilton — McLaren-Mercedes — 1.31.57,403
2. Felipe Massa — Ferrari — +14,925
3. **Kimi Räikkönen** — **Ferrari** — **+16,445**

Chinese GP, qualifying
2. Kimi Räikkönen — Ferrari — 1.36,645

## BRAZILIAN GP

1. Felipe Massa — Ferrari — 1.31.57,403
2. Fernando Alonso — Renault — +13,298
3. **Kimi Räikkönen** — **Ferrari** — **+16,235**

Brazilian GP, qualifying
3. Kimi Räikkönen — Ferrari — 1.12,825

# 2009

## AUSTRALIAN GP

1. Jenson Button — Brawn-Mercedes — 1.34.15,784
2. Rubens Barrichello — Brawn-Mercedes — +0,807
3. Jarno Trulli — Toyota — +1,604
**Kimi Räikkönen retired on lap 55 but was 15th.**

Australian GP, qualifying
9. (7) Kimi Räikkönen — Ferrari — 1.27,163

## MALAYSIAN GP

1. Jenson Button — Brawn-Mercedes — 55.30,622
2. Nick Heidfeld — BMW Sauber — +22,722
3. Timo Glock — Toyota — +23,513
14. **Kimi Räikkönen** — **Ferrari** — **+2.22,841**

Malaysian GP, qualifying
9. (7) Kimi Räikkönen — Ferrari — 1.36,170

## CHINESE GP

| 1. Sebastian Wettel | Red Bull-Renault | 1.57.43,485 |
|---|---|---|
| 2. Mark Webber | Red Bull-Renault | +10,970 |
| 3. Jenson Button | Brawn-Mercedes | +44,975 |
| **10. Kimi Räikkönen** | **Ferrari** | **+1.31,750** |

Chinese GP, qualifying

| 8. Kimi Räikkönen | Ferrari | 1.38,089 |
|---|---|---|

## BAHRAIN GP

| 1. Jenson Button | Brawn-Mercedes | 1.31.48,182 |
|---|---|---|
| 2. Sebastian Wettel | Red Bull-Renault | +7,187 |
| 3. Jarno Trulli | Toyota | +9,170 |
| **6. Kimi Räikkönen** | **Ferrari** | **+42,057** |

Bahrain GP, qualifying

| 10. Kimi Räikkönen | Ferrari | 1.35,380 |
|---|---|---|

## SPANISH GP

| 1. Jenson Button | Brawn-Mercedes | 1.37.19,202 |
|---|---|---|
| 2. Rubens Barrichello | Brawn-Mercedes | +13,056 |
| 3. Mark Webber | Red Bull-Renault | +13,924 |

**Kimi Räikkönen retired on lap 17.**

Spanish GP, qualifying

| 16. Kimi Räikkönen | Ferrari | 1.21,291 |
|---|---|---|

## MONACO GP

| 1. Jenson Button | Brawn-Mercedes | 1.40.44,282 |
|---|---|---|
| 2. Rubens Barrichello | Brawn-Mercedes | +7,666 |
| **3. Kimi Räikkönen** | **Ferrari** | **+13,442** |

Monaco GP, qualifying

| 2. Kimi Räikkönen | Ferrari | 1.14,927 |
|---|---|---|

## TURKISH GP

| 1. Jenson Button | Brawn-Mercedes | 1.26.24,848 |
|---|---|---|
| 2. Mark Webber | Red Bull-Renault | +6,714 |
| 3. Sebastian Wettel | Red Bull-Renault | +7,461 |
| **9. Kimi Räikkönen** | **Ferrari** | **+50,246** |

Turkish GP, qualifying

| 6. Kimi Räikkönen | Ferrari | 1.28,815 |
|---|---|---|

## BRITISH GP

| 1. Sebastian Wettel | Red Bull-Renault | 1.22.49,328 |
|---|---|---|
| 2. Mark Webber | Red Bull-Renault | +15,188 |
| 3. Rubens Barrichello | Brawn-Mercedes | +41,175 |
| **8. Kimi Räikkönen** | **Ferrari** | **+1.09,622** |

British GP, qualifying

| 9. Kimi Räikkönen | **Ferrari** | 1.20,715 |
|---|---|---|

## GERMAN GP

| 1. Mark Webber | Red Bull-Renault | 1.36.43,310 |
|---|---|---|
| 2. Sebastian Wettel | Red Bull-Renault | +9,252 |
| 3. Felipe Massa | Ferrari | +15,906 |

**Kimi Räikkönen retired on lap 34.**

German GP, qualifying

| 9. Kimi Räikkönen | Ferrari | 1.34,710 |
|---|---|---|

## HUNGARIAN GP

| 1. Lewis Hamilton | McLaren-Mercedes | 1.38.23,876 |
|---|---|---|
| **2. Kimi Räikkönen** | **Ferrari** | **+11,529** |
| 3. Mark Webber | Red Bull-Renault | +16,856 |

Hungarian GP, qualifying

| 7. Kimi Räikkönen | Ferrari | 1.22,468 |
|---|---|---|

## EUROPEAN GP

| 1. Rubens Barrichello | Brawn-Mercedes | 1.35.51,289 |
|---|---|---|
| 2. Lewis Hamilton | McLaren-Mercedes | +2,358 |
| **3. Kimi Räikkönen** | **Ferrari** | **+15,994** |

European GP, qualifying

| 6. Kimi Räikkönen | Ferrari | 1.40,144 |
|---|---|---|

## BELGIAN GP

| **1. Kimi Räikkönen** | **Ferrari** | **1.23.50,995** |
|---|---|---|
| 2. Giancarlo Fisichella | Force India-Mercedes | +0,939 |
| 3. Sebastian Vettel | Red Bull-Renault | +3,875 |

Belgian GP, qualifying

| 6. Kimi Räikkönen | Ferrari | 1.46,633 |
|---|---|---|

## ITALIAN GP

| 1. Rubens Barrichello | Brawn-Mercedes | 1.16.21,706 |
|---|---|---|
| 2. Jenson Button | Brawn-Mercedes | +2,866 |
| **3. Kimi Räikkönen** | **Ferrari** | **+30,664** |

Italian GP, qualifying

| 3. Kimi Räikkönen | Ferrari | 1.24,523 |
|---|---|---|

## SINGAPORE GP

| 1. Lewis Hamilton | Brawn-Mercedes | 1.56.06,337 |
|---|---|---|
| 2. Timo Glock | Toyota | +9,634 |
| 3. Fernando Alonso | Renault | +16,624 |
| **10. Kimi Räikkönen** | **Ferrari** | **+58,892** |

Singapore GP, qualifying

| 13. (12) Kimi Räikkönen | Ferrari | 1.47,177 |
|---|---|---|

## JAPANESE GP

1. Sebastian Vettel — Red Bull-Renault — 1.28.20,443
2. Jarno Trulli — Toyota — +4,877
3. Lewis Hamilton — McLaren-Mercedes — +6,472
4. **Kimi Räikkönen** — **Ferrari** — **+7,940**

Japanese GP, qualifying
8. (5) Kimi Räikkönen — Ferrari — 1.32,980

## BRAZILIAN GP

1. Mark Webber — Red Bull-Renault — 1.32.23,081
2. Robert Kubica — BMW Sauber — +7,626
3. Lewis Hamilton — McLaren-Mercedes — +18,944
6. **Kimi Räikkönen** — **Ferrari** — **+33,340**

Brazilian GP, qualifying
5. Kimi Räikkönen — Ferrari — 1.20,168

## ABU DHABI GP

1. Sebastian Vettel — Red Bull-Renault — 1.34.03,414
2. Mark Webber — Red Bull-Renault — +17,857
3. Jenson Button — Brawn-Mercedes — +18,467
12. **Kimi Räikkönen** — **Ferrari** — **+54,317**

Abu Dhabi GP, qualifying
11. Kimi Räikkönen — Ferrari — 1.40,726

# 2012

## AUSTRALIAN GP

1. Jenson Button — McLaren-Mercedes — 1.34.09,565
2. Sebastian Vettel — Red Bull-Renault — +2,139
3. Lewis Hamilton — McLaren-Mercedes — +4,075
7. **Kimi Räikkönen** — **Lotus-Renault** — **+38,014**

Australian GP, qualifying
18. (7) Kimi Räikkönen — Lotus-Renault — 1.27,758

## MALAYSIAN GP

1. Fernando Alonso — Ferrari — 2.44.51,812
2. Sergio Pérez — Sauber-Ferrari — +2,263
3. Lewis Hamilton — McLaren-Mercedes — +14,591
5. **Kimi Räikkönen** — **Lotus-Renault** — **+29,456**

Malaysian GP, qualifying
5. (10) Kimi Räikkönen — Lotus-Renault — 1.36,461

## CHINESE GP

1. Nico Rosberg — Mercedes — 1.36.26,929
2. Jenson Button — McLaren-Mercedes — +20,626
3. Lewis Hamilton — McLaren-Mercedes — +26,012
14. **Kimi Räikkönen** — **Lotus-Renault** — **+50,573**

Chinese GP, qualifying
4. Kimi Räikkönen — Lotus-Renault — 1.35,898

## BAHRAIN GP

1. Sebastian Vettel — Red Bull-Renault — 1.35.10,990
2. **Kimi Räikkönen** — **Lotus-Renault** — **+3,333**
3. Romain Grosjean — Lotus-Renault — +10,194

Bahrain GP, qualifying
11. Kimi Räikkönen — Lotus-Renault — 1.33,789

## SPANISH GP

1. Pastor Maldonado — Williams-Renault — 1.39.09,145
2. Fernando Alonso — Ferrari — +3,195
3. **Kimi Räikkönen** — **Lotus-Renault** — **+3,884**

Spanish GP, qualifying
4. Kimi Räikkönen — Lotus-Renault — 1.22,487

## MONACO GP

1. Mark Webber — Red Bull-Renault — 1.46.06,557
2. Nico Rosberg — Mercedes — +0,643
3. Fernando Alonso — Ferrari — +0,947
9. **Kimi Räikkönen** — **Lotus-Renault** — **+44,036**

Monaco GP, qualifying
8. Kimi Räikkönen — Lotus-Renault — 1.15,199

## CANADIAN GP

1. Lewis Hamilton — McLaren-Mercedes — 1.32.29,586
2. Romain Grosjean — Lotus-Renault — +2,513
3. Sergio Pérez — Sauber-Ferrari — +5,260
8. **Kimi Räikkönen** — **Lotus-Renault** — **+15,567**

Canadian GP, qualifying
12. Kimi Räikkönen — Lotus-Renault — 1.14,734

## EUROPEAN GP

1. Fernando Alonso — Ferrari — 1.44.16,649
2. **Kimi Räikkönen** — **Lotus-Renault** — **+6,421**
3. Michael Schumacher — Mercedes — +12,639

European GP, qualifying
5. Kimi Räikkönen — Lotus-Renault — 1.38,513

## BRITISH GP

1. Mark Webber — Red Bull-Renault — 1.25.11,288
2. Fernando Alonso — Ferrari — +3,060
3. Lewis Hamilton — Red Bull-Renault — +4,836
5. **Kimi Räikkönen** — **Lotus-Renault** — **+10,314**

British GP, qualifying
6. Kimi Räikkönen — Lotus-Renault — 1.53,290

## GERMAN GP

| | | | |
|---|---|---|---|
| 1. | Fernando Alonso | Ferrari | 1.31.05,862 |
| 2. | Jenson Button | McLaren-Mercedes | +6,931 |
| **3.** | **Kimi Räikkönen** | **Lotus-Renault** | **+16,409** |

German GP, qualifying

| | | | |
|---|---|---|---|
| 10. | Kimi Räikkönen | Lotus-Renault | 1.45,811 |

## HUNGARIAN GP

| | | | |
|---|---|---|---|
| 1. | Lewis Hamilton | McLaren-Mercedes | 1.41.05,503 |
| **2.** | **Kimi Räikkönen** | **Lotus-Renault** | **+1,032** |
| 3. | Romain Grosjean | Lotus-Renault | +10,518 |

Hungarian GP, qualifying

| | | | |
|---|---|---|---|
| 5. | Kimi Räikkönen | Lotus-Renault | 1.21,730 |

## BELGIAN GP

| | | | |
|---|---|---|---|
| 1. | Jenson Button | McLaren-Mercedes | 1.29.08,530 |
| 2. | Sebastian Vettel | Red Bull-Renault | +13,624 |
| **3.** | **Kimi Räikkönen** | **Lotus-Renault** | **+25,334** |

Belgian GP, qualifying

| | | | |
|---|---|---|---|
| 4. | (3) Kimi Räikkönen | Lotus-Renault | 1.48,205 |

## ITALIAN GP

| | | | |
|---|---|---|---|
| 1. | Lewis Hamilton | McLaren-Mercedes | 1.19.41,221 |
| 2. | Sergio Pérez | Sauber-Ferrari | +4,356 |
| 3. | Fernando Alonso | Ferrari | +20,594 |
| **5.** | **Kimi Räikkönen** | **Lotus-Renault** | **+30,881** |

Italian GP, qualifying

| | | | |
|---|---|---|---|
| 8. | Kimi Räikkönen | Lotus-Renault | 1.24,855 |

## SINGAPORE GP

| | | | |
|---|---|---|---|
| 1. | Sebastian Vettel | Red Bull-Renault | 2.00.26,144 |
| 2. | Jenson Button | McLaren-Mercedes | +8,959 |
| 3. | Fernando Alonso | Ferrari | +15,227 |
| **6.** | **Kimi Räikkönen** | **Lotus-Renault** | **+35,759** |

Singapore GP, qualifying

| | | | |
|---|---|---|---|
| 12. | Kimi Räikkönen | Lotus-Renault | 1.48,261 |

## JAPANESE GP

| | | | |
|---|---|---|---|
| 1. | Sebastian Vettel | Red Bull-Renault | 1.28.56,242 |
| 2. | Felipe Massa | Ferrari | +20,632 |
| 3. | Kamui Kobayashi | Sauber-Ferrari | +24,538 |
| **6.** | **Kimi Räikkönen** | **Lotus-Renault** | **+50,424** |

Japanese GP, qualifying

| | | | |
|---|---|---|---|
| 8. | (7) Kimi Räikkönen | Lotus-Renault | 1.32,980 |

## KOREAN GP

| | | | |
|---|---|---|---|
| 1. | Sebastian Vettel | Red Bull-Renault | 1.36.28,651 |
| 2. | Mark Webber | Red Bull-Renault | +8,231 |
| 3. | Fernando Alonso | Ferrari | +13,944 |
| **5.** | **Kimi Räikkönen** | **Lotus-Renault** | **+36,739** |

Korean GP, qualifying

| | | | |
|---|---|---|---|
| 5. | Kimi Räikkönen | Lotus-Renault | 1.37,625 |

## INDIAN GP

| | | | |
|---|---|---|---|
| 1. | Sebastian Vettel | Red Bull-Renault | 1.31.10,744 |
| 2. | Fernando Alonso | Ferrari | +9,437 |
| 3. | Mark Webber | Red Bull-Renault | +13,217 |
| **7.** | **Kimi Räikkönen** | **Lotus-Renault** | **+45,227** |

Indian GP, qualifying

| | | | |
|---|---|---|---|
| 7. | Kimi Räikkönen | Lotus-Renault | 1.26,236 |

## ABU DHABI GP

| | | | |
|---|---|---|---|
| **1.** | **Kimi Räikkönen** | **Lotus-Renault** | **1.45.58,667** |
| 2. | Fernando Alonso | Ferrari | +0,852 |
| 3. | Sebastian Vettel | Red Bull-Renault | +4,163 |

Abu Dhabi GP, qualifying

| | | | |
|---|---|---|---|
| 4. | Kimi Räikkönen | Lotus-Renault | 1.41,260 |

## UNITED STATES GP

| | | | |
|---|---|---|---|
| 1. | Lewis Hamilton | McLaren-Mercedes | 1.35.55,269 |
| 2. | Sebastian Vettel | Red Bull-Renault | +0,675 |
| 3. | Fernando Alonso | Ferrari | +39,229 |
| **6.** | **Kimi Räikkönen** | **Lotus-Renault** | **+1.04,425** |

United States GP, qualifying

| | | | |
|---|---|---|---|
| 5. | (4) Kimi Räikkönen | Lotus-Renault | 1.36,708 |

## BRAZILIAN GP

| | | | |
|---|---|---|---|
| 1. | Jenson Button | Red Bull-Renault | 1.45.22,656 |
| 2. | Fernando Alonso | Mercedes | +2,754 |
| 3. | Felipe Massa | Ferrari | +3,615 |
| **10.** | **Kimi Räikkönen** | **Lotus-Renault** | **+1 lap** |

Brazilian GP, qualifying

| | | | |
|---|---|---|---|
| 9. | Kimi Räikkönen | Lotus-Renault | 1.13,298 |

# 2013

## AUSTRALIAN GP

| | | | |
|---|---|---|---|
| **1.** | **Kimi Räikkönen** | **Lotus-Renault** | **1.30.03,225** |
| 2. | Fernando Alonso | Ferrari | +12,451 |
| 3. | Sebastian Vettel | Red Bull-Renault | +22,346 |

Australian GP, qualifying

| | | | |
|---|---|---|---|
| 7. | Kimi Räikkönen | Lotus-Renault | 1.28,738 |

## MALAYSIAN GP

| | | | |
|---|---|---|---|
| 1. | Sebastian Vettel | Red Bull-Renault | 1.38.56,681 |
| 2. | Mark Webber | Red Bull-Renault | +4,298 |
| 3. | Lewis Hamilton | Mercedes | +12,181 |
| **7.** | **Kimi Räikkönen** | **Lotus-Renault** | **+48,479** |

Malaysian GP, qualifying

| | | | |
|---|---|---|---|
| 7. | (10) Kimi Räikkönen | Lotus-Renault | 1.52.970 |

## CHINESE GP

| | | | |
|---|---|---|---|
| 1. | Fernando Alonso | Ferrari | 1.36.26,945 |
| **2.** | **Kimi Räikkönen** | **Lotus-Renault** | **+10,168** |
| 3. | Lewis Hamilton | Mercedes | +12,322 |

Chinese GP, qualifying

| | | | |
|---|---|---|---|
| 2. | Kimi Räikkönen | Lotus-Renault | 1.34.761 |

## BAHRAIN GP

| | | | |
|---|---|---|---|
| 1. | Sebastian Vettel | Red Bull-Renault | 1.36.00,498 |
| **2.** | **Kimi Räikkönen** | **Lotus-Renault** | **+9,111** |
| 3. | Romain Grosjean | Lotus-Renault | +19,507 |

Bahrain GP, qualifying

| | | | |
|---|---|---|---|
| 9. | (8) Kimi Räikkönen | Lotus-Renault | 1.33.327 |

## SPANISH GP

| | | | |
|---|---|---|---|
| 1. | Felipe Massa | Ferrari | 1.31.36,230 |
| **2.** | **Kimi Räikkönen** | **Lotus-Renault** | **+9,338** |
| 3. | Felipe Massa | Ferrari | +26,049 |

Spanish GP, qualifying

| | | | |
|---|---|---|---|
| 4. | Kimi Räikkönen | Lotus-Renault | 1.21.177 |

## MONACO GP

| | | | |
|---|---|---|---|
| 1. | Nico Rosberg | Mercedes | 2.17.52,506 |
| 2. | Sebastian Vettel | Red Bull-Renault | +3,889 |
| 3. | Mark Webber | Red Bull-Renault | +6,314 |
| **10.** | **Kimi Räikkönen** | **Lotus-Renault** | **+44,036** |

Monaco GP, qualifying

| | | | |
|---|---|---|---|
| 5. | Kimi Räikkönen | Lotus-Renault | 1.14.822 |

## CANADIAN GP

| | | | |
|---|---|---|---|
| 1. | Sebastian Vettel | Red Bull-Renault | 1.32.09,143 |
| 2. | Fernando Alonso | Ferrari | +14,408 |
| 3. | Lewis Hamilton | Mercedes | +15,942 |
| **9.** | **Kimi Räikkönen** | **Lotus-Renault** | **+1 lap** |

Canadian GP, qualifying

| | | | |
|---|---|---|---|
| 9. | (10) Kimi Räikkönen | Lotus-Renault | 1.27.432 |

## BRITISH GP

| | | | |
|---|---|---|---|
| 1. | Nico Rosberg | Mercedes | 1.32.59,456 |
| 2. | Mark Webber | Red Bull-Renault | +0,765 |
| 3. | Fernando Alonso | Ferrari | +7,124 |
| **5.** | **Kimi Räikkönen** | **Lotus-Renault** | **+11,257** |

British GP, qualifying

| | | | |
|---|---|---|---|
| 8. | Kimi Räikkönen | Lotus-Renault | 1.30.962 |

## GERMAN GP

| | | | |
|---|---|---|---|
| 1. | Sebastian Wettel | Red Bull-Renault | 1.41.14,711 |
| **2.** | **Kimi Räikkönen** | **Lotus-Renault** | **+1,008** |
| 3. | Romain Grosjean | Lotus-Renault | +5,830 |

German GP, qualifying

| | | | |
|---|---|---|---|
| 2. | (4) Kimi Räikkönen | Lotus-Renault | 1.29.892 |

## HUNGARIAN GP

| | | | |
|---|---|---|---|
| 1. | Lewis Hamilton | Mercedes | 1.42.29,445 |
| **2.** | **Kimi Räikkönen** | **Lotus-Renault** | **+10,938** |
| 3. | Sebastian Vettel | Red Bull-Renault | +12,459 |

Hungarian GP, qualifying

| | | | |
|---|---|---|---|
| 6. | Kimi Räikkönen | Lotus-Renault | 1.19.851 |

## BELGIAN GP

| | | | |
|---|---|---|---|
| 1. | Sebastian Vettel | Red Bull-Renault | 1.23.42,196 |
| 2. | Fernando Alonso | Ferrari | +16,869 |
| 3. | Lewis Hamilton | Mercedes | +27,734 |

**Kimi Räikkönen (Lotus-Renault) retired on lap 25.**

Belgian GP, qualifying

| | | | |
|---|---|---|---|
| 8. | Kimi Räikkönen | Lotus-Renault | 2.03,390 |

## ITALIAN GP

| | | | |
|---|---|---|---|
| 1. | Sebastian Vettel | Red Bull-Renault | 1.18.33,352 |
| 2. | Fernando Alonso | Ferrari | +5,467 |
| 3. | Mark Webber | Red Bull-Renault | +6,350 |
| **11.** | **Kimi Räikkönen** | **Lotus-Renault** | **+38,695** |

Italian GP, qualifying

| | | | |
|---|---|---|---|
| 11. | Kimi Räikkönen | Lotus-Renault | 1.24,610 |

## SINGAPORE GP

| | | | |
|---|---|---|---|
| 1. | Sebastian Vettel | Red Bull-Renault | 1.59.13,132 |
| 2. | Fernando Alonso | Ferrari | +32,627 |
| **3.** | **Kimi Räikkönen** | **Lotus-Renault** | **+43,920** |

Singapore GP, qualifying

| | | | |
|---|---|---|---|
| 13. | Kimi Räikkönen | Lotus-Renault | 1.44,658 |

## KOREAN GP

| 1. | Sebastian Vettel | Red Bull-Renault | 1.43.13,701 |
| 2. | **Kimi Räikkönen** | **Lotus-Renault** | **+4,224** |
| 3. | Romain Grosjean | Lotus-Renault | +4,927 |

Korean GP, qualifying

| 10. | (9) Kimi Räikkönen | Lotus-Renault | 1.38,822 |

## JAPANESE GP

| 1. | Sebastian Vettel | Red Bull-Renault | 1.26.49,301 |
| 2. | Mark Webber | Red Bull-Renault | +7,129 |
| 3. | Romain Grosjean | Lotus-Renault | +9,910 |
| 5. | **Kimi Räikkönen** | **Lotus-Renault** | **+47,325** |

Japanese GP, qualifying

| 9. | Kimi Räikkönen | Lotus-Renault | 1.31,684 |

## INDIAN GP

| 1. | Sebastian Vettel | Red Bull-Renault | 1.31.12,187 |
| 2. | Nico Rosberg | Mercedes | +29,823 |
| 3. | Romain Grosjean | Lotus-Renault | +39,892 |
| 7. | **Kimi Räikkönen** | **Lotus-Renault** | **+1.07,988** |

Indian GP, qualifying

| 6. | Kimi Räikkönen | Lotus-Renault | 1.25,248 |

## ABU DHABI GP

| 1. | Sebastian Vettel | Red Bull-Renault | 1.38.06,1067 |
| 2. | Mark Webber | Red Bull-Renault | +30,829 |
| 3. | Nico Rosberg | Mercedes | +33,650 |

**Kimi Räikkönen retired on lap 1 and withdrew from the last two races of the season.**

Abu Dhabi GP, qualifying

| 5. | (22) Kimi Räikkönen | Lotus-Renault | 1.40,542 |

## 2014

## AUSTRALIAN GP

| 1. | Nico Rosberg | Mercedes | 1.32.58,710 |
| 2. | Kevin Magnussen | McLaren-Mercedes | +26,777 |
| 3. | Jenson Button | McLaren-Mercedes | +30,027 |
| 7. | **Kimi Räikkönen** | **Ferrari** | **+57,675** |

Australian GP, qualifying

| 12. | (11) Kimi Räikkönen | Ferrari | 1.44,494 |

## MALAYSIAN GP

| 1. | Lewis Hamilton | Mercedes | 1.40.25,9741 |
| 2. | Nico Rosberg | Mercedes | +17,313 |
| 3. | Sebastian Vettel | Red Bull Racing-Renault | +24,534 |
| 12. | **Kimi Räikkönen** | **Ferrari** | **+1 lap** |

Malaysian GP, qualifying

| 6. | Kimi Räikkönen | Ferrari | 2.01,218 |

## BAHRAIN GP

| 1. | Lewis Hamilton | Mercedes | 1.39.42,743 |
| 2. | Nico Rosberg | Mercedes | +1,085 |
| 3. | Sergio Pérez | Force India-Mercedes | +24,067 |
| 10. | **Kimi Räikkönen** | **Ferrari** | **+33,462** |

Bahrain GP, qualifying

| 6. | (5) Kimi Räikkönen | Ferrari | 1.34,368 |

## CHINESE GP

| 1. | Lewis Hamilton | Mercedes | 1.33.28,338 |
| 2. | Nico Rosberg | Mercedes | +18,062 |
| 3. | Fernando Alonso | Ferrari | +23,604 |
| 8. | **Kimi Räikkönen** | **Ferrari** | **+1.16,335** |

Chinese GP, qualifying

| 11. | Kimi Räikkönen | Ferrari | 1.56,860 |

## SPANISH GP

| 1. | Lewis Hamilton | Mercedes | 1.41.05,155 |
| 2. | Nico Rosberg | Mercedes | +0,636 |
| 3. | Daniel Ricciardo | Red Bull Racing-Renault | +49,014 |
| 7. | **Kimi Räikkönen** | **Ferrari** | **+1 lap** |

Spanish GP, qualifying

| 6. | Kimi Räikkönen | Ferrari | 1.27,104 |

## MONACO GP

| 1. | Nico Rosberg | Mercedes | 1.49.27,661 |
| 2. | Lewis Hamilton | Mercedes | +9,210 |
| 3. | Daniel Ricciardo | Red Bull Racing-Renault | +9,614 |
| 12. | **Kimi Räikkönen** | **Ferrari** | **+1 lap** |

Monaco GP, qualifying

| 6. | Kimi Räikkönen | Ferrari | 1.17,389 |

## CANADIAN GP

| 1. | Daniel Ricciardo | Red Bull Racing-Renault | 1.39.12,830 |
| 2. | Nico Rosberg | Mercedes | +4,236 |
| 3. | Sebastian Vettel | Red Bull Racing-Renault | +5,247 |
| 10. | **Kimi Räikkönen** | **Ferrari** | **+53,678** |

Canadian GP, qualifying

| 10. | Kimi Räikkönen | Ferrari | 1.16,214 |

## AUSTRIAN GP

| 1. | Nico Rosberg | Mercedes | 1.27.54,976 |
| 2. | Lewis Hamilton | Mercedes | +1,932 |
| 3. | Valtteri Bottas | Williams-Mercedes | +8,172 |
| 10. | **Kimi Räikkönen** | **Ferrari** | **+47,777** |

Austrian GP, qualifying

| 8. | Kimi Räikkönen | Ferrari | 1.10,795 |

## BRITISH GP
1. Lewis Hamilton    Mercedes    2.26.52,094
2. Valtteri Bottas    Williams-Mercedes    +30,135
3. Daniel Ricciardo    Red Bull Racing-Renault    +46,495

**Kimi Räikkönen retired on lap 1.**

British GP, qualifying
20. (18) Kimi Räikkönen    Ferrari    1.46,684

## GERMAN GP
1. Nico Rosberg    Mercedes    1.33.42,914
2. Valtteri Bottas    Williams-Mercedes    +20,789
3. Lewis Hamilton    Mercedes    +22,530
**11. Kimi Räikkönen**    **Ferrari**    **+1 lap**

German GP, qualifying
12. Kimi Räikkönen    Ferrari    1.18,273

## HUNGARIAN GP
1. Daniel Ricciardo    Red Bull Racing-Renault    1.53.05,058
2. Fernando Alonso    Ferrari    +5,225
3. Lewis Hamilton    Mercedes    +5,857
**6. Kimi Räikkönen**    **Ferrari**    **+31,491**

Hungarian GP, qualifying
17. (16) Kimi Räikkönen    Ferrari    1.26,792

## BELGIAN GP
1. Daniel Ricciardo    Red Bull Racing-Renault    1.24.36,556
2. Nico Rosberg    Mercedes    +3,3835
3. Valtteri Bottas    Williams-Mercedes    +28,032
**4. Kimi Räikkönen**    **Ferrari**    **+36,815**

Belgian GP, qualifying
8. Kimi Räikkönen    Ferrari    2.08,780

## ITALIAN GP
1. Lewis Hamilton    Mercedes    1.19.10,236
2. Nico Rosberg    Mercedes    +3,175
3. Felipe Massa    Williams-Mercedes    +25,026
**9. Kimi Räikkönen**    **Ferrari**    **+1.03,535**

Italian GP, qualifying
12. (11) Kimi Räikkönen    Ferrari    1.26,110

## SINGAPORE GP
1. Lewis Hamilton    Mercedes    2.00.04,795
2. Sebastian Vettel    Red Bull Racing-Renault    +13,534
3. Daniel Ricciardo    Red Bull Racing-Renault    +14,273
**8. Kimi Räikkönen**    **Ferrari**    **+1.00,641**

Singapore GP, qualifying
7. Kimi Räikkönen    Ferrari    1.46,170

## JAPANESE GP
1. Lewis Hamilton    Mercedes    1.51.43,021
2. Nico Rosberg    Mercedes    +9,180
3. Sebastian Vettel    Red Bull Racing-Renault    +29,122
**12. Kimi Räikkönen**    **Ferrari**    **+1 lap**

Japanese GP, qualifying
10. Kimi Räikkönen    Ferrari    1.34,548

## RUSSIAN GP
1. Lewis Hamilton    Mercedes    1.31.50,744
2. Nico Rosberg    Mercedes    +13,657
3. Valtteri Bottas    Williams-Mercedes    +17,425
**9. Kimi Räikkönen**    **Ferrari**    **+1.18,877**

Russian GP, qualifying
9. (8) Kimi Räikkönen    Lotus-Renault    1.39,771

## UNITED STATES GP
1. Lewis Hamilton    Mercedes    1.40.04,785
2. Nico Rosberg    Mercedes    +4,314
3. Daniel Ricciardo    Ferrari    +25,560
**13. Kimi Räikkönen**    **Ferrari**    **+1 lap**

United States GP, qualifying
9. (8) Kimi Räikkönen    Ferrari    1.37,804

## BRAZILIAN GP
1. Nico Rosberg    Mercedes    1.30.02,555
2. Lewis Hamiton    Mercedes    +1,457
3. Felipe Massa    Williams-Mercedes    +41,031
**7. Kimi Räikkönen**    **Ferrari**    **+1.03,730**

Brazilian GP, qualifying
10. Kimi Räikkönen    Ferrari    1.11,099

## ABU DHABI GP
1. Lewis Hamilton    Mercedes    1.39.02,619
2. Felipe Massa    Williams-Mercedes    +2,576
3. Valtteri Bottas    Williams-Mercedes    +28,880
**10. Kimi Räikkönen**    **Ferrari**    **+1.27,820**

Abu Dhabi GP, qualifying
7. Kimi Räikkönen    Ferrari    1.42,236

# 2015

## AUSTRALIAN GP
1. Lewis Hamilton    Mercedes    1.31.54,067
2. Nico Rosberg    Mercedes    +1,360
3. Sebastian Vettel    Ferrari    +34,523

**Kimi Räikkönen (Ferrari) retired on lap 40.**

Australian GP, qualifying
5. Kimi Räikkönen    Ferrari    1.27,790

## MALAYSIAN GP

| 1. | Sebastian Vettel | Ferrari | 1.41.05,793 |
|---|---|---|---|
| 2. | Lewis Hamilton | Mercedes | +8,569 |
| 3. | Nico Rosberg | Mercedes | +12,310 |
| **4.** | **Kimi Räikkönen** | **Ferrari** | **+53,822** |

Malaysian GP, qualifying

| 11. | Kimi Räikkönen | Ferrari | 1.42,173 |
|---|---|---|---|

## CHINESE GP

| 1. | Lewis Hamilton | Mercedes | 1.39.42,008 |
|---|---|---|---|
| 2. | Nico Rosberg | Mercedes | +0,714 |
| 3. | Sebastian Vettel | Ferrari | +2,988 |
| **4.** | **Kimi Räikkönen** | **Ferrari** | **+3,835** |

Chinese GP, qualifying

| 6. | Kimi Räikkönen | Ferrari | 1.37,232 |
|---|---|---|---|

## BAHRAIN GP

| 1. | Lewis Hamilton | Mercedes | 1.35.05,809 |
|---|---|---|---|
| **2.** | **Kimi Räikkönen** | **Ferrari** | **+3,380** |
| 3. | Nico Rosberg | Mercedes | +6,033 |

Bahrain GP, qualifying

| 4. | Kimi Räikkönen | Ferrari | 1.33,227 |
|---|---|---|---|

## SPANISH GP

| 1. | Nico Rosberg | Mercedes | 1.41.12,555 |
|---|---|---|---|
| 2. | Lewis Hamilton | Mercedes | +17,551 |
| 3. | Sebastian Vettel | Mercedes | +45,342 |
| **5.** | **Kimi Räikkönen** | **Ferrari** | **+1.00,002** |

Spanish GP, qualifying

| 7. | Kimi Räikkönen | Ferrari | 1.26,414 |
|---|---|---|---|

## MONACO GP

| 1. | Nico Rosberg | Mercedes | 1.49.18,420 |
|---|---|---|---|
| 2. | Sebastian Vettel | Ferrari | +4,486 |
| 3. | Lewis Hamilton | Mercedes | +6,053 |
| **6.** | **Kimi Räikkönen** | **Ferrari** | **+14,345** |

Monaco GP, qualifying

| 6. | Kimi Räikkönen | Ferrari | 1.16,427 |
|---|---|---|---|

## CANADIAN GP

| 1. | Lewis Hamilton | Mercedes | 1.31.53,145 |
|---|---|---|---|
| 2. | Nico Rosberg | Mercedes | +2,285 |
| 3. | Valtteri Bottas | Williams-Mercedes | +40,666 |
| **4.** | **Kimi Räikkönen** | **Ferrari** | **+45,625** |

Canadian GP, qualifying

| 3. | Kimi Räikkönen | Ferrari | 1.15,014 |
|---|---|---|---|

## AUSTRIAN GP

| 1. | Nico Rosberg | Mercedes | 1.30.16,930 |
|---|---|---|---|
| 2. | Lewis Hamilton | Mercedes | +8,800 |
| 3. | Felipe Massa | Williams-Mercedes | +17,573 |

**Kimi Räikkönen (Ferrari) retired on lap 1.**

Austrian GP, qualifying

| 18. | Kimi Räikkönen | Ferrari | 1.12,867 |
|---|---|---|---|

## BRITISH GP

| 1. | Lewis Hamilton | Mercedes | 1.31.27,729 |
|---|---|---|---|
| 2. | Nico Rosberg | Mercedes | +10,956 |
| 3. | Sebastian Vettel | Ferrari | +25,443 |
| **8.** | **Kimi Räikkönen** | **Ferrari** | **+1 lap** |

British GP, qualifying

| 5. | Kimi Räikkönen | Ferrari | 1.33,379 |
|---|---|---|---|

## HUNGARIAN GP

| 1. | Sebastian Vettel | Ferrari | 1.46.09,985 |
|---|---|---|---|
| 2. | Daniil Kvyat | Red Bull Racing-Renault | +15,748 |
| 3. | Daniel Ricciardo | Red Bull Racing-Renault | +25,084 |

**Kimi Räikkönen (Ferrari) retired on lap 55.**

Hungarian GP, qualifying

| 5. | Kimi Räikkönen | Ferrari | 1.23,020 |
|---|---|---|---|

## BELGIAN GP

| 1. | Lewis Hamilton | Mercedes | 1.23.40,387 |
|---|---|---|---|
| 2. | Nico Rosberg | Mercedes | +2,058 |
| 3. | Romain Grosjean | Lotus-Mercedes | +37,988 |
| **7.** | **Kimi Räikkönen** | **Ferrari** | **+55,703** |

Belgian GP, qualifying

| 14. (16) | Kimi Räikkönen | Ferrari | no time |
|---|---|---|---|

## ITALIAN GP

| 1. | Lewis Hamilton | Mercedes | 1.18.00,688 |
|---|---|---|---|
| 2. | Sebastian Vettel | Ferrari | +25,042 |
| 3. | Felipe Massa | Williams-Mercedes | +47,635 |
| **5.** | **Kimi Räikkönen** | **Ferrari** | **+1.08,860** |

Italian GP, qualifying

| 2. | Kimi Räikkönen | Ferrari | 1.23,631 |
|---|---|---|---|

## SINGAPORE GP

| 1. | Sebastian Vettel | Ferrari | 2.01.22,118 |
|---|---|---|---|
| 2. | Daniel Ricciardo | Red Bull Racing-Renault | +1,478 |
| **3.** | **Kimi Räikkönen** | **Ferrari** | **+17,154** |

Singapore GP, qualifying

| 3. | Kimi Räikkönen | Ferrari | 1.44,667 |
|---|---|---|---|

## JAPANESE GP

| 1. | Lewis Hamilton | Mercedes | 1.28.06,508 |
|---|---|---|---|
| 2. | Nico Rosberg | Mercedes | +18,964 |
| 3. | Sebastian Vettel | Ferrari | +20,850 |
| **4.** | **Kimi Räikkönen** | **Ferrari** | **+33,768** |

Japanese GP, qualifying

| 6. | Kimi Räikkönen | Ferrari | 1.33,347 |
|---|---|---|---|

## RUSSIAN GP

| 1. | Lewis Hamilton | Mercedes | 1.37.110,24 |
|---|---|---|---|
| 2. | Sebastian Vettel | Ferrari | +5,953 |
| 3. | Sergio Pérez | Force India-Mercedes | +28,918 |
| **8.** | **Kimi Räikkönen** | **Ferrari** | **+1.12,358** |

Russian GP, qualifying

| 5. | Kimi Räikkönen | Ferrari | 1.38,348 |
|---|---|---|---|

## UNITED STATES GP

| 1. | Lewis Hamilton | Mercedes | 1.50.52,703 |
|---|---|---|---|
| 2. | Nico Rosberg | Mercedes | +2,850 |
| 3. | Sebastian Vettel | Ferrari | +3,381 |

**Kimi Räikkönen (Ferrari) retired on lap 25.**

United States GP, qualifying

| 8. | (18) Kimi Räikkönen | Ferrari | 1.59,703 |
|---|---|---|---|

## MEXICAN GP

| 1. | Nico Rosberg | Mercedes | 1.42.35,038 |
|---|---|---|---|
| 2. | Lewis Hamilton | Mercedes | +1,954 |
| 3. | Valtteri Bottas | Williams-Mercedes | +14,592 |

**Kimi Räikkönen (Ferrari) retired on lap 21.**

Mexican GP, qualifying

| 15. | (19) Kimi Räikkönen | Ferrari | 1.22,494 |
|---|---|---|---|

## BRAZILIAN GP

| 1. | Nico Rosberg | Mercedes | 1.31.09,090 |
|---|---|---|---|
| 2. | Lewis Hamiton | Mercedes | +7,756 |
| 3. | Sebastian Vettel | Ferrari | +14,244 |
| **4.** | **Kimi Räikkönen** | **Ferrari** | **+ 47,543** |

Brazilian GP, qualifying

| 5. | (4) Kimi Räikkönen | Ferrari | 1.12,144 |
|---|---|---|---|

## ABU DHABI GP

| 1. | Nico Rosberg | Mercedes | 1.38.30,175 |
|---|---|---|---|
| 2. | Lewis Hamilton | Mercedes | +8,271 |
| **3.** | **Kimi Räikkönen** | **Ferrari** | **+19,430** |

Abu Dhabi GP, qualifying

| 3. | Kimi Räikkönen | Ferrari | 1.41,051 |
|---|---|---|---|

# 2016

## AUSTRALIAN GP

| 1. | Nico Rosberg | Mercedes | 1.48.15,565 |
|---|---|---|---|
| 2. | Lewis Hamilton | Mercedes | +8,060 |
| 3. | Sebastian Vettel | Ferrari | +9,643 |

**Kimi Räikkönen retired on lap 21.**

Australian GP, qualifying

| 4. | Kimi Räikkönen | Ferrari | 1.25,033 |
|---|---|---|---|

## BAHRAIN GP

| 1. | Nico Rosberg | Mercedes | 1.33.34,696 |
|---|---|---|---|
| **2.** | **Kimi Räikkönen** | **Ferrari** | **+10,282** |
| 3. | Lewis Hamilton | Mercedes | +30,148 |

Bahrain GP, qualifying

| 4. | Kimi Räikkönen | Ferrari | 1.30,244 |
|---|---|---|---|

## CHINESE GP

| 1. | Nico Rosberg | Mercedes | 1.38.53,891 |
|---|---|---|---|
| 2. | Sebastian Vettel | Ferrari | +37,776 |
| 3. | Daniil Kvyat | Red Bull Racing-TAG Heuer | +45,936 |
| **5.** | **Kimi Räikkönen** | **Ferrari** | **+1.05,872** |

Chinese GP, qualifying

| 3. | Kimi Räikkönen | Ferrari | 1.35,972 |
|---|---|---|---|

## RUSSIAN GP

| 1. | Nico Rosberg | Mercedes | 1.32.41,997 |
|---|---|---|---|
| 2. | Lewis Hamilton | Mercedes | +25,022 |
| **3.** | **Kimi Räikkönen** | **Ferrari** | **+31,998** |

Russian GP, qualifying

| 4. | (3) Kimi Räikkönen | Ferrari | 1.36,663 |
|---|---|---|---|

## SPANISH GP

| 1. | Max Verstappen | Red Bull Racing-TAG Heuer | 1.41.40,017 |
|---|---|---|---|
| **2.** | **Kimi Räikkönen** | **Ferrari** | **+0,616** |
| 3. | Sebastian Vettel | Ferrari | +5,581 |

Spanish GP, qualifying

| 5. | Kimi Räikkönen | Ferrari | 1.23,113 |
|---|---|---|---|

## MONACO GP

| 1. | Lewis Hamilton | Mercedes | 1.59.29,133 |
|---|---|---|---|
| 2. | Daniel Ricciardo | Red Bull Racing-TAG Heuer | +7,252 |
| 3. | Sergio Pérez | Force India-Mercedes | +13,825 |

**Kimi Räikkönen retired on lap 10.**

Monaco GP, qualifying

| 6. | (1) Kimi Räikkönen | Ferrari | 1.14,732 |
|---|---|---|---|

## CANADIAN GP

| 1. | Lewis Hamilton | Mercedes | 1.31.05,296 |
|---|---|---|---|
| 2. | Sebastian Vettel | Ferrari | +5,011 |
| 3. | Valtteri Bottas | Williams-Mercedes | +46,422 |
| **6.** | **Kimi Räikkönen** | **Ferrari** | **+1.03,017** |

Canadian GP, qualifying

| 6. | Kimi Räikkönen | Ferrari | 1.13,579 |
|---|---|---|---|

## EUROPEAN GP

| 1. | Nico Rosberg | Mercedes | 1.32.52,366 |
|---|---|---|---|
| 2. | Sebastian Vettel | Ferrari | +16,696 |
| 3. | Sergio Pérez | Force India-Mercedes | +25,241 |
| **4.** | **Kimi Räikkönen** | **Ferrari** | **+33,102** |

European GP, qualifying

| 5. | (4) Kimi Räikkönen | Ferrari | 1.44,269 |
|---|---|---|---|

## AUSTRIAN GP

| 1. | Lewis Hamilton | Mercedes | 1.27.38,107 |
|---|---|---|---|
| 2. | Max Verstappen | Red Bull Racing-TAG Heuer | +5,719 |
| **3.** | **Kimi Räikkönen** | **Ferrari** | **+6,024** |

Austrian GP, qualifying

| 6. | (4) Kimi Räikkönen | Ferrari | 1.09,901 |
|---|---|---|---|

## BRITISH GP

| 1. | Lewis Hamilton | Mercedes | 1.34.55,831 |
|---|---|---|---|
| 2. | Max Verstappen | Red Bull Racing-TAG Heuer | +8,250 |
| 3. | Nico Rosberg | Mercedes | +16,911 |
| **5.** | **Kimi Räikkönen** | **Ferrari** | **+1.09,743** |

British GP, qualifying

| 5. | Kimi Räikkönen | Ferrari | 1.30,881 |
|---|---|---|---|

## HUNGARIAN GP

| 1. | Lewis Hamilton | Mercedes | 1.40.30,115 |
|---|---|---|---|
| 2. | Nico Rosberg | Mercedes | +1,977 |
| 3. | Daniel Ricciardo | Red Bull Racing-TAG Heuer | +27,539 |
| **6.** | **Kimi Räikkönen** | **Ferrari** | **+49,044** |

Hungarian GP, qualifying

| 14. | Kimi Räikkönen | Ferrari | 1.25,435 |
|---|---|---|---|

## GERMAN GP

| 1. | Lewis Hamilton | Mercedes | 1.30.44,200 |
|---|---|---|---|
| 2. | Daniel Ricciardo | Red Bull Racing-TAG Heuer | +6,996 |
| 3. | Max Verstappen | Red Bull Racing-TAG Heuer | +13,413 |
| **6.** | **Kimi Räikkönen** | **Ferrari** | **+37,023** |

German GP, qualifying

| 5. | Kimi Räikkönen | Ferrari | 1.15,142 |
|---|---|---|---|

## BELGIAN GP

| 1. | Nico Rosberg | Mercedes | 1.44.51,058 |
|---|---|---|---|
| 2. | Daniel Ricciardo | Red Bull Racing-TAG Heuer | +14,113 |
| 3. | Lewis Hamilton | Mercedes | +27,634 |
| **9.** | **Kimi Räikkönen** | **Ferrari** | **+1.01,109** |

Belgian GP, qualifying

| 3. | Kimi Räikkönen | Ferrari | 1.46,910 |
|---|---|---|---|

## ITALIAN GP

| 1. | Nico Rosberg | Mercedes | 1.17.28,089 |
|---|---|---|---|
| 2. | Lewis Hamilton | Mercedes | +15,070 |
| 3. | Sebastian Vettel | Ferrari | +20,990 |
| **4.** | **Kimi Räikkönen** | **Ferrari** | **+27,561** |

Italian GP, qualifying

| 4. | Kimi Räikkönen | Ferrari | 1.22,065 |
|---|---|---|---|

## SINGAPORE GP

| 1. | Nico Rosberg | Mercedes | 1.55.48,950 |
|---|---|---|---|
| 2. | Daniel Ricciardo | Red Bull Racing-TAG Heuer | +0,488 |
| 3. | Lewis Hamilton | Ferrari | +8,038 |
| **4.** | **Kimi Räikkönen** | **Ferrari** | **+10,219** |

Singapore GP, qualifying

| 5. | Kimi Räikkönen | Ferrari | 1.43,540 |
|---|---|---|---|

## MALAYSIAN GP

| 1. | Daniel Ricciardo | Red Bull Racing-TAG Heuer | 1.37.12,776 |
|---|---|---|---|
| 2. | Max Verstappen | Red Bull Racing-TAG Heuer | +2,443 |
| 3. | Nico Rosberg | Mercedes | +25,516 |
| **4.** | **Kimi Räikkönen** | **Ferrari** | **+28,785** |

Malaysian GP, qualifying

| 6. | Kimi Räikkönen | Ferrari | 1.33,632 |
|---|---|---|---|

## JAPANESE GP

| 1. | Nico Rosberg | Ferrari | 1.26.43,333 |
|---|---|---|---|
| 2. | Max Verstappen | Mercedes | +4,978 |
| 3. | Lewis Hamilton | Ferrari | +5,776 |
| **5.** | **Kimi Räikkönen** | **Ferrari** | **+28,370** |

Japanese GP, qualifying

| 3. | (8) Kimi Räikkönen | Ferrari | 1.30,949 |
|---|---|---|---|

## UNITED STATES GP

| 1. | Lewis Hamilton | Mercedes | 1.38.12,618 |
|---|---|---|---|
| 2. | Nico Rosberg | Mercedes | +4,520 |
| 3. | Daniel Ricciardo | Ferrari | +19,692 |

**Kimi Räikkönen (Ferrari) retired on lap 38.**

United States GP, qualifying

| 5. | Kimi Räikkönen | Ferrari | 1.36,131 |
|---|---|---|---|

## MEXICAN GP

| 1. | Lewis Hamilton | Mercedes | 1.40.31,402 |
|---|---|---|---|
| 2. | Nico Rosberg | Mercedes | +8,354 |
| 3. | Daniel Ricciardo | Red Bull Racing-TAG Heuer | +20,858 |
| **6.** | **Kimi Räikkönen** | **Ferrari** | **+49,376** |

Mexican GP, qualifying

| 6 | Kimi Räikkönen | Ferrari | 1.19,376 |
|---|---|---|---|

## BRAZILIAN GP

| 1. | Lewis Hamilton | Mercedes | 3.01.01,335 |
|---|---|---|---|
| 2. | Nico Rosberg | Mercedes | +11,455 |
| 3. | Max Verstappen | Red Bull Racing-TAG Heuer | +21,481 |

**Kimi Räikkönen (Ferrari) retired on lap 19.**

Brazilian GP, qualifying

| 3. | Kimi Räikkönen | Ferrari | 1.11,404 |
|---|---|---|---|

## ABU DHABI GP

| 1. | Lewis Hamilton | Mercedes | 1.38.04,013 |
|---|---|---|---|
| 2. | Nico Rosberg | Mercedes | +0,439 |
| 3. | Sebastian Vettel | Ferrari | +0,843 |
| **6.** | **Kimi Räikkönen** | **Ferrari** | **+18,816** |

Abu Dhabi GP, qualifying

| 4. | Kimi Räikkönen | Ferrari | 1.39,604 |
|---|---|---|---|

# 2017

## AUSTRALIAN GP

| 1. | Sebastian Vettel | Ferrari | 1.24.11,672 |
|---|---|---|---|
| 2. | Lewis Hamilton | Mercedes | +9,975 |
| 3. | Valtteri Bottas | Mercedes | +11,250 |
| **4.** | **Kimi Räikkönen** | **Ferrari** | **+22,393** |

Australian GP, qualifying

| 4. | Kimi Räikkönen | Ferrari | 1.23,033 |
|---|---|---|---|

## CHINESE GP

| 1. | Lewis Hamilton | Mercedes | 1.37.36,158 |
|---|---|---|---|
| 2. | Sebastian Vettel | Ferrari | +6,250 |
| 3. | Max Verstappen | Red Bull Racing-TAG Heuer | +45,192 |
| **5.** | **Kimi Räikkönen** | **Ferrari** | **+48,076** |

Chinese GP, qualifying

| 4. | Kimi Räikkönen | Ferrari | 1.32,140 |
|---|---|---|---|

## BAHRAIN GP

| 1. | Sebastian Vettel | Ferrari | 1.33.53,374 |
|---|---|---|---|
| 2. | Lewis Hamilton | Mercedes | +6,660 |
| 3. | Valtteri Bottas | Mercedes | +20,397 |
| **4.** | **Kimi Räikkönen** | **Ferrari** | **+22,475** |

Bahrain GP, qualifying

| 5. | Kimi Räikkönen | Ferrari | 1.29,567 |
|---|---|---|---|

## RUSSIAN GP

| 1. | Valtteri Bottas | Mercedes | 1.28.08,743 |
|---|---|---|---|
| 2. | Sebastian Vettel | Ferrari | +0,617 |
| **3.** | **Kimi Räikkönen** | **Ferrari** | **+11,000** |

Russian GP, qualifying

| 2. | Kimi Räikkönen | Ferrari | 1.33,253 |
|---|---|---|---|

## SPANISH GP

| 1. | Lewis Hamilton | Mercedes | 1.35.56,497 |
|---|---|---|---|
| 2. | Sebastian Vettel | Ferrari | +3,490 |
| 3. | Daniel Ricciardo | Red Bull Racing-TAG Heuer | +1.15,820 |

**Kimi Räikkönen (Ferrari) retired on lap 1.**

Spanish GP, qualifying

| 4. | Kimi Räikkönen | Ferrari | 1.19,439 |
|---|---|---|---|

## MONACO GP

| 1. | Sebastian Vettel | Ferrari | 1.44.44,340 |
|---|---|---|---|
| **2.** | **Kimi Räikkönen** | **Ferrari** | **+3,145** |
| 3. | Daniel Ricciardo | Red Bull Racing-TAG Heuer | +3,745 |

Monaco GP, qualifying

| 1. | Kimi Räikkönen | Ferrari | 1.12,178 |
|---|---|---|---|

## CANADIAN GP

| 1. | Lewis Hamilton | Mercedes | 1.33.05,154 |
|---|---|---|---|
| 2. | Valtteri Bottas | Mercedes | +19,783 |
| 3. | Daniel Ricciardo | Red Bull Racing-TAG Heuer | +35,297 |
| **7.** | **Kimi Räikkönen** | **Ferrari** | **+58,632** |

Canadian GP, qualifying

| 4. | Kimi Räikkönen | Ferrari | 1.12,252 |
|---|---|---|---|

## AZERBAIJAN GP

| 1. | Daniel Ricciardo | Red Bull Racing-TAG Heuer | 2.03.55,573 |
|---|---|---|---|
| 2. | Valtteri Bottas | Mercedes | +3,904 |
| 3. | Lance Stroll | Williams-Mercedes | +4,009 |

**Kimi Räikkönen (Ferrari) retired on lap 46 but was 14th.**

Azerbaijan GP, qualifying

| 3. | Kimi Räikkönen | Ferrari | 1.41,693 |
|---|---|---|---|

## AUSTRIAN GP

| 1. | Valtteri Bottas | Mercedes | 1.21.48,5236 |
|---|---|---|---|
| 2. | Sebastian Vettel | Ferrari | +0,658 |
| 3. | Daniel Ricciardo | Red Bull Racing-TAG Heuer | +6,012 |
| **5.** | **Kimi Räikkönen** | **Ferrari** | **+20,370** |

Austrian GP, qualifying

| 4. | (3) Kimi Räikkönen | Ferrari | 1.04,779 |
|---|---|---|---|

## BRITISH GP

1. Lewis Hamilton   Mercedes   1.21.27,430
2. Valtteri Bottas   Mercedes   +14,063
3. **Kimi Räikkönen**   **Ferrari**   **+36,570**

British GP, qualifying
2. Kimi Räikkönen   Ferrari   1.27,147

## HUNGARIAN GP

1. Sebastian Vettel   Ferrari   1.39.46,713
2. **Kimi Räikkönen**   **Ferrari**   **+0,908**
3. Valtteri Bottas   Mercedes   +12,462

Hungarian GP, qualifying
2. Kimi Räikkönen   Ferrari   1.16,444

## BELGIAN GP

1. Lewis Hamilton   Mercedes   1.24.42,8206
2. Sebastian Vettel   Ferrari   +2,358
3. Daniel Ricciardo   Red Bull Racing-TAG Heuer   +10,791
4. **Kimi Räikkönen**   **Ferrari**   **+14,471**

Belgian GP, qualifying
4. Kimi Räikkönen   Ferrari   1.43,270

## ITALIAN GP

1. Lewis Hamilton   Mercedes   1.15.32,312
2. Valtteri Bottas   Mercedes   +4,471
3. Sebastian Vettel   Ferrari   +36,317
5. **Kimi Räikkönen**   **Ferrari**   **+1.00,0825**

Italian GP, qualifying
7. Kimi Räikkönen   Ferrari   1.37,987

## SINGAPORE GP

1. Lewis Hamilton   Mercedes   2.03.23,544
2. Daniel Ricciardo   Red Bull Racing-TAG Heuer   +4,507
3. Valtteri Bottas   Mercedes   +8,800

**Kimi Räikkönen (Ferrari) retired on lap 1.**

Singapore GP, qualifying
4. Kimi Räikkönen   Ferrari   1.40,069

## MALAYSIAN GP

1. Max Verstappen   Red Bull Racing-TAG Heuer   1.30.01,290
2. Lewis Hamilton   Mercedes   +12,770
3. Daniel Ricciardo   Red Bull Racing-TAG Heuer   +22,519

**Kimi Räikkönen (Ferrari) did not drive the GP.**

Malaysian GP, qualifying
2. Kimi Räikkönen   Ferrari   1.30,121

## JAPANESE GP

1. Lewis Hamilton   Mercedes   1.27.31,194
2. Max Verstappen   Red Bull Racing-TAG Heuer   +1,211
3. Daniel Ricciardo   Red Bull Racing-TAG Heuer   +9,679
5. **Kimi Räikkönen**   **Ferrari**   **+32,622**

Japanese GP, qualifying
6. (10) Kimi Räikkönen   Ferrari   1.28,498

## UNITED STATES GP

1. Lewis Hamilton   Mercedes   1.33.50,991
2. Sebastian Vettel   Ferrari   +10,143
3. **Kimi Räikkönen**   **Ferrari**   **+15,779**

United States GP, qualifying
5. Kimi Räikkönen   Ferrari   1.33,577

## MEXICAN GP

1. Max Verstappen   Red Bull Racing-TAG Heuer   1.36.26,552
2. Valtteri Bottas   Mercedes   +19,678
3. **Kimi Räikkönen**   **Ferrari**   **+54,007**

Mexican GP, qualifying
5. Kimi Räikkönen   Ferrari   1.17,238

## BRAZILIAN GP

1. Sebastian Vettel   Ferrari   1.31.26,262
2. Valtteri Bottas   Mercedes   +2,762
3. **Kimi Räikkönen**   **Ferrari**   **+4,600**

Brazilian GP, qualifying
3. Kimi Räikkönen   Ferrari   1.08,538

## ABU DHABI GP

1. Valtteri Bottas   Mercedes   1.34.14,062
2. Lewis Hamilton   Mercedes   +3,899
3. Sebastian Vettel   Ferrari   +19,330
4. **Kimi Räikkönen**   **Ferrari**   **+45,386**

Abu Dhabi GP, qualifying
5. Kimi Räikkönen   Ferrari   1.36,985

# 2018

## AUSTRALIAN GP

1. Sebastian Vettel   Ferrari   1.29.33,283
2. Lewis Hamilton   Mercedes   +5,036
3. **Kimi Räikkönen**   **Ferrari**   **+6,309**

Australian GP, qualifying
2. Kimi Räikkönen   Ferrari   1.21,828

## BAHRAIN GP
1. Sebastian Vettel — Ferrari — 1.32.01,940
2. Valtteri Bottas — Mercedes — +0,699
3. Lewis Hamilton — Mercedes — +6,512

**Kimi Räikkönen (Ferrari) retired on lap 35.**

Bahrain GP, qualifying
2. Kimi Räikkönen — Ferrari — 1.28,101

## CHINESE GP
1. Daniel Ricciardo — Red Bull Racing-TAG Heuer — 1.35.36,380
2. Valtteri Bottas — Mercedes — +8,894
3. **Kimi Räikkönen** — **Ferrari** — **+9,637**

Chinese GP, qualifying
2. Kimi Räikkönen — Ferrari — 1.31,182

## AZERBAIJAN GP
1. Lewis Hamilton — Mercedes — 1.43.44,291
2. **Kimi Räikkönen** — **Ferrari** — **+2,460**
3. Sergio Pérez — Force India-Mercedes — +4,024

Azerbaijan GP, qualifying
6. Kimi Räikkönen — Ferrari — 1.42,490

## SPANISH GP
1. Lewis Hamilton — Mercedes — 1.35.29,972
2. Valtteri Bottas — Mercedes — +20,593
3. Max Verstappen — Red Bull Racing-TAG Heuer — +26,873

**Kimi Räikkönen (Ferrari) retired on lap 25.**

Spanish GP, qualifying
4. Kimi Räikkönen — Ferrari — 1.16,612

## MONACO GP
1. Daniel Ricciardo — Red Bull Racing-TAG Heuer — 1.42.54,807
2. Sebastian Vettel — Ferrari — +7,336
3. Lewis Hamilton — Mercedes — +17,013
4. **Kimi Räikkönen** — **Ferrari** — **+18,127**

Monaco GP, qualifying
4. Kimi Räikkönen — Ferrari — 1.11,266

## CANADIAN GP
1. Sebastian Vettel — Ferrari — 1.28.31,377
2. Valtteri Bottas — Mercedes — +7,376
3. Max Verstappen — Red Bull Racing-TAG Heuer — +8,360
6. **Kimi Räikkönen** — **Ferrari** — **+27,184**

Canadian GP, qualifying
5. Kimi Räikkönen — Ferrari — 1.11,095

## FRENCH GP
1. Lewis Hamilton — Mercedes — 1.30.11,385
2. Max Verstappen — Red Bull Racing-TAG Heuer — +7,090
3. **Kimi Räikkönen** — **Ferrari** — **+25,888**

French GP, qualifying
6. Kimi Räikkönen — Ferrari — 1.31,057

## AUSTRIAN GP
1. Max Verstappen — Red Bull Racing-TAG Heuer — 1.21.56,024
2. **Kimi Räikkönen** — **Ferrari** — **+1,504**
3. Sebastian Vettel — Ferrari — +3,181

Austrian GP, qualifying
4. Kimi Räikkönen — Ferrari — 1.03,660

## BRITISH GP
1. Sebastian Vettel — Ferrari — 1.27.29,784
2. Lewis Hamilton — Mercedes — +2,264
3. **Kimi Räikkönen** — **Ferrari** — **+3,562**

British GP, qualifying
3. Kimi Räikkönen — Ferrari — 1.25,990

## GERMAN GP
1. Lewis Hamilton — Mercedes — 1.32.29,845
2. Valtteri Bottas — Mercedes — +4,535
3. **Kimi Räikkönen** — **Ferrari** — **+6,732**

German GP, qualifying
3. Kimi Räikkönen — Ferrari — 1.11,547

## HUNGARIAN GP
1. Lewis Hamilton — Mercedes — 1.37.16,427
2. Sebastian Vettel — Ferrari — +17,123
3. **Kimi Räikkönen** — **Ferrari** — **+20,101**

Hungarian GP, qualifying
3. Kimi Räikkönen — Ferrari — 1.36,186

## BELGIAN GP
1. Sebastian Vettel — Ferrari — 1.23.34,476
2. Lewis Hamilton — Mercedes — +11,061
3. Max Verstappen — Red Bull Racing-TAG Heuer — +31,372

**Kimi Räikkönen (Ferrari) retired on lap 8.**

Belgian GP, qualifying
6. Kimi Räikkönen — Ferrari — 2.02,671

## ITALIAN GP

1. Lewis Hamilton      Mercedes      1,16.54,484
2. **Kimi Räikkönen**      **Ferrari**      **+8,705**
3. Valtteri Bottas      Mercedes      +14,066

Italian GP, qualifying
1. Kimi Räikkönen      Ferrari      1.19,119

This broke Juan Pablo Montoya's record for the fastest lap in F1 history. The previous record stood at 262.242 km/h; Räikkönen averaged 263.587 km/h.

The Italian GP in September 2018 was the last one that could be incorporated in the book.

**301**

# KIMI RÄIKKÖNEN'S CAREER 1988-2018

**1988**    Karting in classes A, B and C until 1991.

**1991**    Class Mini.

**1992**    Class Racket Junior.

**1993**    Class Racket Junior Finnish Cup, 9th place.

**1994**    Class Racket Junior Finnish Cup, 2nd place.

**1995**    Class Formula A Monaco Cup, retired from 4th place.

**1996**    European Series GP, World Championship (WC) and Nordic Championship (NC). Finnish Champion of Class Formula A.

**1997**    Wins Finnish Championship (FC) of Formula A; wins NC of Class Formula Intercontinental A; comes 2nd in European Karting GP Class Super A; 3rd in Monaco Cup. Takes part in WC series of Formula Super A.

**1999**    2nd in FC series of Class Formula A; 10th in WC series of Class Formula Super A. First race in

Formula Renault with Haywood Racing, 3rd place. Wins so-called winter series of Formula Renault.

**2000** Wins British Formula Renault 2000 series for Manor Motorsport team. Takes part in two European Formula Renault championship races.

**2001** F1 for Sauber Petronas, 10th in WC.

**2002** Moves to McLaren Mercedes, 6th in WC.

**2003** 2nd in WC; first GP win in Malaysia.

**2004** 7th in WC series.

**2005** 2nd in WC series.

**2006** 5th in WC series.

**2007–10** Contract with Ferrari.

**2007** Wins WC.

**2008** 3rd in WC.

**2009** 6th in WC.

**2010–11** Takes a year out from F1; rally driver in WC series.

**2010** 10th in rallying WC series.

**2011** 19th in rallying WC series. Drives in two NASCAR races: 15th (Trucks) and 27th (Nationwide).

**2012** Returns to F1; contract with Lotus Renault, 3rd in WC.

**2013** 5th in WC.

**2014** Moves back to Ferrari, 12th in WC.

**2015** 4th in WC.

**2016** 6th in WC.

**2017** 4th in WC.

**2018** In August, 3rd in WC.

# BONUS TRACKS

**Kimi Räikkönen has said** so little that many of the few words are still remembered. He has also spoken out of turn and been in your face. Some of his utterances have become well-known sayings, though they weren't meant to be. The phrases are eruptions, mainly blurted out in awkward situations, perhaps hasty reactions by someone in a defensive mode. In any case, they were uttered. They can't be taken back and there they are, on the net and YouTube for all the world to see.

'Leave me alone, I know what to do' is not an aphorism hatched slowly in the silence of a forest, but a phrase let out by an experienced and impatient driver to an engineer in the middle of the Abu Dhabi GP in 2012. After the race, neither the driver nor the race engineer bore a grudge, and had probably forgotten the incident. In this sport, an altercation between two colleagues can be heard by the whole world and become an indelible tattoo.

This section, called 'Bonus Tracks', features a few of Kimi's sayings. The driver can be proud of some of them; some of the others might have been better left unsaid. He can't take them back.

————

'F1 without the press would be a paradise.'

————

'Makes no difference if it rains or not.'

————

Question: 'What do rallying and
Formula 1 have in common?'
Kimi's reply: 'You use a steering wheel in both.'

————

'I'm not interested in what people think
about me. I'm not Michael Schumacher.'

————

Kimi missed a ceremony at which the legendary footballer Pelé handed over a special award to Michael Schumacher before the last race of Schumacher's F1 career. Martin Brundle, who compered the occasion, asked in a live broadcast the reason for Kimi's absence. Kimi: 'I was taking a dump.'

———

Question: 'Many drivers have rituals associated with their helmets. Have you got any?'
Kimi: 'I give it a wipe, so I can see better.'

———

'I don't intend to go to a language school to learn Italian; it's not why I came to Ferrari.'

———

Question: 'What was the most exciting situation during this race weekend?'
Kimi: 'The start.'
Question: 'And the most boring?'
Kimi: 'This.'

Kimi was asked after the qualifying in
Hockenheim: 'What do the tyres feel like?'
Kimi: 'They go round as you'd expect.'

———

Question: 'Do you think you're a good neighbour?'
Kimi: 'Of course. Because of the
job, I'm never at home.'

———

Lewis Hamilton was celebrating his first
GP win and said it felt better than sex. The
reporter asked for Kimi's opinion on the matter.
Kimi's reply: 'Perhaps he's never done sex.'

———

Question: 'Are you happy with the
result?' [Kimi didn't get any points]
Kimi: 'Do you think I am?'

———

Question: 'What can you do in Finland?'
Kimi: 'Well, in summer you can fish and
fuck, but in winter fishing isn't so good.'

———

Question: 'Have you got any hobbies?'
Kimi: 'I gather nuts.'

———

'Let's see what we can do.' [This is the
sentence Kimi almost always repeats when a
reporter asks about the next day's race.]

———

Question: 'Where do you plan to deploy your
car's KERS [Kinetic Energy Recovery System]?'
Kimi: 'On that track.'

———

Question: 'What advice would you give
newcomers Nico Rosberg and Scott Speed?'
Kimi: 'I hope they give way nicely.'

'You don't drive a race on paper.'

———

Kimi is asked about losing weight before
the start of the season. Kimi's answer:
'I don't know, I haven't got scales.'

———

Question: 'What's the fifth place on
the grid like to start from?'
Kimi: 'It's the fifth place.'

———

'Don't talk to me in the middle of a corner!'
Kimi's response to Ferrari's race engineers
on the team radio at the practice session
in the 2009 Malaysian Grand Prix.

———

'Yes, yes, yes, yes. I'm doing all the tyres. You don't have to remind me every second!' Kimi's reply to a radio message from Lotus's race engineers in the Abu Dhabi GP in 2012.

―――――

Baku GP, 2017. Kimi comes back from Ferrari's pit garage. All is well, except that the car has no steering wheel. The worker holding the steering wheel runs alongside Kimi's car but, for some reason, initially fails to pass it to the Finn. Kimi shouts: 'Steering wheel. Pass the steering wheel here! Hey, hey! The steering wheel! Somebody tell him to give it to me! Come on, move!'

# INDEX

Racing Service Jaatinen, 70
Räikkönen (née Dahlman), Jenni,
159
and divorce, 268
Kimi's engagement to, 128
and marriage breakdown, 206
and Masa's death, 161
and Masa's fall, 160
Räikkönen, Kimi, 205
and alcohol consumption, 108–9,
138, 190, 212–13, 218, 240
Alén's will to win shared by, 150
and army service, 77, 105–6,
108–12
Arrivabene on, 250–1
asleep in drying cupboard, 203
binge-drinking given up by, 140
birth of, 52–3
and blood and urine tests, 179
body temperature of, 10
breathalysed, 110
Camilleri on, 251–2
career of, 1988–2018, 303–4
and car's power loss, 28–9
and celebrity, coping with, 36
Chigwell arrival of, 102–3
childhood home improved by, 129
childhood sports played by, 56
children loved by, 140
choice of rallying by, 149
as citizen of two countries, 105
damaged vocal cords of, 38
in detailed statistics, 277–301
door that bears name of, 176
at Down by the Laituri rock
festival, 104
drinking habits of, 28
driving in traffic by, 55–6
dyslexia of, 68
engine failures of, 28–9, 40, 129,
133, 134

England move by, 97, 99–100
'enigmatic' tag applied to, 52
events entered by, *see individual
competitions by name*
and father's clay shooting, 159–60
father's role of, 33–4
and fear, 44
Ferrari dedicates book to, 41
and FIA monitoring, 225–6
and filming for sponsors, 237,
241–2
and financial help from parents,
67
first F1 race of, 116, 125
first race of, as child, 69
first season of, 25
first speed test of, 79–80
first-year wages of, 125
forename of, 6
Formula 1 entered by, 35, 81
and Formula Renault series,
35, 36
four successive winter races won
by, 108
Grönholm's will to win shared by,
150
and gym exercises, 75, 236, *254*,
255–6
helmet collection of, 51, 135, 164,
242
and ice hockey, 188
'Iceman' nickname of, 34, 131–2
improved English acquired by, 132
and instinct, 45–6
Jenni's engagement to, 128
Kankkunen's will to win shared
by, 150
and karting, 56
and karting towards Europe, 73
and Kidman, 41
Kulta on, 243–4